PRAISE FOR *U CHIC*

"Get ready to be empowered. This isn't just a ~~[obscured]~~ but to life!"

—Stephanie Elizondo Griest, author of
100 Places Every Woman Should Go

"Lots of clever strategies on how to have a fabulous time at college, combined with wise advice on how to avoid all-too-common mistakes. A great resource for anyone who wants to be a chic college coed."

—Kim Clark, Senior Writer,
U.S.News & World Report

"Full of fun, sassy advice on how to make the most of a great time of life, *U Chic* makes me yearn for my college days!"

—Marcy McGinnis, Associate Dean, School
of Journalism, Stony Brook University

"From the sisterhood of girlfriends who've been there, *U Chic* answers everything a college girl really wants to know."

—Tracey Wong Briggs, former coordinator of
USA TODAY's All-USA Academic and Teacher Teams

UPDATED 3RD EDITION

THE COLLEGE GIRL'S GUIDE TO EVERYTHING

Christie Garton

Published by Sourcebooks, Inc.
P.O. Box 4410, Naperville, Illinois 60567-4410
(630) 961-3900
Fax: (630) 961-2168
www.sourcebooks.com

Garton, Christie.
  U chic : the college girl's guide to everything / Christie Garton. — 3rd ed.
    p. cm.
  Includes index.
1. College student orientation—United States. 2. Women college students—United
States—Life skills guides. I. Title.
  LB2343.32.G39 2013
  378.1'98—dc23

                        2012046645

            Printed and bound in the United States of America.
                VP 10 9 8 7 6 5 4 3 2 1

To the women of UChic.com,
the true inspiration behind this book.

contents

foreword

. . . .

From Christie Garton, founder and publisher, UChic.com

Without an older sister growing up, I occasionally had to learn things the hard way. There are advantages to not having to stand in anyone's shadow, but there were many times when a little tried-and-true advice could have helped, especially during my first few years in college. I definitely would have not registered for 18 credit hours my first semester in school! After a few detours, roundabouts, and restarts, I eventually found my way through college and into the real world, but things would have been a whole lot easier with the right advice.

This was the inspiration behind this book and UChic.com. I wanted to create a place where college women could come together to find support and advice during one of the most important times of a girl's life. We worked tirelessly to recruit a group of contributors with a diverse range of experience for the book that you now hold in your hands. I want to thank all of the contributors for being completely open and honest in sharing their personal stories. It is my sincere hope that what you will discover in reading *U Chic* is that we are all sisters in the end.

welcome to *u chic: the college girl's guide to everything!*

. . . .

*W*hether you're headed to college or are already there, one thing is certain: college is the time to expand your horizons. You need to experience college in your own way, and our guide is here to help you discover it!

With the endless choices you'll face in college, you'll often have questions and find yourself in need of a little advice. Our hope is that you find your answers here. We asked college women across the country to dish about their collegiate experiences, challenges, and successes. The result? A guide that provides you with exclusive advice that could only come from those who have experienced it for themselves. From preparing to move, to dating advice, to balancing that all-important budget, to finding the right balance of school and fun, you will find answers and insights to your important questions in these shared experiences from college women around the country. This is a book that you can turn to throughout your entire college career. In that spirit, don't feel like you need to sit down and read the book cover-to-cover (though that certainly won't hurt anything!). Each of our contributors has answered specific questions, so you can turn right to the section you need, when you need it.

With *U Chic*, the conversation doesn't stop at the last page.

Let's say you have a specific question that is not directly addressed. We've created an online chat area at UChic.com exclusively for readers, where you can comment on things that you've read in the guide, seek further advice, or read more about or even contact the guide's writers. This guide is truly the start of a conversation that can last throughout your entire college career.

So what are you waiting for? Turn the page and be on your way to your own fabulous college experience!

xoxo,
Christie Garton
Founder, UChic.com

CHAPTER 1

Getting Started

S tarting to get serious about where you'd like to go to college? Or maybe you were already accepted and are packing for your new home now. Either way, this chapter has you covered. You probably are already well aware that the transition to college is a major stress. Besides maybe summer camp, when else have you packed up your entire life's belongings into several boxes and suitcases to head off to an unknown place to live with some random stranger? To help smooth your path, this chapter is filled with insider advice on making this transition with confidence and style. As Carrie Bradshaw might say, we wish we were in your Choos, starting the college experience all over again!

getting in

I had known from the age of 12 that I was destined to attend Brown University. This had been decided before I had even visited the campus. I'd just read about it in one of my brother's college brochures, but regardless, I knew I was going to Brown to study theater and to be a free spirit under a requirement-free curriculum. And maybe join a naked protest or two.

Six years and a $70 application fee later, my hopes were dashed. *I didn't get in.* When I received that thin, impersonal rejection letter, I went through the Kübler-Ross cycle of grief faster than you can say "safety school." First there was denial. *No way, I totally got in; they got the wrong Allison Davis.* Then anger. *Those jerks—what do they know about college admissions?!* Followed by bargaining. *I'll retake my SATs, do 600 more hours of community service—anything!* Next, depression. *My world has ended.* And, finally, acceptance.

Did You Know?

The schools with the lowest acceptance rates are actually music schools—Philadelphia's Curtis Institute of Music and New York's Juilliard School have acceptance rates less than 8 percent. Harvard comes in next at 9 percent.

Honestly, the rejection letter stung. A lot. You spend 4+ years slaving over SATs, GPAs, APs, extracurriculars, and enough community service to be on par with a Peace Corps member just to qualify for consideration at your dream school—the only university or college that you fervently believe matches who you are and, more importantly, who you want to become. It's almost like an unhealthy romantic relationship; your whole self-worth becomes involved in impressing "the one." It is disappointing to be so brusquely rejected by what was your collegiate soul mate.

HOW TO COPE

So you did not get a fat acceptance package from your first choice school. Disappointing? Absolutely. But devastating? No. If you get rejected from your first (or second or third) choice school, give yourself some time to be upset, but remember there are about 6 billion different possible reasons for an admission decision. There is almost no way to understand the why, which is really frustrating. Rather than wallow over the unanswerable "why" by tearing yourself and your application apart, focus on what you do have—other college choices.

When I got my rejection letter from Brown, I cried, threw things, tore up the letter, but then I got some sanity back. Brown was 1 school out of 13 that I applied to. And at the end of the whole ordeal, I may not have gotten into Brown, but I ended up with 12 other acceptances and eventually was accepted to the school that I now proudly call my alma mater, Barnard College.

Once you've been rejected, you may feel a little lost as to what to do next. Since we can't all create our own fake colleges like Justin Long did in the movie *Accepted*, considering other *real* schools is the logical next step.

What Not to Do When You Get Your College Acceptance Letter

Kylie Thompson, Harvard University

Congrats! You made it through college acceptance and rejection season. Whether or not this was the year your own fate was up to the admissions gods, I'm sure you ran into a few obnoxious Facebook statuses, lost prefrosh on your campus's visiting weekend, or saw tears from family friends whose hearts were set on a particular school. While the days leading up to finally finding that letter in your mailbox may be some of the most nerve-wracking in a student's high school career, it's important to remember not to over share when those acceptances do roll in.

Case in point: Recently college blogs were all abuzz when one student took his excitement at being accepted to a number of great schools a little too far. Updating his Facebook status one night, he wrote: *"I just got my admittance letters into Yale, Duke, Northwestern, Penn, and Columbia. Now Harvard is begging my ass to go to their school. FULLY PAID SCHOLARSHIP. LOL. Hmmmm…Ahahahah naw kiss my ass. F@!k Harvard! I don't need no Harvard or no scholarship HAHA! No really though, I'm going to Harvard guys. Wooooooo =D."*

This is unacceptable on many levels. First off, admissions decisions had not yet been mailed out to students by the night he wrote those fateful words (I should know since I work there). Secondly, NO Ivy League school offers scholarships to students, only financial aid made up of need-based grants. Thirdly, this is just a post in poor taste. Rumor has it, Harvard rescinded this student's admission, and in my opinion, deservedly so.

While it's great to be proud of your achievements, Facebook, or any social media site for that matter, is not the venue for shameless boasting of this nature. That should probably be saved for immediate family, grandma and grandpa, or the teacher who gave you a C– in Algebra I in the eighth grade.

WHAT TO DO IF YOU APPLIED EARLY DECISION

If you applied early decision, or early action, and didn't make it in, go talk to the college counselor at your high school. You have a nice stretch of time to reconsider schools and find new ones. Before you go, make a list of the reasons you fell in love with First Choice University. Was it the rural environment? The ivy-covered brick buildings? The out-of-this-world biochemistry department? Well, guess what? Other campuses have the same things. Your college counselor can help you find other schools with similar criteria and whose admissions standards more closely fit what you have to offer.

Something else to consider is the *tabula rasa* approach to looking for new schools. By weighing your original reasons for choosing your first choice school, you also have a second chance to evaluate what you actually want out of a college. In high school, especially, it is so easy to be pushed into a neat little box with a concise label. I'm sure you can hear it now: you are "the really athletic girl" or "the really brainy girl." But maybe there is another girl inside you that you need to explore. College gives you that opportunity. Consider applying to a school that has what you know you are interested in (like a good badminton team) but may also have a strong reputation in something you want to pursue in the future.

A WHOLE NEW SET OF POSSIBILITIES

I always considered myself the quirky, alternative-theater girl. I thought I wanted to be in a small town where most of your life revolved around the campus. I also wanted a campus with a strong academic history and, yes, with ivy-covered buildings. Once I didn't get into Brown, I considered other schools just like it—Vassar and Bowdoin were my next top candidates. My college counselor reminded me that I was an active writer and that maybe I should consider schools that had strong writing programs. It was a great suggestion. I had always intended to go to school for theater—something that I had done almost my entire life. But by expanding my college search to those with well-known writing programs, I began to see a whole new set of options, and what I had thought I had wanted out of a school changed. Suddenly, I was attracted to schools in bigger cities, like Barnard. And though I still have my ivy-covered buildings, campus life is no longer the focal point of my social activities. Truly, Barnard helped me discover my real passion and develop into a person I didn't even know I could be. And maybe this would have happened at Vassar or Bowdoin as well, but the reevaluations I did during my second admissions process opened a lot of possibilities.

FOR REGULAR DECISION APPLICANTS

If you applied regular decision and didn't get in, you'll have other admissions decisions coming at the same time, meaning there are likely several acceptance letters to look forward to. Even though you really wanted to go to First Choice University, there were reasons you liked all the other schools you applied to. Go back and reconsider those reasons. If you have the time, go spend a weekend at one or two of the schools that are your remaining top choices. The most important thing to remember is to stop comparing it to First Choice University. It's fine to say, "Well, I really liked how that school had eco-friendly dorms." But if you are comparing the linoleum of the dorm room floors, you are setting yourself up for disappointment in the end. Look at the positive aspects of each school rather than considering what it doesn't have.

U Chic Tip!

Once you find a school (or schools) you want to apply to, go back to your college counselor and ask for application hints. For instance, let's say that you play varsity lacrosse during your four years of high school but you also sing in the chorale. Your college counselor can help you work both of those unique experiences into your personal essay. Or maybe you'll find that your application is perfect already, but chances are, with a reevaluation and some helpful hints from your high school's resident college expert, you can find some way to better your chances for the second round of applications.

I know it's cheesy to remind you of the old saying that you'll end up where you were meant to be, but it's kind of true. Somehow, even if the school you end up going to isn't the one you thought you wanted, it may end up being the best fit.

U Chic Tip! Ivy or Not? That Is the Question!

Jill Ravae Scherr, Academy of Art University

Did you get into an Ivy but are still trying to figure out how to pay for it? Did another non-Ivy institution offer you a better financial aid package or even a full ride?

There is so much to worry about when attending college from choosing courses to picking majors to making new friends. These are supposed to be some of the best years of your life and you don't need financial burdens keeping you down and affecting your overall health and performance. That is why it is essential for you to make smart financial decisions today that will allow you to successfully graduate on time and be able to pursue the career of your dreams without back-breaking debt.

If you can't afford to attend the Ivy League institution, it may not be the best option. Sure, it is wonderful to attend a prestigious university and call it your alma mater, but it is not the end all, be all. Also, studies show that there really isn't that much proof that an Ivy education gets you more ahead in life than an education from a state or trade school. Certainly, some extra prestige and clout may initially open up doors for you, but ultimately it is up to you to keep them open and prove yourself and your abilities.

Don't be afraid to choose the non-Ivy school that offered you a great financial aid package. You can always transfer to an Ivy location at a later time or attend grad school at an Ivy, if it ends up being something you still aspire to do. The bottom line? Getting an education of any kind from a private or public university—or even trade school—in an area you are passionate about is a wonderful accomplishment.

FINAL THOUGHTS

After three years at Barnard, I knew that I loved where I was, but I always wondered, "What if I had gone to Brown?" Well, I went to visit a friend of mine who attends Brown last year. The campus was as beautiful as I had remembered. Providence is a great town, and I really liked the people. But there was something missing for me this time I went back. If I had gone to Brown, I never would have been able to take a writing class where Rachel Weiss made an appearance so we could learn the art of interviewing. I would never have been able to spend my semesters interning at the *New York Times*, and I would not have been able to hop on a subway and see a Tony-winning play and then come back to campus and hang out at a dorm party later in the evening. I would have missed out on so many different and wonderful opportunities.

And the funny part of this story is that my friend who goes to Brown chose it because she hadn't gotten into Columbia University in New York City. After I had been going on and on about how much I loved going to school in the city and how much I love Barnard, she said, "If I had gone to Columbia, I would have been lost. Brown was such a better fit." So, case in point: sometimes the things we ask for aren't really the things we need. If your first choice university took a pass, be grateful because your second (or third or fourth) choice will most likely be the better choice in the end.

Insights provided by Allison Davis, Barnard College

how to survive and thrive when in the minority

Growing up in a small town where every fourth name in the school directory was Feldman or Cohen, it is easy to assume that being Jewish is just as common as having brown hair. But you know what they say about assuming things: it's bad. So when you finally hit college—an overwhelming occasion in itself—what do you do when you find out how very much in the minority you may be?

DON'T PANIC

First of all, don't panic. Check out opportunities on campus. Attend new student fairs and collect pamphlets, or go to the student life office on campus where you'll find lists of clubs and organizations. And let us not forget, the mother of all information sources—Facebook. From the local Temple to Hillel (the largest Jewish student organization in the world), there were plenty of Judaism-affiliated opportunities for me at UC–Davis to choose from. Bottom line: All I had to do was look around.

Why I Chose a Historically Black College or University (HBCU)

Briana Peppers, Spelman College

What I love most about attending a black college is that I can be whoever I desire to be. I can embrace any style or social outlet wholeheartedly and be welcomed. In fact, when it comes to personal style, the more different, the better. I exit my residence hall to regularly see hairstyles from the '80s paired with classic pearls and '70s dress. On other days, I exit my residence hall to see suits and laptops. For the males, it's not uncommon to see the bow tie, and I absolutely love it! It is, indeed, a Southern gentleman's necessity.

What I'm referring to here is more than just fashion. The style reflects a deeper truth in that the students are always so poised and well versed. They are genuine "Renaissance" women and men. I knew that I wanted to earn the same title. I wanted to be refined and perfected. This is what compelled me most to attend Spelman College.

What to expect

Overall, life at a black college can be described as peaceful hysteria. It is full of constant excitement and passion but also comfort and support. To make things even more exciting, a social or academic event is always going on at a black college. Every Friday, Spelman hosts an outdoor celebration complete with music and food and vendors. We call it Market Friday.

Other great aspects of HBCUs are the experiences and traditions that are specific to black colleges. For example, every year during freshman orientation each member of the freshman class must experience an "initiation" into the Spelman sisterhood. I am not referring to anything dangerous or illegal. I am only referring to a memory that links every Spelman student and every Spelman woman together!

There really is genuine sisterhood. The bond is somewhat like being in a sorority without the pledging and initiation process. No matter what stage you are at in life, there will always be a group of people everywhere—ranging in all ages and social hierarchies— who are willing to give their last to you just because you, too, are a student or alumna of their alma mater. What I'm referring to is being a family. Just saying the name of the school can immediately turn a stranger into a family member. For example, a Spelman alumna once told me how she actually chased a vehicle with a Spelman College sticker just so she could say hello. Once she got close, filled with excitement, she jumped out of her own car to shout, "My Sister!"

Be prepared for a challenge

Students in a black college must be ready to combat the belief that our education is not as challenging as other college academic programs. It most definitely is. Our academics are equally as challenging and serve as an equivalent preparation for life.

What is different are the unique academic offerings that you'll find at an HBCU. A black college is one of the few places where knowledge and empowerment can come from titles such as *Gender as Analytical Category* by Beverly Guy-Sheftall or Aimé Césaire's *Discourse on Colonialism*. This knowledge is a rarity and a treasure. We are so fortunate at HBCUs for this kind of enlightenment to be our foundation. When I was a senior in high school, a recruiter from Tuskegee University shared this fact with me. At the time, I understood the message, but now, attending Spelman, I understand its truth.

There is something really unique and special about students at an HBCU that no one adjective can pinpoint. The one thing that binds us together the most is not race but our potential and vision. Some may argue that all college students are bound for something great in their future. This is probably true, but the future for students in Historically Black Colleges and Universities is more than a future. It is a destiny. Everything we do is powerful. Your time in a Historically Black College or University will be incredible! There is a persona and a mystique that will be with you forever, and it cannot be found anywhere else. So welcome. We are waiting.

SHOW UP

As lame as it sounds to be the new kid in five different clubs, sometimes just showing up will demonstrate that you are really serious about making connections. Go somewhere and join something that is related to your religion or ethnic heritage. When I went to my first sorority recruitment event, I had no clue that sorority membership would help me connect to the Jewish community at my school. Nevertheless, I wound up attending Friday night services once a month (which I had never done before), hosted my own Shabbat dinners, and did much more for the Jewish community than I'd ever done before in my life. And now, I'm the president of a Jewish-interest sorority. Go figure.

Why I Chose a Women's College

Rebecca E. Mill, Sweet Briar College

Searching for the perfect college was one of the most difficult things I have ever done (second only to actually graduating from high school!).

I don't mind admitting that I visited over 15 schools and that I applied to at least 10 of them. I visited every kind of school: private, public, coed, all-women's, in the North, in the South, in the city, and in the middle of nowhere.

After having spent four years at an all-girls' high school, I was shocked when I visited schools where women didn't hold every leadership position, and where women weren't constantly being told that they were able to do anything their male peers were able to do. Although I was expecting college to be different—and I would have happily welcomed a number of changes—this, however, did not bode well with me.

Needless to say, applying to and eventually choosing to attend a women's college seemed like the only logical choice for my college career.

I could go on to share some statistics about how women learn better in a single-sex environment or how there are fewer distractions without males in the classroom, but you can already find this information from other sources. I'm here to share my personal experience as a student at a women's college.

When I first shared the news of my decision with friends and family, I heard the various comments ranging from "Are you a lesbian?" to "Another all-girls' school?"

Sure, the comments were harsh, but picking the "perfect" college is a very personal decision. After stepping on campus for the first time, I instantly knew that the school I had chosen—Sweet Briar College—was the right choice for me.

At single-sex institutions, female students are shown from day one that they can do anything. Women serve as presidents, chairwomen, captains, interns, researchers, performers, and most of all—intellects. We see that we can do anything.

In the year that I have been at Sweet Briar, I've been pushed in every direction. I've taken advantage of probably more opportunities than I should have. I don't regret any of my choices, and I certainly wouldn't change anything.

Choosing an all-women's college meant more than a community of learners with at least one thing in common—our gender, of course. To me, a women's college is a family—a *sisterhood*. I'm sure you could find a great group of friends at any college, but how often is it that you can say you found your sisters?

In addition to academics, you may be wondering about what the social scene is like at a women's college. Most of you are probably used to sitting in a classroom full of boys, if you attended a coed high school. Although that is not exactly the case at a women's college, I don't want you to think that you're never going to see guys. Most, if not all, women's colleges have ties with area coed colleges. It's also easy to find and hang out with guys. It's entirely up to you!

Women's colleges certainly aren't for everyone, but it was the best choice for me. If you're thinking about it or are on the fence, I recommend that you visit at least one to see if it might be right for you, too.

REMEMBER, MINORITY DOESN'T MEAN LONELY

It can be hard being in the minority for any reason—political, ethnic, or religious. But remember that even though you're not the majority, that does not mean you are alone. Think about it this way: if all the minorities got together, we would likely rival the majority. Take solace in that fact, and remember that if you're feeling alone, someone else is probably feeling the same. Perhaps you can help each other out so that neither of you have to be sad in your perceived solitude.

HAVE FAITH

When it comes to surviving and thriving, being yourself is the only thing to hold on to. If your beliefs come under siege, having faith is mandatory. People can try to threaten your beliefs through hurtful words, vandalism, or just general meanness. I wish I could say that never happens, but it does. However, no one can take away your beliefs or your sense of self worth. End of story.

Staying True to Your Roots

Raneisha Williams, Ripon College

The instant I set foot on campus my first day in college, I could hardly believe what I had gotten myself into. I was truly in the minority—an African American female on a predominantly white campus. I knew that this would be outside my comfort zone. But my desire to learn encouraged me to conquer any fears that I had about going. I simply wanted a good education. Certainly, I have come across racial stereotypes along the way. However, what I've found is that those generalizations are based on ignorance rather than hate. Instead of getting upset when people have questioned my abilities or counted me out, I have worked harder to prove myself. This means that I always have to be on my toes, but the funny thing is, I have been doing that my whole life.

So here I am, and I'm not backing down. Instead of accepting how things currently are, I am constantly searching for ways to alleviate racial tension and discrepancies. And, because of this, I feel powerful. If you're in a similar situation, it's completely normal to feel that people may not quite understand where you're coming from at times. But if you stay true to yourself, work hard, and make an effort to educate others about where you come from and how you see things, you are taking the best steps forward in getting a great education while helping educate the world.

AND JUST REMEMBER...

If it's important to you, don't lose sight of your identity. Hang on to your values, your traditions, and the connections that you have to your religion and heritage. Create your own community, whether that means joining an existing one or starting from scratch.

Insights provided by Emily Kaplan, University of California–Davis

put an end to homesickness!

I fear change—and college is a big change. So it was no surprise that I spent the majority of my summer before college *freaking out* about the thought of being in a new place without my friends, without my boyfriend, without my family. As if preparing for a coming storm, I went around buying everything that I could think of to start a "home" emergency kit—a stash of items that would remind me of home when I was stuck in a tiny dorm room. Why wouldn't I? In my mind, the dorm was that weird place that conjured up images of girls-gone-wild meets summer camp. I even went so far as to ask my mother to get custom-made bedding inspired by my bedding at home. Sadly, she declined, so to cope I instead bought dorm accessories with the same purple and gold color scheme as my childhood bedroom.

Well, despite all of my numerous breakdowns in the Target store, my first week of college was fine. I think I even had fun during first week's orientation! The wonderful thing about orientation is that they keep you busy with so many activities that you forget to be homesick. And most of these activities are the special kind of lame that have you instantly bonding with members of your orientation group just to survive. Voila! Instant friendships.

AFTER THE FIRST WEEK

But the real challenge during your transition to college is after orientation—your first unstructured weekend. I almost couldn't handle it. Who was I supposed to hang out with? These people weren't really my friends; I'd known them for only five days! And communal bathrooms? I was so over it after the first time some random guy caught me shaving my legs in the sink.

I just wanted to go home and see my best friend, watch a movie with my boyfriend, and pee in the privacy of my own bathroom. Between you and me, I almost did. I was about 5 minutes away from booking a train ticket home for the first weekend when I gave myself a pause. I realized that if I went running for the comforts of suburbia every time things became uncomfortable, I'd spend my college experience in a friendless black hole with nothing but my books to keep me company. So, against my instincts to cut and run, I decided to stay. Looking back, that decision was the best one I have made over the course of my 4 years at school. In fact, I met some of the girls who would become my best friends at school that weekend.

Renee and I were both terminally bored at a tropically-themed Alpha Epsilon Pi frat party (read: warm jungle juice and underdeveloped shirtless frat boys). We both decided to leave the party in exchange for a band's live show elsewhere on campus.

That was one of the best nights of my college career. After that, Renee and I started going out to events that interested us rather than the ones that felt "college-y," and eventually found a lot of people were interested in doing the same. Once I started finding things I liked to do and inviting people, I made friends.

Once I started making more friends and building a life by taking risks and going out with new people, the homesickness went away. If you're concerned that you may, too, experience a difficult transition, there are several things you can do to make the transition a little bit easier and get yourself out of the funk a little bit faster.

> And communal bathrooms? I was so over it after the first time some random guy caught me shaving my legs in the sink.

TRY SOME PREEMPTIVE PEP TALK

Just take a deep breath and accept it: you are probably going to get homesick. It may vary in degrees of awfulness, but at some point, you are going to miss the people and places that you encountered every day for the past 18 years. Don't suppress these feelings: it's completely natural and pretty common. If you go into college thinking you are never going to miss anyone or anything, you are setting yourself up for a fall and may be caught off guard, unable to deal with the unexpected sad feelings. By taking the time to accept the fact that you may get lonely or begin to miss home a time or two, you can prepare yourself rather than being surprised by these feelings of homesickness. It may be hard to deal with these emotions, but it isn't impossible. This preemptive pep talk goes a long way.

IT'S OK TO BRING THINGS THAT REMIND YOU OF HOME, BUT DON'T BRING *HOME*

Sure, bring a few pictures of your friends and family, your favorite stuffed animal, and maybe even a special tchotchke. (The ceramic pony my dad gave me when I was 7 will always be on my desk regardless of what anyone says.) They are even good conversation starters. It makes complete sense that you want to surround yourself with familiar things, but there is a limit to how much. Filling up your new space with remnants of the past makes it really difficult to enjoy the present. (Plus your roommate may not appreciate all your trinkets from home.) It is probably not a good idea to bring all of your yearbooks from high school, your collection of sweatshirts from old boyfriends, or that sweater you haven't worn since you were 7 but swear you can still smell your first grade teacher's perfume on.

You're in college to make new memories and develop into a well-rounded person. How to do this? Make sure your 8 x 10-foot cell of a dorm room has space for your new life. It will fill up before you know it.

It is probably not a good idea to bring all of your yearbooks from high school, your collection of sweatshirts from old boyfriends, or that sweater you haven't worn since you were 7 but swear you can still smell your first grade teacher's perfume on.

GET YOURSELF OUT THERE

It may be easier to go to bed early or spend hours in the library in order to get ahead in your classes, and these are good habits in most cases, but taking it to the extreme can lead to a dangerous pattern. Even worse, you could have done the very same thing at home! You're ignoring the perks and pleasures of college life, and that's not healthy.

Take advantage of being in college by seizing those opportunities to socialize and meet people you would not have met otherwise. It might feel like you're putting yourself out on the line by trying to hang out with new people, so to make it easier, simply join a new club, write for the student newspaper, or strike up a conversation with someone in your freshman seminar course. What do you have to lose? For the first few weeks, everyone is looking to make friends, so people will be receptive. After you introduce yourself, it's only awkward for the first few minutes of conversation, or until you find out that Sarah in your Intro to Poli Sci course also shares your love of obscure Austrian electro hip-hop.

Once you start talking, you'll be amazed at how much you have in common with and have to learn from the new people around you.

After you introduce yourself, it's only awkward for the first few minutes of conversation, or until you find out that Sarah in your Intro to Poli Sci course also shares your love of obscure Austrian electro hip-hop.

KEEP IN TOUCH WITH FRIENDS AND FAMILY, BUT TO A REASONABLE DEGREE

Thanks to the communication age we live in, you can call, text, email, instant message, Skype, or Facebook all the people you left behind for hours on end. But try not to. It's hard at first, but spending hours talking to people via whatever your preferred communication method might mean that you are losing precious hours of face-to-face conversation with people at your college. A good rule of thumb: until you have started building a niche for yourself at school, avoid spending more time talking to people from home than you do talking to your classmates.

My freshman-year roommate talked to her boyfriend for about 8 hours a day. I really wasn't surprised when she transferred to her boyfriend's college after first semester because she felt so alone.

It makes it harder to create a home at school when you're constantly talking to people from home. Plus your best friend is trying to make friends at her own school, so give her—and yourself—a chance to create a new life for yourselves at college.

U Chic Tip! Relying on Old and New Friends
Melanie Harris, Virginia Tech

Let's say that you're having a difficult time and need to chat with your old friends for some support. Go for it. Don't hesitate to call your besties from high school, but do so only when you need to or have something particularly great to share—definitely not every day. I can't emphasize enough how important it is to work on building a new life, and you can't move on when you're too much in touch with your old pals. And really, it's not fair to be calling or texting them all the time.

As an alternative to calling old friends *all* the time, reach out to your new friends. The National Mental Health Association encourages students to seek support from a roommate or a friend from class. Friendships can help make a strange place feel more friendly and comfortable. Sharing your emotions reduces isolation and helps you realize that you are not alone. This way, you're working on making a new life for yourself and moving on in a healthy way. Before you know it, these new bonds and connections will change your whole outlook on the college experience for the better, and your old friends might happily end up wondering why you're not calling as often as you used to.

REALIZE THAT MOST STUDENTS ARE GOING THROUGH THE SAME THING

It may seem like everyone is having an easier time making friends and having a life than you—but they aren't. Most of the time, people like to act like they're partying every night and have thousands of friends. This is actually a fact you may learn in your first psychology course—if you act popular, people are more likely to perceive you as popular. But deep down, everyone feels a little lost and alone at the start of school. It's just that people show it in different ways. If you are feeling really alone, reach out to someone—your roommate or a hall-mate—and say, "I'm feeling a little alone. How are you coping with all of this?" If you think that is lame, just take solace in the fact that everybody is feeling a little disoriented and may appreciate the opportunity to share their feelings. I guarantee that you will quickly discover that you are not the only one feeling alone. Think of it this way: if someone confided their feelings, you would hear them out without hesitation.

Skype Away the Homesick Blues

Victoria Reitano, Quinnipiac University

I became a fan of Skype while living in Italy. It helped me talk to my mom every day (something we've always done) and still keep the costs low. Skype also helps me keep in touch with my friends now that I've graduated. We all moved around the East Coast for jobs and family obligations, and it's hard to travel to see one another on a weekly basis. Our solution? We Skype. It's the same as "seeing" the other person, and if you schedule it at lunch or dinner, it's like you're having a meal together. Train your parents, boyfriend, and friends on how to use it, and you'll never have to worry about being homesick.

GET SOME STRUCTURE

The first week of college feels like a scene out of *Camp Nowhere* where everyone can run around and do whatever they want, whenever they want. That's kind of cool after having your life scheduled down to the minute in high school. But trust me: it takes almost a week, but this kind of freedom does lose its novelty. Don't forget that your goal is to build a life at school, not to become a professional spring-breaker. Once you start classes, join clubs, become active, and find people to join you at the dining hall, you'll find that all these things require a schedule, and a structured schedule is your best friend. You'll waste hours wondering what you are going to do and who you are going to do it with if you're not careful, so embrace your fabulously busy life with a fabulous schedule.

STAY TRUE TO YOURSELF

There are some tempting shortcuts to getting over homesickness, including things like drinking a lot, sleeping with random boys, or joining the chess club even though it bores you to tears. In short, it is easy to silence who you really are for the sake of having companions. But remember, if you build false relationships now, they won't last, and you'll find yourself lonely again. It may suck to feel alone during the early stages, but it's going to suck more when you find yourself friendless at the end of second semester because you feigned an interest in being in a sorority. Or conversely, you shunned sororities because a friend told you to, even though you knew it was right for you. Take the time to build true friendships that are based on your real interests at the very beginning of school. I promise it will pay off later.

U Chic Tip! Care Packages Go a Long Way

My mom sends me care packages for everything; it has been the one saving grace of my college experience. I went to London to study abroad for a semester and she sent me packages filled with Oreos and American peanut butter. I was the most popular Yank in my flat! If you are feeling sad, ask your parents for a care package—it's a nice way to be reminded that people out there love you. And offers of your mom's chocolate chunk cookies are great icebreakers for making new friends.

TRY NOT TO GO OVERBOARD

For every girl who thinks staying in her room doing nothing is the best way to cure homesickness, there will be another that has to join every club, get every person's number, and knock on everyone's door. Don't be that girl either. She generally ends up burned-out and friendless because she annoys people. It is great to put yourself out there to make a big network of friends and activities, but don't force it to happen right away. Bottom line: it's about the quality, not quantity, of friendships. So what if you only play one sport or only have one or two really good friends at first? If these friends are fun and worth your time, you only need a few. And definitely don't worry about winning any popularity contest. By the end of college you will have tons of friends and way too many activities; just give it time.

IF IT DOESN'T GET BETTER, TALK TO A COUNSELOR

There is a difference between being a little (or even a lot) sad about missing home and being depressed. If months go by and you still really hate school, your grades suffer, you can't stop crying, and you sleep too much or not enough, go talk to someone. There are counseling centers on every college campus that are there to help students cope with homesickness or any other issues on your mind. Going to college means a lot of new and wonderful opportunities, but it also means a lot of changes that we aren't always equipped to handle.

If you are lucky enough to never be homesick, I certainly envy you. But if you are, these tips are a surefire way to beat homesickness. Once you do that, you're ready for four unforgettable years.

Insights provided by Allison Davis, Barnard College

U Chic Essentials—Getting Started

Stay true to yourself

It is tempting to silence who you really are for the sake of having companions. But remember, if you build false relationships now, they won't last, and you'll find yourself lonely again.

Limit too much contact with your past

Until you have started building a niche for yourself at school, avoid spending more time talking to people from home than your new classmates.

Get some structure

The best remedy for homesickness? Getting out and getting involved. As soon as you hit the campus pavement, start looking for opportunities to get involved and meet new people. And before you know it, there won't be any time in your schedule to miss home.

Looking for more great advice? Head to www.UChic.com for our fave resources and websites—they come highly recommended from our guide's contributors and editors. Be sure to leave your suggestions as well!

CHAPTER 2

Sharing Space

*T*he previous chapter was all about making the transition to college. In this chapter, our writers dish on another early-stage college experience—sharing space with a roommate. Sharing a room in the dorms—especially when the room is an itty-bitty hole in the wall—is no easy feat. For those of you who were privileged with pimped-out bedrooms and private baths back home, get ready for a change. Before you even arrive, common questions you may face include: Should I room with my BFF from high school? What if my roommate is a freak? Where do I find extra-long bed sheets? Are coed dorms the way to go? Is the scholarship hall or sorority house for me? It's normal to have all of these concerns and questions when it comes to sharing space.

Here's the low-down on how to "live it up" in college no matter what your living situation may be.

the preliminaries

Once I received that fateful acceptance letter detailing my dorm information the summer before my freshman year, I immediately assigned all my new roommates code names. I knew very little about them at this point, just their first and last names, hometowns, and pretty much all the information I could gather from their Facebook profiles.

For the three weeks leading up to freshman move-in day, my future roomies and I spent a lot of time messaging each other back and forth about who would bring stuff like the fridge, TV, etc. I told all of my friends back home how I would be living with "Nineties Girl" (who flashed a peace sign and wore ripped, faded jeans and a black crop top in her profile picture), "The Party Nerd" (who had a profile picture of her aiming for a beer pong cup preceded by a profile picture of her wearing a Science Olympiad tee), and the "Tomboy" (the tough-looking lacrosse and hockey pics said it all).

Sure, me and my friends from high school found the whole thing amusing, but imagine my shock when I met them in the flesh and all my expectations and prejudgments flew right out the window. Here we were, these four girls, trapped together in the middle of a huge storm during a power outage, forced to camp out in a makeshift space at the giant science center on campus. We had no choice *but* to bond! (Trust me, breaking the ice isn't that hard when you're trapped in a strange place, in all your messy hair and smeared makeup glory, with nothing to do but chat it up until the powers-that-be figure out a way to get the backup generators running again.)

By the time the electricity came back on, I had a pretty good sense of who I would be living with, and *they* had a pretty good idea as to who and what I was all about. Like the storm that brought us together, we had weathered the worst, and our relationships with each other proved better for it.

ICEBREAKERS THAT WON'T LEAVE YOU OUT IN THE COLD

The key to getting to know your new roommate is to be proactive. Don't wait until a few weeks before school starts to drop her a line—do it as soon as you have her information sitting right in front of you. Introduce yourself via email/Facebook, chat up your background a bit (keep it brief), and start facilitating a conversation about the logistics of living together. Something as simple as offering to bring your DVD player can spark a dialogue about which movies you both like (just one surefire way to get a sense of who and *what* your new roomie is all about).

Tip 1: Break the ice

While it's fine to talk a bit about yourself, do make sure to ask *her* questions and genuinely think about the responses you get before you make any judgments. If she's your total carbon copy, great. But if not, that doesn't mean the two of you won't get along. Keep in mind, this is just as weird and awkward for her, so it might take a little while before she warms up and starts sharing more personal things.

Tip 2: Dip your toes in

Once you've established an email relationship, take the next step and suggest a weekly phoner. This is your chance to talk about more in-depth topics like class schedules, room decor options, likes, dislikes, and personal pet peeves. Be honest—not brutal. If she's obsessed with Hello Kitty and has her heart set on an all-pink bedroom, this is the time to gently let her know that's not your thing, but you're open to compromise. The same thing goes for any obvious personality quirks that may derail your relationship down the road. If she's the ultimate social butterfly and you're a total bookworm, don't be afraid to speak up and let her know you prefer not to have any guests over while you're trying to study.

Tip 3: Dive in headfirst

Meeting your new roommate is like going on a date—first impressions are everything. Before you even hit the dorms, turn off your cell phone, slip on a smile, and vow to give her your full attention. Still nervous? Why not bring something special like a batch of your mom's cookies to share, or a movie or book she's been meaning to buy. In each instance, a simple gift shows you're not only excited about living with her, but also invested in the idea of making it a positive experience.

Insights provided by Kylie Thompson, Harvard University

bringing some sanity to dorm-room chaos

When you're entering college as a freshman, it can seem that the classes and the countless hours studying, preparing presentations, and writing papers are the defining focal points of your new life. But an equally important part of the college experience involves your living situation. Whether you're required to live in a dorm as a first-year student or you opt for off-campus housing, here's some advice on how to manage dorm-room chaos while making the best out of any living situation.

CONTACT YOUR ROOMMATE-TO-BE

Many colleges will allow you to choose your roommate ahead of time—like your best friend from high school who's attending the same college. This may seem like a no-brainer. But a word of advice here: while choosing to live with a current friend can be a good choice because she's someone you already know and love (it's comfortable!), living with someone that you've never met can be a great way to become exposed to an entirely new set of friends.

I didn't have many high school friends who were going to the same college, so I opted to allow the university to choose a roommate for me. My new roommate, Grace, was completely different from me in family background, music tastes, clothing, and pretty much everything else under the sun. At first, I was worried that we wouldn't get along, considering my abiding love of Britney Spears and celebrity gossip websites and her complete distaste for these "frivolous" things. But for the most part, it was a great experience. Yes, she liked to listen to the Aquabats and hang slides from her presentation on leprosy in our window, but these initial annoyances taught me to be tolerant of others and be open to someone else's tastes. Because I kept an open mind, I was exposed to films, music, and people I would probably never have encountered if left to my own devices. Since she was a junior—a couple years older than me—Grace was also a good source of information on important things, from where to grab a bite on campus to negotiating the vast library system. She was virtually

> a stranger to me when we met, but over time and with an open mind,
> we came to enjoy each other's company.

For those of you who decide to live with someone entirely new, your college will usually send you the contact information for your new roomie and vice versa. A great way to break the ice is to contact her before you even arrive on campus. Connecting via Facebook, Twitter, email, or even by phone can set you up for an easier go of it once you actually move in. Introduce yourself and find out what each of your expectations are for living together. This is also a great chance to get to know each other. Who knows? You may already form a bond before you move in! You can get a general idea of what your roommate will be like from these conversations. No matter what, keeping an open mind is really important when you first start out.

A FEW THINGS TO CONSIDER ASKING YOUR ROOMIE-TO-BE

- **What is she planning to bring?** Being able to decide who is bringing what and when you are moving in makes life easier once you get there. Items that are usually split between roommates can be things such as futons, TVs, mini refrigerators, microwaves, rugs, etc. If you talk before move-in day, you can decide who will bring what items and then you won't have two TVs and no futon. Splitting the costs of these items can also help alleviate the financial strain as you begin the new school year.

- **When is she planning to move in?** It might be a good idea to coordinate your move on the same day, as this prevents one person from claiming their part of the room without consulting the other. Also, the two of you can configure the furniture and decorate the room in a way that is mutually acceptable.

- **Is she a morning person or a night owl?** Differences in sleeping schedules can pose a problem when on the first night you find out that she keeps the lights blazing 'til 1 a.m. and you're in bed by 9 p.m. sharp. Knowing her personal schedule beforehand can prevent an unexpected surprise when it's time to get some shut-eye. Consider buying a sleep mask and some high-quality earplugs. These can block the light of your roomie's desk lamp and the "ping" of her instant messaging when you're trying to catch some much-needed z's.

- **Would she like to grab coffee or lunch the first day you meet?** If you can't move in on the same day, no worries. As soon as the dust settles, invite your roommate to go to coffee, have lunch, or just take a walk through campus. By making an effort to get to know her, you show that you care about being a good roommate and possibly even friends.

MOVE-IN DAY

Moving is stressful for anyone, and it seems as if the move from home to college is the most stressful of the bunch. Not only are you worried about physically moving your things from home to your dorm room, but you also are nervous about meeting new people, especially your roommate. Add in the emotion that goes along with leaving your family, and it just might put you over the edge. Remembering to keep calm and maintain a good attitude while moving may be your saving grace. Don't let your emotions get the best of you! If you're really anxious, get in touch with an older family member or friend who has just been through the process. Share how you're feeling, and ask for their advice. Simply getting these feelings off your chest with someone will go miles in helping you de-stress about the big day.

Some universities and colleges assign you to a side of the room, but if not, try to communicate in advance with your roommate on options. Even if they say they don't care, giving them the option to be involved in the decision makes them feel like a part of the team and gets you off on the right foot. But realize they may choose the side you really wanted. So if you are partial to a particular side, let it be known as soon as possible. Also, splitting the space as evenly as possible is important. And last but not least, try to unpack your things in a timely manner, making the space feel like home as soon as possible. This will help the transition to college feel more real without all those distracting boxes sitting around. After all, once class begins, you won't have much time to take care of this important chore.

KNOW AND MAKE KNOWN YOUR BOUNDARIES

So you've moved in your stuff and shared some pizza slices and a chat. But what happens when you discover some red flags about your roommate? Maybe you find out that she has a long-term boyfriend who's big on PDA and wants to hang in your room on a nightly basis. Or does she listen to Evergreen Terrace and Avenged Sevenfold while you're an Alicia Keys and Sara Bareilles fan? Worst-case scenario: she's allowing drugs or alcohol in the room and, through guilt by association, you could potentially get in trouble.

Though you generally can't control what other people do, being clear about what is or isn't acceptable will make it easier for you to voice your opinions without having to second-guess yourself.

A few BIG things to remember:

Do not borrow your roommate's things without asking

I know it is tempting when you don't have any clean clothes (or even when you do have clean clothes) to hop over to your roommate's closet and borrow her favorite sweater because luckily it looks great on you too! But unless you've asked, I urge you to stay away. Walking on campus and seeing your roommate scoot by in your clothes when she didn't even take a second to ask you may be grounds for an argument.

If, by chance, you do borrow your roommate's things without asking, make sure to return the item(s) in their original condition, washed (if worn), and in a timely manner. If she asks about it, apologize and tell her it won't happen again…then don't let it happen again. Remembering how you would feel in that situation is important because you should treat others as you would like to be treated.

Do your part around your dorm room

Splitting the chores, such as dusting, sweeping, and taking out the trash, is a crucial part of living on campus and with a roommate. Make sure once you've decided who is doing what, you really stick to that deal. If your roommate is constantly the one cleaning up the mess, she may start to resent you and that is the last thing you want while living together. Just do your part and chip in to buy cleaning supplies when needed.

U Chic Tip! Your RA Is Your Best Ally

If drugs are involved, go speak with your Resident Assistant immediately. These things are illegal, and you should not have to put up with them.

DEALING WITH TENSION AND CONFLICT

People do not always get along. Even if you initially hit it off with your roommate, it does not mean that later down the road, after spending so much time together, you may not get into an argument or two. There are many reasons why arguments begin but if you handle them correctly, you may be able to avoid some major blowouts.

If there are situations with your roommate that are bugging you, talk to her about it. Don't let the little things build up. Your roommate may not have any idea that what she's doing is bothering you. Some people simply have a higher threshold as to what is acceptable behavior around others. For instance, she might not think that having her friend lean his greasy bike against your bed frame is offensive, while you may be deeply disturbed.

If you feel uncomfortable with something that's happening, let your roommate know. Don't be afraid that you're being inconsiderate by voicing your concerns. It's like that famous line in a wedding ceremony: "Speak now or forever hold your peace." Think about it: there's never a "right" time to bring up a topic that's bothering you. But trust me. It'll go better if you speak your mind early on rather than suffering in silence and having that influence your attitude towards her.

Also, if you are having problems with your roommate, talk to her instead of talking about her behind her back. If your roommate hears that you've been talking about her instead of to her, it may cause more trouble than you had before. Everyone needs to vent, but venting to your mom or to your pillow—rather that to fellow classmates—will be less harmful in the long run.

Same goes for the online world. Many people resort to social media as a way to vent. But posting pictures of your roommate's messy side of the room or tweeting about how annoying she is may get you into trouble. After all, you may be potentially violating her privacy to do this, which can get you into a lot of trouble down the road. Talking to your roommate about the problem, instead of venting on Facebook, will allow you to work things out before they blow up. Something is bothering you, but where to begin? Start by speaking up.

Are the Dorms Going to the Dogs?

Have a pet you can't live without? Your dog or cat could be able to live with you at school if you pick a college with pet-friendly dorms. PetSide.com ranked the Top 10 most pet-friendly colleges in 2009. Eckerd College in Florida won the top spot because of its advantageous areas for pets.

Here's an excerpt from Eckerd College's pet policy:

1. Regardless of the circumstances, the pet owner is ultimately responsible for the actions of the pet.

2. All dogs and cats must wear their Eckerd College identification tag and a current rabies vaccination tag at all times.

3. All pets must live with their owners.

4. Unless approved by the Pet Council, visiting pets are not allowed to stay overnight on campus.

5. All dogs and cats must be housebroken before arriving on campus.

6. Pets are not allowed inside academic and administration buildings, except Brown Hall. All pets must be on a leash at all times. And your pet must be under vocal command. Under no circumstances are pets allowed to run around outside unsupervised. Pets are not permitted in residence hall bathrooms.

7. Owners must clean up after their pets.

8. Facilities staff may not enter a room to make repairs or spray for bugs if a pet is inside. Pet owners should call Facilities Management to make arrangements in this case.

9. Owner negligence or mistreatment of a pet will not be tolerated. The Pet Council may refer the case to the Student Community Standards Board for conduct action.

10. Pets attacking other animals or humans will not be tolerated. The Pet Council may refer the case to the Student Community Standards Board for conduct action.

11. Failure to remove a pet from campus will result in a $500 fine and/or conduct action.

Still interested in having your pet with you after reading this policy, which is common to most pet-friendly dorms? For more information on how you can bring your pet with you to college, visit PetSide.com.

COME PREPARED

Since you're sharing a room, each inhabitant is entitled to equal space in said room. However, dorm rooms, being as small as they are, become even smaller once you move in TVs, microwaves, stereo systems, and minifridges. Be considerate of your roommate by not taking up too much of the communal floor space. If you have a bike, store it in a bike room to keep your bedroom clear and prevent dirt from tracking in. Put your laundry basket on top of your closet if there's space, or under your bed.

If you opt for a shared fridge, make sure you don't take up more than your half. Free up even more space by foregoing items like microwaves and mini-ironing boards. Many dorms have kitchenettes on each floor that contain essentials such as microwaves, sinks, ovens, and ironing boards. You can also make an impromptu ironing board by putting a towel on your bed. Basically, it all boils down to coming prepared and being resourceful. Only bring items into the dorm room that you know you will use, and if you're in doubt, leave it at home. It can always be shipped to you later or you can get it during a visit home over the holidays. Space is at a premium, so pack light and enjoy your clutter-free environs.

U Chic Tips for Dorm-Room Bliss!

Tip 1: Must-have furnishings

There are just some things you do not want to neglect bringing, including a file cabinet or several storage bins to keep your papers organized; a rug for those cold dorm-room floors; and tall shelves so you can store a lot without taking up space.

Tip 2: A comfortable bed makes for a comfortable room

You must get extra-long twin sheets. That's the number-one rule for dorm-room bedding because dorm-room beds are notorious for being extra-long. Also, bring several sets of sheets. There will be times when you want clean sheets at 2 a.m. but are obviously not in the mood to do the laundry. Finally, a mattress pad will ensure your much-needed beauty rest.

Tip 3: Utilize every inch of space

Consider lofting your bed. You can usually get lofting kits from maintenance or the front desk of your residence hall. When finished, the area under your bed can become a great place for a comfy chair and a reading lamp, creating another sitting area besides your bed and desk. To additionally free up some space, add hooks to the backs of doors. You'll be surprised how an extra towel or two on the ground can really detract from the room's overall good vibe.

Tip 4: Go green!

If protecting the environment is of concern to you (of course it is!), you can introduce eco-friendliness to your dorm room through green furniture, a recycling bin, and energy-saving items like compact fluorescent light bulbs.

I also recommend making your toiletries as easy to carry as possible by investing in a good shower caddy with holes for water to drain. I made the mistake of buying one that didn't have holes in the bottom, causing water to puddle in the bottom and mold until I had to stab a hole in it myself with a pair of scissors. Also, consider decanting your shampoo, conditioner, body wash, and the like into travel-size bottles. This will lighten your load considerably when you're making morning and nightly treks to the bathroom.

Coed Dorms on the Rise: What You Need to Know

Despite what your parents may say, campus life has changed quite a bit since their college days. With new living arrangements popping up across campuses nationwide, you could be in for a surprise when deciding where to live your freshman year.

Though the traditional view of dorms is same-sex floors or same-sex buildings, many colleges offer alternatives. A majority of colleges, mine included, offer places where members of the opposite sex can live on the same floor.

This has even expanded to coed suites and bedrooms. According to a recent article in *The Sacramento Bee*, there are more than 50 colleges that offer "gender neutral" dorms where members of the opposite sex can share dorm rooms and suites. Though this sounds like an intriguing idea, there are definitely pros and cons to the situation.

Pros:

- Hang with the boys: Want someone to watch the game or play soccer with? You might not have to look any further than your roommate.

- Meet new people: Since you'd be living with a guy, that definitely means there will be more opportunities to meet new boys through his group of friends.

- A guy's perspective: Guys can shed light on our problems in a sincere way and give really good advice. From BFF troubles to boyfriend drama, some guys can really help you work through your problems.

Cons:

- Awkward moments: Since you'd be living in the same room as a guy, you are going to run into some awkward encounters. You'll have to think more about changing in the room or what to do after you hop out of the shower.

- Possible mess alert: If you are a perfectionist about your room staying neat and tidy, make sure the guy you room with is the same way. Guys are typically stereotyped as being messy, so unless you're comfortable with that, ditch the coed dorm room.

- Lack of sensitivity: Guys are usually a lot less sensitive than their female counterparts in most facets of life. If you're not going to miss the dramatic elements of living on a female floor, then this could be for you. However, you're not going to get a lot of sympathy from your boy roomie when you cry for hours and hours over the jerk who dumped you.

UTILIZE OTHER AREAS

So you've talked to your roommate and have made sure that everything fits in your tiny living space. But what to do when she has unexpected guests over? That's one of the great and, at times, most irritating things about the dorms: you're constantly surrounded by people. Certainly, there will be times when you or your roommate will want to invite others to your room to watch movies, eat, or just hang out. This is fine until the day comes when you have to study for an exam and your roommate and her four closest friends want to play *Guitar Hero*. This is a perfect time to check out the other amenities your dorm has to offer. Some dorms have study rooms, usually a windowless room set up with a table and a chair where you can take your laptop and books to read or write in solitude. Maybe there's a lounge on your floor with couches and tables where you can study in relative peace and quiet. Keep in mind, though, since it's a shared space, you may have to vacate if a group decides they want to watch TV.

OTHER AMENITIES TO CONSIDER

Don't forget that you can always leave the dorm and check out a library on campus. Many schools have at least one library that's open late or even 24 hours. If you go after dark, stay safe by taking the bus or call campus security and have someone come and escort you to your destination. Another reason to get out of the dorm: sometimes all you need is a break from your roommate and from your regular surroundings to reset your outlook. We all have to take a break from others at times, even the people we love the most.

When all is said and done, there are going to be moments of great fun and frivolity in dorm life and also some frenzy and frustration, too. Knowing and accepting this ahead of time will make the transition to dorm living a whole lot easier than coming unprepared. Expect that there will be some situations that may catch you off guard or test your annoyance threshold, but overall, the dorm can be a great place to make friends and lay your head down at night.

Insights provided by Madeline Greene,
Minnesota State University, and Anna Prestek,
University of Washington–Seattle

a fashionista's tips
on fitting it all in

How do you fit a roomful of clothing, shoes, and accessories into a tiny 4 x 3-foot cube? No, it isn't a riddle or a math problem; it's the dilemma faced by every fashion-loving college-bound student. Unless you've been blessed with living accommodations that provide you with the luxury of a walk-in closet—and if you have, I seriously doubt you're at college—you face the task of devising a plan to keep your clothes from overflowing into your tiny dorm room or apartment. You need to stock it with the essentials that keep you looking fashionable and fresh, essentials that are practical for both your climate and your busy life as a college student.

Read on to find several easy tips for evaluating your style. Knowing exactly what you like will help you decide what's essential to have in your tiny room and what can be left behind, while at the same time keeping your wardrobe in top shape.

TIP 1: RECOGNIZE THAT YOU CAN'T TAKE IT ALL

I know, it's tough, but unless you've already pared your wardrobe down to favorites and essentials, there's no way you're going to fit every pair of jeans, every purse, or every shoe into your new closet. Some things are going to have to stay behind. But fear not: the next couple steps will help you to make wise decisions about what to bring and what to leave behind.

TIP 2: LIST YOUR FAVORITES

Make a short list of the items in your closet that you turn to again and again, the ones you love to wear. My list includes such things as a plain white peasant top from American Eagle, my black Puma yoga pants, a chunky cream-colored cardigan, my dark skinny jeans, and a pair of chocolate ballet flats, to name a few. Keep your list short, but honest: try to include the things you actually wear often (and not ones you keep meaning to wear often…), and make sure you include items that work together in different combinations to make a wide array of outfits. Finally, classify each favorite by the season in which you would wear it—you can swap out wardrobes for summer and winter—and make sure you've included at least a few seasonless items.

TIP 3: LIST YOUR NECESSITIES

These are the things you wear because you have to: plain black, white, tan, and brown camis, workout clothes, sweats for lazy days, and the obvious socks, underwear, and bras. Depending on where you're going to school, you may also need boots and a winter coat.

TIP 4: EVALUATE YOUR STYLE

Look at your list of favorites and think about the things you wear every day. Women in their late teens and early twenties often do not have a single, developed style and instead toy with various trends and looks, but identifying patterns in the way you dress will make it easier to choose other items to complement those favorites and necessities with old clothes and new. After you identify some of your patterns, try writing a short explanation of your style or making a collage of pictures from magazines and the Internet. This will not only provide some guidance as you expand your list and shop for new items, but may also spark new ideas on how to wear old items as the school year goes on.

TIP 5: GO SHOPPING!

Now that you know what necessities and favorites you'll be bringing along, and have an idea of the sort of style you are aiming for, it's time to go shopping. This may seem counterintuitive as most college living arrangements provide little space for clothing, but shopping smart will actually allow you to bring less, buy less later, and look better more often.

Look for gaps in your lists and fill them with versatile items that fit into the style you're going for. Personally, I'm lacking in the dressy-top department, especially when it comes to fall and winter pieces, and could use a few new pairs of comfortable walking shoes. I will definitely stock up on these things and will look for items that fit into the new earthy, richly detailed style I seem to be gravitating toward lately.

I'll also look for items that will complement those things I'm already sure to bring and wear—things like neutral-colored cardigans and shrugs, simple silver jewelry, and leather belts that will keep the same outfits looking new and fresh, even if I have to repeat them twice in one week. If you're on a budget or just want to save some money (we are college students, after all), check out stores like T.J.Maxx, Filene's Basement, or Saks Off 5th, where great deals and unique pieces can always be found.

TIP 6: PLAN FOR THE SEASONS

If you're attending a school in a climate where you'll see all four seasons, you'll need to plan accordingly. However, if you will be making it home during or before Thanksgiving break, this may not be a horrible problem. Pack those things that you would wear in summer and early fall—and a few warmer items—along with a winter coat in case temperatures drop early. But plan to switch your warmer weather clothes out for your winter ones when you return home in November.

If you're far away from Mom and Dad's house, consider setting aside your cool-weather clothes and arrange to have your parents ship them to you at a certain date, at which time you'll ship back some of the lighter things you'll no longer need. If neither of these things seems to be an option, Space Bags (www.spacebag.com) can be a good alternative for storing bulky things like coats and sweaters until they are needed.

TIP 7: GET THE GEAR

Finding a way to utilize your closet space is essential when living in a dorm or apartment. Before you head off to school, consider picking up a second rod for your closet (it hangs from the built-in rod and doubles your hanging space), a belt hanger (doubles as a purse hanger), quality plastic-tube hangers, and a hanging shoe rack. Also, make sure you check with your school as to what sort of drawer space you'll be provided. Plastic drawer towers can be a great addition or alternative to a traditional dresser.

TIP 8: LEARN BY TRIAL AND ERROR

Even with the amount of planning I put into my college wardrobe before moving into my dorm, I still ended up overpacking and devoting a significant space in my 4 x 8-foot closet to clothes I didn't wear all semester.

Many of us, myself included, are chronic overpackers, exceeding the weight limit on our bags every time we fly even if we're just taking a five-day vacation. For people like us, entirely avoiding the curse of too many clothes may not be possible, but this general rule of thumb will help us overpackers stay on track: if it's too much to fit in the trunk of a normal-sized car (not a station wagon or SUV), it's probably too much. After seeing my roommate's family's eyes pop when my dad carried my clothes from our car to my dorm room, I realized I should have adhered a bit more strongly to this rule.

Even those who don't overpack are still likely to end up with at least a few items that never get worn. Many girls change their style a bit after spending a few weeks or months on campus, and some (like myself) simply realize that those cute leather flats aren't friendly to their feet during their daily treks to class. You'll learn what works and what doesn't as the year goes on, and when it becomes clear that an item has lost its place in your closet, you have several options. If it's possible, send whatever you aren't wearing at school home. You can also consider trading unwanted items with other girls in your dorm, or sending them off to a thrift store. If you're getting rid of brand-name clothing that is still in good condition, you may be able to find a resale or consignment shop that will either pay you for your used clothing or allow you to buy space to sell it within their store and make a little money off your oldies but goodies.

The more time you spend at college, the more you'll start to understand your college style, and the easier it will become to figure out what you truly need and what you can trash.

And with a little planning and creativity, you'll be able to create a college wardrobe that meets your lifestyle needs and keeps you looking stylish, even when space is limited.

Insights provided by Alyssa Vande Leest, University of Wisconsin

sloppy roommates?
simple solutions

We've all dealt (or will soon deal!) with messy living quarters—overflowing trash cans, mildew-ridden shower floors, piled-high plates in the kitchen sink. Whether your freshman roommate was randomly chosen by the school or you live with your best friend who turns out to be a total slob, messy roommates can really ruin a room's mood and possibly ruin friendships if not dealt with properly. And aside from the strain that messiness can put on relationships, it can really affect your schoolwork thanks to its drain on your motivation to stay organized.

MAKING THE MOST OF COMMUNAL LIVING AREAS

Learning to cope with other people's lifestyles is one of the major stresses you'll face during your transition to college. Start out by agreeing on some rules and making sure that everyone is clear on how the communal space should look. My senior-year suite had one bathroom, a living room, and three very tiny bedrooms for six girls. The word "messy" was an understatement. The first weekend, we each had our own idea of "fun" in the suite. Before heading out to the bar, Tracy and I decided to have our friends over for a party. Our other roommate, "Denise," was a little less enthusiastic about our fun, and I guess I can't blame her. The littered floor and the loud music coming from our bedroom probably did not make for a welcoming first weekend for her. Needless to say, Denise called a suite meeting soon after to go over some "ground rules." The meeting caught me off guard, because the last thing I wanted was someone telling me how to live. But once it started, I realized it was a positive thing for all of us.

First, each person got a chance to share her pet peeves no matter how silly they sounded to say out loud, and then we discussed ways to avoid each other's pet peeves. One roommate, "Jesse," had a real pet peeve about the trash not being emptied in a timely manner. Funny, though, we quickly learned that trash was the *least* of our problems.

One roommate—I never did find out who—had a terrible habit of leaving her birth-control patch stuck to the shower wall. No one ever admitted to the deed, but addressing it in the meetings actually made the mystery stop. Apparently the embarrassment of an open discussion was enough to make the patch bandit rethink the error of her ways. Sometimes, just addressing common issues can help put an end to them. The meeting was such a success that we held similar ones on a regular basis all year to keep us all on track. I'd highly suggest that you follow a similar strategy with your roommates.

Funny, though, we quickly learned that trash was the least of our problems.

MESS = STRESS

For me, exam time equals major stress. I tend to look for anything and everything else to do before I sit down to study. I need complete silence to concentrate, and if there is any clutter around me, I can't focus. In fact, I use the clutter as an excuse not to study, and it's usually my own piles of clothes and dirty dishes that need to be picked up before I hit the books.

Poor organizational skills really affect my study sessions. When I was in high school and couldn't find my notebooks, books, pens, and paper, I could enlist my mom's help. She stayed on my back about being organized, and if I didn't do it, she usually did. Probably not a good thing because once I arrived at college, it was up to me to find my way and learn a whole new set of skills that I didn't have at the time. My first semester was rough. From the new dorm to new friends to new classes, I was a mess. Literally. The stress of all the change finally made me realize that I needed to change, too. With my roommate's help, the two of us became more organized together. Simple things like designating a spot for common items made a world of difference. Assigning a spot for my books, jacket, keys, and bag helped me start organizing the rest of my life.

If the mess in your room is unavoidable, try going to the library to study. As discussed, most dorms also have a study lounge on each floor. It will serve as a night getaway from the clutter of your room and a great place to focus on your exams.

WAYS TO ESTABLISH ORDER

Now, holding meetings does not necessarily ensure that all will go smoothly. Some people are stubborn and may not be willing to change their bad habits—like ordering pizza and leaving the box and uneaten slices on the table overnight. Ants or no ants, some people refuse to modify their behavior. Also, it can be tricky if you are living with someone you barely know, but don't let this make you give up. If cleanliness is important to you, let them know, but do so without nagging them. No one wants to feel like she's being parented by one of her peers. I've had roommates in the past who ambushed me with cleaning "rules." This approach will surely add to the already-existing tension in your 10 x 12-foot dorm room. Rather than jumping on your roommates, try being polite to start the communication process.

A way to avoid the appearance of nagging is to try to compromise with a sloppy roommate. Don't like the way your roommate leaves her shoes lying around the room? Set up a space for both of you to put your stuff away. That way, your roommate won't feel as though she is being told what to do, but that you're both working together to keep things in order.

Take advantage of the relationship that you've built, and appreciate the fact that you know your roommate on a different level than most people do. Don't put a strain on this unique relationship because of something silly like a pile of clothes on the ground.

> If you, your roommate, and your RA can't find a solution for how to live with one another, it may be time to request a new roommate.

ROOMMATES WHO REFUSE TO MEND THEIR MESSY WAYS

I'm notorious for complaining about other people's bad habits and not noticing that I, too, am guilty of the same thing. Before flying off the handle about your roommate's messy tendencies, take a deep breath and look at your own side of the room. Make sure that you are respectful of your roommate's space before you start complaining about her mess.

If all else fails, never be afraid to turn to your Resident Assistant (RA) for help. They are trained to deal with the common and uncommon issues that arise between roommates. If you, your roommate, *and* your RA can't find a solution for how to live with one another, it may be time to request a new roommate.

That's not to say that every roommate experience will work itself out. Friends of mine have had roommates who did drugs in the room, and some even stole from them. These things are not acceptable. It's up to you to know when you've reached your limit. There is always a solution, and if need be, don't be afraid to ask for a new roomie. RAs are used to these kinds of issues, and most are happy to help you find a roommate that better suits you.

When I was a freshman in college, my boyfriend went to another school, so when he came to visit, he was always in my room. Not only was it cramped and crowded for the two of us, but also for my poor roommate. She didn't exactly want a sleep-in guest all weekend long. It's a huge adjustment, and it's really important to be aware of not only your own needs and your guy's, but also how your roommate feels about having your guy around all the time. And if your roommate is unhappy with the situation, you need to ask your boy to leave soon.

THE OPPOSITE SEX

Try not to be the girlfriend who is always around—no one likes that girl. Give your guy some space, and ask that he do the same for you. Don't leave your junk lying around his room, and if he's being messy in your room, talk about it and work through it together. Communicate, communicate, communicate! If necessary, your or his RA can regulate how many nights people are staying over and put a stop to anything that is making you uncomfortable.

MAKING IT WORK

When a bunch of different personalities are thrown into one small living space, friends or not, people are bound to butt heads. Take responsibility for your own actions and belongings. If something's bothering you, talk about it. It's important to remember that you're living in a shared space, and rules that existed at home don't always follow you to college. But if you respect one another, your roommate situation will be a success.

Insights provided by Katie Reynolds,
Central Connecticut State University

making the move off campus

You may reach a point in your college career where you want to explore ditching the dorms and moving off campus. Many students do this as a way to solve the problem of warring roommates, being stuck with a party animal, or just wanting more personal space.

Considering an off-campus move but can't decide? Try making a list of the pros and cons to moving off campus to help guide the decision. Here is a list that I came up with to help get you started.

PROS

- You have complete control over your own space to arrange and decorate as you see fit. And it's always nice to have your own personal space, so you don't have to hide behind a closet door so your dorm-mate doesn't see you change.

- You have the opportunity to establish a rental history—valuable when you apply for other apartments down the road.

- It's not the most responsible reason, but once you're off campus you can throw parties without worrying about Resident Assistants breaking them up.

- Because you're the one cooking the food, it's likely a million times better than what's being served in the dining hall.

- There's something to be said for a bathroom where you don't have to wait in line for the shower and the outlets don't short out because 16 girls are trying to blow-dry their hair at the same time.

- Student apartments are usually pretty reasonable price-wise. I paid a mere $550 per month for a decent-sized room (it's probably a bit more expensive these days) that had its own bathroom, a covered parking space, and all utilities included. Yes, the apartment had lime green shag carpeting that was probably originally installed when Nixon was in office, but it was so worth it to have my own space when it came to studying and sleeping.

CONS

- Unlike in the dorm, you no longer have a built-in network of friends. You're lucky if you even see your neighbors, let alone meet them. This was something I had to deal with as an apartment-dweller; it seemed lonely without the constant flow of people coming in and out.

- You now have to deal with apartment management. Mine was a strange, senile man who would come into our apartment with no advance notice and ask, "Do you live here?" as if he had forgotten we had ever moved in. Some apartment managers seem to go out of their way to take advantage of inexperienced college student renters. Take what happened to us: our manager "lost" the list where we noted all the preexisting damages upon moving in, and my roommates and I had to pay for things that were broken long before we got there. Word to the wise: always, always make a copy of any document between you and the management and always send correspondence regarding legal matters, such as giving notice of moving out, via certified mail. Having a documented paper trail will save you from a lot of potential headaches in case something gets "lost."

- Those meals you cook? You also have to clean them up. Including the kitchen. And the bathroom. And the living room. Tasks that were once performed by a janitorial service, such as taking out the trash, are now yours. Although to a lesser degree, you still have to deal with roommates and their annoying quirks. Maybe someone doesn't take their turn doing the dishes or shortchanges you on a utility payment; whatever it is, there may still be problems with your roommate, they'll just be different problems.

- If you throw parties, the dorm staff won't break them up—but the police will.

SO YOU'VE DECIDED TO MAKE THE MOVE

If you've already decided to head off campus, now it's time to get serious about looking for your new home. The best places to look for an apartment are classifieds in student newspapers, Craigslist (www.craigslist.org), and word of mouth. Walk around the neighborhood you want to live in and look for vacancy signs. Check out a few places with your potential apartment-mates and make sure everyone agrees on a place before signing anything. Take pictures of each potential unit to compare later; after looking at, say, five units, it will be difficult to distinguish one from another. Talk to parents who have been down this road and friends who are already renting to make sure you know what to look for before you sign on the dotted line. Is it a year's lease or month-to-month? Is the damage deposit refundable? When is the rent due and where is it due? Just make sure you read everything before signing the lease, and if you're unsure, ask if you can read it over and then fax or mail back after signing.

Whether you decide to stay in the dorms until graduation or leave after your first cafeteria meal, you will encounter situations there that will make you wheeze with laughter, roll your eyes in frustration, or thank the Almighty that it didn't happen in your room. If you move off campus, you do have to take on more responsibility, but you also gain a better understanding of what it takes to make it in the post-collegiate world. And no matter where you live in college, you're in for a once-in-a-lifetime experience!

Insights provided by Anna Prestek,
University of Washington–Seattle

U Chic Essentials—Sharing Space

A fabulous dorm design

Your dorm room—a place where you'll be spending lots of time—should reflect who you are as a person. Love music? Try a rock icon motif. A future Anna Wintour? Deck your walls with vintage *Vogue* covers. Don't be afraid to truly express yourself in your surroundings no matter how girlie you want or do not want to go.

Accessorize it!

We all know how that right accessory can make an outfit perfect. The same goes for your dorm room. It's the special touches like some bright-colored window treatment or a funky lampshade that can really make a space your own.

Speak up

Good relationships with your roommates can go a long way in making dorm living tolerable. If things aren't going well, don't be afraid to speak up. And also be open to listening to any grievances that a roommate may have. Most problems can be resolved if both parties are willing to listen and work together.

Looking for more great advice? Head to www.UChic.com for our fave resources and websites—they come highly recommended from our guide's contributors and editors. Be sure to leave your suggestions as well!

CHAPTER 3

Head of the Class

Valedictorian in high school? Honor roll every semester? Maybe neither of these things were you. But guess what: even if you weren't at the head of your class in high school, you can still be a star in college. As any academic advisor will tell you, your high school performance does not determine your potential success in college because college is the time to pursue the things that you are good at. Bottom line: getting to the head of the class is something that everyone can do in college. The secret is that you just have to want it bad enough.

Now, before we dive into the secrets of success in school, we need to set the record straight: getting an A is not everything. It doesn't hurt, of course, but sometimes what you do outside of class matters just as much as what you do in it. Striving to do your best in school while maintaining balance with an active social and extracurricular life will help you succeed in both college and in life. So where to start in the quest to be at the head of the class? Start by reading this chapter!

tips and tricks for making the perfect class schedule

Scheduling your classes is the hardest and most important thing you will probably do all semester. Scheduling bad or great courses can really affect you academically and can impact other things like whether or not you will keep a scholarship or make the Dean's List.

The classes you take will also help you develop your world view, so it is important that you choose wisely and take the classes you need to graduate as well as classes that interest you.

So how to create the perfect schedule? First, realize that a typical college schedule for a full-time student is anywhere between 12 to 16 credit hours, but that is just the tip of the iceberg. College students are usually involved in so much more than just class. They have club activities, sports, part-time jobs, and friends to keep them busy, so it is crucial that a great schedule reflects not only time spent in class but time spent outside of class as well.

Once you've evaluated what extracurriculars you're likely to be involved in outside of class, you should then make a draft list of the classes you want to take. To make this list, you have to evaluate yourself on a few essential questions:

1. **What time of day do I achieve my best work?**

   Are you a morning or a night person? Do you get more done before 8 a.m. than most people get done all day, or are you a night owl who loves to stay up all night and work on projects while the rest of the world is sleeping? Take this into consideration when you are figuring out your schedule. It is also good to note that night classes in college usually only meet once a week. So be careful if you decide to choose mostly night classes, as you could end up in one class three hours in one night, which can be long and tiring at that time of day.

2. **How many hours am I willing to go to class?**

   Do you want to take 12 hours or do you want to turn up the heat and do 18? It just depends on how much time you are willing to devote to going to class. Sometimes, you can balance it out so that you take more courses in one semester than another and will still be able to graduate on time.

3. **How difficult do I want my classes to be?**

   Do you mostly want to fill your schedule with hard classes, easy ones, or a mix of both? You should never make a schedule too hard or too easy, because you don't want a particular semester to be so hard that it ends up being a GPA buster or too easy so that your next semester is harder. Balance is key.

4. **How spaced out are my classes from one another?**

Each school has a different time period in between classes, depending on the size of the school. Most schools usually allot somewhere between 10 to 15 minutes. When making your schedule, it's important to block out which class is where to make sure you can get to your class on time. Try to avoid running across campus, if possible!

Now that you have a good feel for what works best for you in terms of timing for classes, it is time to start making a schedule.

WHAT DO YOU WANT TO TAKE?

First things first, gather all of your necessary materials. This includes general education checklists, major and minor checklists, and any other necessary sheets that tell you more about class listings. Find the classes you want to take that semester, as well as some backup classes that you would be willing to take in case your first choices don't go through.

Be sure to schedule an appointment with your advisor at this point. Usually you need to see your advisor before you can register for classes, so while you are there, you can review the classes you plan to take or ask for their advice on what classes to take. Even if your school doesn't require a meeting with an advisor, still seek out his or her input, as advisors are great for alerting you to any potential pitfalls or classes you may want to avoid taking at a certain time in your college career.

SCHEDULING IN THE DIGITAL AGE

Log on to your school's website to find information about the classes you want to take. The website can tell you if they are available to be taken, how many spots are in those classes, who teaches them, and where they are located. Jot down as much of this information as possible. If one class has so many teachers and time slots available it makes your head spin, consider narrowing that specific class down to a specific timeslot or two. This way you won't have as many classes to evaluate or look at.

There are also several different websites out there that can be used to help planning make more sense. Automatic schedule planners and professor rating sites make planning today easier than it ever was before. To learn more about your potential professors, check out RateMyProfessors.com. It's a website where other students rate the teachers they had and can write reviews on them. It is extremely helpful because you can get so much more feedback about a professor than you could ever get from just asking everyone in your group of friends. If you are looking for a device to plan your schedule for you, a site like MyEdu.com can take information from your school and turn the mass amounts of schedules available into a schedule that is tailored to your needs.

DON'T PUT ALL YOUR EGGS IN ONE BASKET

Always have backup courses ready, especially if you go to a large school, know a class is really popular, or you are one of the last people to register. If you think a class that focuses on a cool topic or has a well-respected professor is the one to take, chances are others will, too. To be safe, come up with alternative classes in case the worst happens and you don't get your first picks. It also saves time later, if all the sections are full.

REGISTRATION DAY HAS ARRIVED

So after you have your perfect schedule in place and registration day is right around the corner, it is time to get prepared to go online to sign up for classes. If you are an incoming freshman, you will usually register during your freshman orientation.

Here are some tips to make your registration day run more smoothly:

1. **Wake up early.** It is good to wake up about 15 minutes early to get together any needed materials, wake up, get your computer up and running, etc.

2. **Have your course registration numbers on hand.** You can usually write them all down on a sticky note and attach it to your computer the night before. Or, to make things quicker, you can save it all in a Word document on your laptop so you can copy and paste. It is just important to do this so you can register as quickly as possible.

3. **Don't fret.** Sometimes the system will crash or not work because of an overload of people getting on to register. Stay calm and don't freak out. If you really need a class and couldn't get it, consider directly petitioning the professor or dean, depending on how your school operates, to see if you can get a seat.

CRISIS! ALL OF THE CLASSES YOU NEED ARE FULL!

The big problem here that you absolutely want to avoid is not having enough credit hours to be considered a full-time student. Why? If you're not a full-time student, it may end up jeopardizing the loan money you were relying on to pay your tuition. Take a deep breath. There is a solution. You may not be able to get into the classes that you need right away, but remember, you can always petition for them later or you can simply sign up for your backup classes.

The first step to preventing this potential disaster is getting into any classes that are available as soon as possible. Many students make the mistake of solely relying on the petitioning process and not registering for the classes that are still open. This is not a smart decision because teachers are not required to let you into a full class, potentially leaving you without the minimal amount of units required to receive your loans. Any class is better than no class. Keep this in mind, and look to your backup list of courses for replacements. You can always rearrange your schedule after teachers add you to their roster.

PARTING ADVICE

Making a schedule can be a stressful process. The key is to take it one step at a time, plan far in advance, and register as soon as possible. Don't sit around working on your schedule for longer than you should. And it doesn't have to be done in one night! Remember that you can always go back in and move things around later, if needed.

Insights provided by Amanda Cross, University of Central Arkansas, and Kelly Leslie, San Francisco State University

which major is for me?

Do you remember those multiple-choice tests that were supposed to tell you what you should be when you grew up? I wish that choosing a major in college was as simple as filling in a few circles and waiting for a machine to do the deciding for you.

The first thing to understand and accept about choosing a major is that your first choice may backfire on you and, more important, not to be discouraged if it does. Sometimes, you find that a certain major is too hard, or too easy, or just isn't what you want to do anymore. And that's OK: it's better that you switch than study (and get an expensive degree in!) something that makes you miserable.

Maybe you are afraid of an extra semester or two in school. While you should keep the costs of an extra year of school in mind, think of it this way: what is more important, graduating in four years or getting yourself set up for a job that you love? I have plenty of friends who came into college with a specific path in mind, but ended up changing after finding their true calling. College offers a lot of ideas and courses, and what you fall in love with may be something you hadn't even heard of in high school.

WHEN TO DECIDE

If you're on a strict four-year college timeline, you should not wait longer than spring semester of sophomore year to decide on your major. It is very likely that your school will have an application process and deadline to meet (generally spring semester of sophomore year) in order to be accepted into the program, and you'll likely need as much time as possible to take all the required classes for the major. An added benefit of selecting your major your sophomore year is that you have more time to meet with an advisor or counselor in that major and discuss classes and careers.

U Chic Tip!

Once you've met with your advisor, don't forget to consult the course guide each semester. It is easier than you think to forget to take that one random class required for graduation.

What if you waited until your junior year? Although it will require more effort, you still can complete your major in four years. To see just how much effort it will take, you will need to sit down soon with an advisor in your new major. If you find out during the meeting that you cannot finish the major in the next two school years, you should look into taking summer classes. In almost every case, you only have to pay per each class that you take, and it may end up being cheaper in the long run than an extra semester or two of school. And be sure to look for other ways to complete your major on time. Some colleges have a "speedy" summer session after your fourth year. At my school, UNC–Chapel Hill, this summer session is affectionately known as "Maymester." You can still walk at graduation, but you have to finish the summer classes in order to get your official diploma.

HOW DO YOU FIND A MAJOR?

The answer to this question depends entirely on your situation.

For freshmen, I can share some general advice based on my own experiences as a student. Most college students will have general education requirements. It may seem like an unimaginative and controlled system, but there are great benefits: you'll get a taste of everything, allowing you to discover a subject and potential career you might never have considered. So, for those of you who don't know what major to pursue, go for a well-rounded educational experience the first semester of your freshman year while simultaneously getting some of these requirements out of the way. Try taking intriguing classes in each area you're interested in—and some you're not!—and you may end up finding your true passion just by chance.

For nonfreshmen, start by printing out a list of all of the classes that you have taken thus far. Go through the list and cross off the names of classes that made you want to scream. Next, look to see if you can spot any trends in your course selection. If you find that you mostly enjoyed your English classes, maybe you should consider a major in English. What about science? This is a pretty broad category, so you'll have to narrow the choices down. So take some more science classes! Another approach to picking a major for nonfreshmen is to peruse the entire list of degrees that your school offers. There may be a major that is perfect for you that you didn't know existed. For example, I had a friend who loved her English classes and her foreign language class. And voila! With a little extra effort in looking into her options, she discovered that she could use both of these skills if she majored in Comparative Literature.

Whether you're a freshman or not, after choosing a major, you should immediately meet with an advisor or counselor that the school provides. They will help you figure out what classes you have left to take, and they will give you a general course timeline to help you graduate on time. It is always good to continually check on your progress with an advisor before signing up for classes each semester. Some schools may have specific advisors assigned to you while others may have certain advisors for specific majors. And don't be afraid to pick your own advisor. You may have really clicked with one professor who may end up being the best advisor you could have ever asked for, regardless of their specialty. The better the advisor knows you, the better they can assist you with making the right academic decisions and even help guide you toward scholarships, fellowships, and training that can enhance your overall education.

YOU KNOW WHAT YOU WANT TO BE, BUT NOT WHAT TO STUDY

If you come into college with a specific career in mind and you are unsure what to major in, talk to people who are working in that particular field. See what they studied in college and get advice on how they landed your future dream job. Most people are more than happy to answer questions about "how they got there," especially when you tell them that you hope to pursue a similar career path. Some schools have online databases of alumni networks that are available for student use. Don't be shy. Get in touch with these alums—and find out how they did it.

After you make a connection, keep up with them throughout school and even after your college years. These individuals can become mentors who will help guide you along your career path. Keep them updated on your progress and be sure to write thank-you notes. And don't forget: one important key to getting jobs after college is connections. Knowing someone in the field who is aware of your work ethic and commitment (and who is from your school) can be incredibly helpful. So, make an effort to stay in touch.

Most people are more than happy to answer questions about "how they got there," especially when you tell them that you hope to pursue a similar career path.

WARNING! YOU MAY HAVE PICKED THE WRONG MAJOR

If you are getting bad grades in classes and you are not feeling motivated to do the work, you may be going down the wrong path. If your GPA is below 2.0 for a semester and you put in an honest effort, it could be an indication that you're pursuing the wrong major. (If it's something else, like too much drinking and partying, be honest with yourself about it.) You should not have to struggle just to get through the major that is right for you. I am not saying that every class is going to be wonderful and completely stress-free, but you should feel like it is worth the effort that you're putting into it.

CHANGING YOUR MAJOR

If you discover halfway through college that you were not meant to be a chemical engineering major, for example, get out fast. But be sure to call your parents or whoever is helping fund your education to loop them in on the decision and to logically explain why you have to switch majors. Explain that it would be a total waste of your abilities to stick with a course of studies that is making you cry every night and that you're likely to fail. Your parents will (probably) understand, because in the end, they want you to be happy.

Once you have decided to change your major and have made the necessary phone calls, you need to make an appointment with an advisor. Some of you may even have to go to the advisor within your current major to get their approval to change. Get started as soon as possible. You are initially going to have to do a lot of paperwork to change your major, but just remember why it's so important to you and that you'll soon be studying a subject you love.

GOING FOR A MINOR

If there is an additional area of study that you find yourself interested in but don't have the time to pursue as a major, why not go for a minor? I'm studying graphic design, but I also enjoy writing, so I've decided to minor in creative writing. Why did I go for it? I was writing so much in my free time that I thought, "Why not get credit for it?"

It is also possible that if you've taken lots of classes in a specific area (i.e., if you changed majors halfway through), you may end up with enough credits or close to enough credits to minor in that topic. My older brother was surprised to find out his senior year that he had enough credits to minor in history if he took one more class. No surprise, he decided to go for it. Having a minor shows ambition and well-roundedness to future employers or grad schools, and it can add fun and variety to your education.

THE END GOAL

Would you rather have a career that you love or finish school on time? Yes, doing both would be ideal, but sometimes that's just not realistic. The real reason you go to college is to help you discover your life's path—but this doesn't happen overnight. In fact, on average, it usually takes a college student more than four years to graduate. So don't be afraid if you are going to have to stay a little bit longer to pursue a course of study that you are totally passionate about. Choosing a major is not easy, but once you have figured it out, you've already made a "major" accomplishment in discovering your path to success in college and in life.

Insights provided by Kathryn Lewis,
University of North Carolina–Chapel Hill

how to get to the top

There are many different ways to get top grades. For one, you could literally sit at the head of the class—in the front of the classroom. This actually works for many reasons. You're forced to pay more attention to the professor, you'll always have an unobstructed view, and there is no one to hide behind during class discussions.

But sitting in the front row will not guarantee you top grades: there's no way to avoid the work and responsibility that comes along with being a top student these days. Hard work is the only way to get ahead. Lucky for me, my high school prepared me well. I was ready to buckle down as a college student after facing the challenges of high school and going through the college application process. But it was not just my high school preparation that put me at the top. I also had a strategy to be successful from the start. Want to get to the head of the class? Read on to find out how.

THE STRATEGY

When you're going for top honors, let's be honest—it's competitive. Would you head into a sporting competition without a success strategy? That is why I highly recommend devoting some time to developing a plan for your study and achievement. With a little effort, this strategy will help you, at a minimum, keep up with the competition. At its best, you'll be at the top.

THE GOOD, THE BAD, AND THE UGLY

After you've attended all your courses the first week of the semester (btw, this advice applies to all semesters going forward—going to class is the best way to make sure you pass), take a couple of hours over the weekend to devise your "strategy" for the semester. Try to determine which courses seem like they'll be fairly easy for you or won't require too much work and which ones could end up being a nightmare. Some things to look out for in separating the tough from the easy courses: the existence or frequency of quizzes, number of required papers, midterms, term papers, and yes, the final. If a particular course has more of these items than not, you're most likely dealing with a class that's going to keep you really busy.

Once you've categorized your classes, figure out a schedule that will have you spending the right amount of time on each course in order to keep up with all of the readings and assignments without completely stressing yourself out. Also, be ready to revise this strategy along the way if necessary. With a good schedule, you will not be surprised by any pop quizzes, you will stay on track for any midterm or term papers, and finals preparation will be a whole lot easier than if you waited until the last minute to catch up.

IF ANYTHING, JUST GO

Attendance is a major factor in being successful in school. Students who attend class often are far more likely to succeed than students who do not attend class. Any professor whom you speak with will back this up. At some point you'll probably hear something along these lines: "Ninety percent of success is showing up," because for a lot of students the hard part is getting to class. If you have to be absent from a class, pair up with someone who is also in it. This way, there is someone to contact about what was assigned and discussed that day and even to get notes from. Also, make up any missed work as soon as possible. Being absent is an easy way to fall behind and lose a spot at the head of the class. From my own experience, showing up on time and being ready to learn is the only real way to get ahead.

U Chic Tip! When to Drop a Class

Madeline Greene, Minnesota State University

While there are a lot of great aspects to college, the academic side of college (after all, we are here to get a degree and graduate!) is not always easy.

I know what it feels like to be overwhelmed with my schoolwork. Yes, I was *that student* who piled on the credits to graduate on time.

Now, I'm not saying that all classes should be easy. If college didn't challenge us, why go? However, there comes a point in each semester when you realize that you've either taken too little credits, the right amount, or far too many. Sounds like a case of Goldilocks and the Three Bears!

In the case of *far too many*, how do you know when the right time is to say when and drop a class? Well, there is likely one course that is causing all the trouble, so take time to identify it. Before you make the final decision to drop it, first talk to your academic advisor to ensure that this will not mess up important things like financial aid or your graduation plan.

Take time to also get personal with yourself before pulling the trigger. Are you being lazy or do you really have too much on your plate? If you are up until all hours of the night and you cannot physically get through the next day because you were finishing homework, you probably should consider dropping the class.

However, if the class is really hard and is just a hassle to take, don't give up on it yet. College is meant to challenge you, and if you're being challenged (in a good way), take a deep breath and stick with it. On the other hand, if a challenging class is taking you away from your other studies, that's probably a toss-up. So, you'll want to check with your academic advisor.

One last piece of advice: you don't always have to drop a class to lighten the load. There are other options. For instance, "pass/fail" is an option where, instead of taking a college course for a grade, you take it with the option of passing or failing. While you still receive credit for the course, it isn't counted in your GPA. However, as it will still show up on your transcript, you should use this option sparingly, as this does not always look good to future employers.

When it comes to the decision of whether to drop a course, remember that college is the time to challenge and push yourself. You just don't want to push yourself too far.

PAY ATTENTION TO YOUR COMMUNICATION STYLE

While your communication style is hugely important in your social life, it also has a specific role in getting good grades. Sure, tests and quizzes also have a significant role in getting that coveted A on the report card, but take a look at your syllabus that covers the grading scale in your classes and you'll often find that a percentage of your grade is tied to that elusive "classroom participation" factor.

So what does this mean for your strategy? For anyone who aspires to be at the top, you first have to understand your communication preferences. Ask yourself, "Am I a good listener who is somewhat shy in a public setting, or am I someone who enjoys speaking up and debating from time to time on subjects that interest me?" Understanding your personal preferences for classroom involvement is key to figuring out how to stand out in the classroom regardless of whether you're shy or on the chatty side. If you're shy, make an effort to speak at least once a week on a subject that you either know a lot about or are somewhat passionate about. The knowledge or passion will help carry you through your shyness. Also, take time to go visit your professor during office hours so that he or she can get to know who you are and come to appreciate your efforts even if you're not speaking up on a daily basis. And if you're the gregarious type, by all means, speak up! However, you need to be careful that you're not speaking simply in order to hear your own voice. Your classmates and professor will know the distinction. Make sure that your comments are thoughtful and either advance the discussion or introduce a new idea. By planning your strategy for communication inside the classroom, you're guaranteeing that you're meeting your professor's expectations for A-worthy classroom participation.

VOLUNTEER

We all know that community service is an important component of being a college student. Guess what? Volunteering in class can also help you get ahead. When the professor asks for someone to volunteer for *anything*, be the first to take the assignment. Taking the initiative is a great tool for success. I had a professor in college who gave extra credit to anyone who volunteered to do something for the class.

WHAT YOU CAN DO OUTSIDE OF CLASS

Now that you've got a strategy for success, it's time to focus on how you'll conduct yourself outside of the class in order to ensure your success.

Make a study schedule—and stick to it

Besides attending class, a few hours per week must be dedicated to homework and studying. There is just no way around it. Most likely, quizzes and exams will make up the majority of a class grade, so good study skills are crucial to graduating at the top of the class. A few nights before the test or quiz, reread any notes and material that will be covered. It may also be a good idea to write a summary of the notes that were taken in class. From my experience, it takes an average of one to two hours of studying per week for each class to get a good grade (although this varies with different majors). This advice, however, does not apply to midterms and finals. These items are special and are discussed further below.

Find your favorite study place

For most people, the best place to study is a quiet environment that will have zero distractions. Instead of your dorm room, where you can easily slack off to take a nap or surf the Web, opt for the library or a designated study area on campus. If you're more extroverted and get more done with people around you, a coffeehouse can be a good place to hit the books—especially since you'll have quick access to caffeine to keep you going. It's OK (in fact encouraged!)

to treat yourself to a snack while studying. It will give you more energy, and is an incentive to get through the material.

It's OK (in fact encouraged!) to treat yourself to a snack while studying. It will give you more energy, and is an incentive to get through the material.

Form a study group

This tip doesn't work for everyone. Some of us are more social, and others prefer a more isolated environment. But if you like studying with other people, it can be useful to have them to interact with. For example, you can ask for their help if you're having difficulty with the material. Also, you might feel more inspired to study if your fellow students are in the trenches with you, and you can help each other stay motivated. I was never part of a study group. I get distracted too easily by other people, especially if there happens to be someone attractive in the group! I find that the more people involved, the more likely studying will turn into socializing. However, if you can find a group of people who share your dedication to staying on task, it can be a great experience.

Treat yourself right

Good preparation for class involves allowing yourself a good night's sleep, getting regular exercise, and making an effort to eat healthy. These activities are proven to help classroom performance. Exercise is also of great importance. There are tons of scientific studies showing how good exercise is for your brain. I suggest reading some of them if you ever need some motivation to go to the gym! While weightlifting and walking are good, it is generally thought that vigorous cardiovascular exercise (30 minutes or more of running or biking, for example) is the best workout for your mind.

Success can be dependent on what you eat

And finally, a couple key points on eating healthy. Breakfast is the most important meal of the day! It sets your mood and energy level every morning for the whole day. Stay away from the sugary coffee drinks—if you need them, at least save them for an afternoon break. Try not to become a caffeine addict—save it for when you need it. If you are a Starbucks fiend, consider that a regular tall coffee (12 oz.) has almost 6 times as much caffeine as a 12-oz. Diet Coke. If you love your caffeine, at least have it in moderation.

Did You Know?

A 12-oz. coffee from your favorite nearby coffee shop could have nearly as much caffeine as a 6-pack of 12-oz. Diet Coke.

Start the day with anything that has a decent amount of protein in it, because protein decreases your hunger better than carbs and provides a steady energy source all morning. Eggs, nuts, health bars, and many other foods are perfect for this. Just find what you like and make sure it has some protein.

Fat also provides a steady energy source and decreases your appetite more than carbs do; just don't overdo the trans fats and saturated fats that are in donuts, creams, and the like. Also remember that with too many carbs, you will get an energy high and crash a couple hours later, which is no good for learning. If you still need your bread or bagel, try to make it wheat or whole grain, which will help keep your energy level more even over a longer period of time.

AFTER-HOURS

No, I'm not talking about partying here (but of course you should have fun too!). A student does not need to be failing to want to improve a grade. Extra help is available for anyone who simply wants to do better. There are usually tutors or study sessions on campus. This could add an hour or two on top of what you're already doing outside of class, but it will be well spent.

Also, make an effort to get to know your professors. They like to see that their students are interested in their class. Make time to talk to professors about their material. Discuss anything of interest and ask them any questions about the subject. If your effort was sincere, they will most likely take this into consideration when it comes time to give you a final grade.

STAY ORGANIZED

Every semester you receive so many handouts and take so many notes for each class that it can be hard to keep track of all of them. Many of my teachers recommended a three-ring binder that is categorized by date and subject. This way, notes can be easily located when it comes to preparing for a test or quiz. Students who are disorganized waste time looking for notes instead of preparing for the exam itself. I also use highlighters to keep track of any important information. Note cards and Post-its can also be useful.

Another way to keep organized is to keep an assignment book. List each assignment's due date and make sure to refer to it every day. Then, check off each assignment as it is completed; it's a great way to make sure everything gets done on time. Make sure to prioritize since the workload can get heavy at times.

TRY STAYING AHEAD OF THE GAME

Completing assignments a few days before they are due is a good idea. It allows you extra time to make any last-minute changes or revisions in the work before it's graded. In general, make sure you are consistently knowledgeable about the coursework as the semester progresses rather than cramming the day before a test, midterm, or final. By staying on top of things, you will save time (and your sanity!) when it comes to studying for a difficult exam, midterm, or final since there won't be as much to review.

STAYING AHEAD DOES NOT INCLUDE CHEATING

The statistics are overwhelming. In 1940, only 20 percent of students admitted to cheating. Flash-forward to the present, and those numbers have swelled to 75–98 percent. Cheating on tests and assignments isn't just on the rise—it's a widespread epidemic that's plaguing American high schools and college campuses at almost every level. Blame it on extreme pressure to succeed from parents, or even a heightened fear of failure from the students themselves. Whatever the case, schools are taking drastic action to ensure that cheating becomes a thing of the past. Thought about plagiarizing your research paper or cheating during an exam? You might want to think twice.

To catch a cheat

In a recent *New York Times* article, an associate dean from the University of Central Florida highlighted some of the highly covert methods the school was using to track and penalize cheaters in the classroom. Testing is now computerized and computers are recessed into desks so camera phones can't photograph other students' work. Gum isn't allowed (since chewing can muffle the sound of someone coaching a student through a hands-free device), and while scratch paper is provided, it must be dated and handed in to the professor at the end of the test or exam.

If a student is suspected of cheating, a professor can tag his or her work on the computer, burn it to a CD as evidence, and then direct an outside security team to videotape the student while taking the test so they can later analyze the results to determine if the person was in fact cheating. Obviously this is an extreme measure, but certainly a growing trend among colleges and universities is an effort to remind students they are watching and you will be caught if you attempt to scam your way to an A.

Plagiarism on campus

Cruise your local Craigslist on any given day and you're sure to encounter at least one or two ads offering to pay for writing "services" on a term paper or school project. Not discreet enough for you? Just Google the phrase "term paper help" and see how many links come up for companies that provide term papers and essays in exchange for money (that's not including all the additional links for "essay help," "custom term papers," and "research paper help"). Sadly, the line between stealing and creating original work has become somewhat blurred. Schools like Duke and Bowdoin have implemented plagiarism surveys and testing materials for this year's crop of incoming freshmen.

Meanwhile, other schools are taking an extremely hard-line approach and are using plagiarism software like that provided by Turnitin.com. The software measures word algorithms and phrases to determine if content was lifted from common research sites like Wikipedia or other published pieces found online. To date, 9,500 colleges and high schools around the country are now employing Turnitin, and those numbers continue to grow as students try new and complicated ways to beat Turnitin's system (the irony here is obvious—for all the time and initiative students take to try to find cracks in Turnitin's software, they could just as easily be channeling their energy into researching, studying, and creating their own unique work).

The bottom line? Cheating is becoming harder to do, so you might want to try another approach…like actually doing the work. After all, the only person you're really cheating is yourself.

REGISTER FOR COURSES ASAP!

Another thing to do ahead of time is register for classes as soon as possible. Be sure to pick up a catalog as soon as you can, even before you get to school, and browse through the classes to see which seem the most interesting. You will find that the good courses (those that are either easy or have fantastic professors) fill up quickly—as do the courses that everyone in your major needs to graduate.

Even if it means waking up early to get in line and register for those classes, it's completely worth losing a few extra hours of sleep. It's a lot easier to get ahead when classes are genuinely interesting and enjoyable. Also take note of any professors who were recommended by your friends. People who have taken the class before definitely have the inside scoop. To see what students on your campus are saying about a particular course or professor at your school, visit a website like RateMyProfessors.com. The site collects ratings from hundreds of students at your school and provides you instant access to this data. And don't forget that you can also rate your previous professors and courses while you're there.

ACTUALLY DO THE READING

Reading is another way to get ahead and be more knowledgeable about a subject. By actually reading your textbooks and other materials, you'll gain a deeper understanding of the subject. Many students do not want to dedicate the time to read or even purchase their college textbooks, but it's foolish to try to rely solely on a professor's notes and lectures. Reading books is the only way to be fully prepared for class, since the professor assigns those books for specific reasons. And it is impossible for the professor to discuss everything that will be covered on the tests or quizzes. Therefore it is your responsibility to read everything you are assigned when it's assigned and be ready to discuss it or take a quiz on it.

Did You Know?

If your parents tell you they studied more than you do, they could be right. According to the *Boston Globe*, researchers from California have found that today's average college student studies only 14 hours a week, compared to 1961, when students studied 24 hours a week. The article states many different theories for the decline, including a "breakdown of the professor-student relationship."

MIDTERMS AND FINALS

Midterms and finals can seem overwhelming, especially since they usually cover a lot of information. Don't try to study the material for each course all at once or else it will be too much to remember and possibly overwhelm you. Start early and study a little bit at a time. Take it chapter by chapter and slowly begin to become familiar with the information. Only at the very end will everything be integrated. Also, one strategy that worked for me was to focus on one test at a time. If I had two tests in one week, I would study nothing else except the material for these courses. This kept my stress level down to a minimum, and I was able to go into each exam feeling very confidently prepared.

FINALLY, REPUTATION MATTERS

Work on building a reputation for being one of the most dedicated and responsible students in your class. Your professor will greatly appreciate it, and this can also serve as a deciding factor when it comes to grades.

U Chic Tip!

Many students hand things in late or ask for an extension. If you want to get ahead, don't do this. If you really are spending too much time on an assignment, it is time to ask for help. Work hard to stay on top, but if for some reason your efforts aren't paying off, talk

> with your professor to make sure that you understand the material. This will prevent you from falling behind and possibly even failing a course.

No one said that it's easy to be on top. As you'll find, it can take a lot of time to get ahead. But, if you follow some of the advice above, this is definitely an achievable goal. Graduating with high honors and an impressive grade point average is something you can be proud of after graduation, as well as something that will help you get ahead in the future. The hard work and determination you will need are worth it.

Insights provided by Jennifer Rubino, Kean University

f.i.n.a.l.s.: fudge, I never actually learned squat!

Make a list. Check it twice. Maybe three times. Maybe even four. Where did the semester go? Where did those simple days of just worrying about homework go? Times have changed, and all of a sudden you find yourself cramming for that dreaded final exam.

STUDY STYLES

One of the most important steps in successfully studying for a final exam is finding out your study style. Study styles vary depending on what kind of learner you are and how well you remember important information. Another thing to take into consideration is how good of a note-taker you've been all semester and if you've been following the reading.

For the "I love to take obsessive notes/I've done all my reading" student

For those good note-takers out there, the obsessive-compulsive ones who write down everything the professors say, the challenge is narrowing things down. Grab that nice, big highlighter and your note-filled notebook and find a comfortable chair to curl up in. *It's time to power through it.* In getting started, first ask yourself, "What's on the exam?" If there's a list of terms or ideas or even chapters, make sure that, as you go through your notes, you're collating your lists and highlighting only the most important stuff. The next step depends on what you like to do. If you're one of those people who loves index cards with a passion—you know, one of those people who buys index cards in different colors, shapes, sizes, and maybe even with a spiral going through them—grab that stack of blank note cards and write out all the highlighted terms from your notebook.

U Chic Tip!

If your laptop is with you wherever you go, like mine is, open a Word document and get cracking on retyping out the important sections of your notes—a condensed crib sheet.

Writing things down and rereading them again and again, at least three times, will immerse your mind in the key terms and ideas you need to know. And before you know it, the knowledge you will need to ace the test will just be there.

For the "I fell asleep during lecture/I prefer doodling to notes" student

For those of you who fell asleep on that severely uncomfortable wooden lecture desk or daydreamed about the boy sitting in the front row, or just forgot to write things down because you needed to finish that elaborate design on the corner of your spiral notebook, it might be a bit harder to catch up. But don't give up; it can be done.

Here's what you need to do to quickly get on track. Take whatever is left of your doodled notebook (or just get a new one), head to the library, and take the books you were supposed to read for class. Since you are short on time, there is no way you can read through all the required material in time for the exam. Not to worry. Actually, the worst thing you can do right now is to freak out.

Now that you know what might be on the exam (especially if your professor told you during a review session or handed you some sort of study guide), your catch-up reading can be *very* focused. Go through and skim the chapters that are relevant. Make sure to make good use of the table of contents and the index to focus your reading. Once you've read what you needed to and have taken some quality notes, start making a study guide.

Since you still might not be sure that you have all the notes you need, your best option is probably to opt for a study group. For a lot of people, the best way to learn is to explain concepts to your friends and classmates, and have them explained to you.

The worst thing you can do right now is freak out.

So, get your fellow classmates together—they'll likely come willingly, as they're already studying for the test, too. A good group session in the student union or outside (depending on the weather) is a perfect way to get a lot of work done in the precious few days (or even hours!) that you have to catch up before the exam.

For a lot of people, the best way to learn is to explain concepts to your friends and classmates.

IT'S OK TO TAKE A BREAK

A good study session involves some necessary breaks. Breaks can involve food, drink, and sometimes even a little fun. Sometimes the best study break is taking a moment, stepping away from the books and the computer, and blasting your favorite dancing tune of the week. It's like having a mini dance party. Close your eyes, dance your little heart away, and then get back to work. Jumping jacks also work.

When it comes to food, make sure to have a balance of healthy snacks and complete crap food. Proteins and healthy fats are a good way to start a long study session (a peanut butter sandwich on wheat bread is simple and healthy), but it's OK to throw in an apple or banana when you need that extra burst of energy.

When it comes to drinks, I know coffee is certainly a tempting option and so is that can of Monster or Red Bull staring down at you from your bookshelf. Resist. When it comes to coffee— and I am sure you've heard it a million times—the higher you climb, the harder you fall. It might give you that initial boost, but when you are trying to stay awake during your exam and the floor starts spinning, those cups of coffee won't seem like such a great idea anymore.

The best and most often underestimated option is actually water. Buy a massive bottle of water or two and just keep drinking it. If the liquid keeps going through your system, it will revitalize and keep you awake without the negative or counterproductive effects of caffeine or taurine, the stuff that gives you wings but turns you into a monster later.

The Power of a "Power Nap"

Procrastinated writing your research paper or studying for a test? During your all-nighter, pass on the latte and hit your pillow for a power nap instead. Education.com reported on a study that found power naps can be a more effective way of staying focused and concentrating better. And if that isn't enough to sway you, according to the University of Georgia's Student Health Center, students who get seven to eight hours of sleep have higher GPAs than students who get six hours or less. Want to get more sleep? Experts say establishing regular sleep routines and avoiding caffeine at night can help.

SETTING GOALS

Reward yourself for a job well done—or just done. When I was a kid, my mom used to make me do my math homework at the kitchen table. Lucky for me, she is a math teacher. She used to make me a nice snack or put a chocolate bar in front of me and she would say, "*Olya* (my Russian name), *finish this page of math problems and then you can reward yourself.*"

I hated it. So when she walked out of the room, I would sneak a bite. Why should I wait? I used to hate having to miss swim practice because I was not done with my homework or because my room wasn't clean. Why did I have to finish it first? Why couldn't I just go to practice and then finish my work when I got home?

As I grew older, however, I learned the value of these lessons and have turned them into a sort of self-discipline. Granted, there is a good deal of procrastination that goes into that equation, but I am less inclined to procrastinate when I know that I can go out to that party on Saturday night only if I have my final study guide ready. Also, let's face it: Facebook stalking and messaging friends on AIM is not as appealing as the reward at the end of the road.

Just tell yourself, if I finish reading through four chapters tonight, I can go meet my friend for coffee tomorrow. This way, you get part of your work done and you also get to take a well-deserved break.

FIND OUT HOW YOU STUDY

Alert, Alert! Tempting beds operating in your area! Move away from all pillows and couches immediately! Your safety depends on it...or at least your studying does.

Where you choose to study, once again, depends on what kind of studier you are. One piece of advice that I feel definitely applies to everyone is to get out of your room! Don't fall into the trap of, "Oh I'll just read my sociology book in my bed, it's so comfortable." No matter how enthralling your world history or philosophy book is, reading about fascist dictators or the Socratic method will not keep you awake if you are surrounded by the cloud of your comforter. I'm not saying you won't fall asleep at the library, but most likely the wooden desk where your head would rest is not anywhere near as cushiony, soft, or inviting. If you fall asleep, you most likely won't be there for long.

U Chic Tip!

How to make the library work? First, some libraries have more social floors and areas that you can seek out when you head over with your laptop bag and a handy study buddy. Find a nice place to sit with your friends and once in a while stop to ask questions or maybe even chat a little. The best thing about bringing a study buddy with you is that you can pop out to take an ice cream break without having to completely pack up and get off track. You can leave your precious laptop with your trusty friend. When you're studying solo, head to the quieter floors or areas to get some serious studying done.

Library

Your school's library is a good place to get some studying done. Not only are you surrounded by other students who share your study woes, but you are also surrounded by bookshelves. Even if you don't feel the need to grab one of those books for some extra prefinal reading, the sheer power of all of those books should inspire you to get down and dirty with your studies. The library might not be appealing to those who prefer to be invisible during finals time because it will be filled with people, but remember they are all there for the same reason. If you want a good balance between social life and intense studies, the library always works.

Loud/social areas

If you are one of those people who find silence way too quiet in a creepy kind of way, perhaps you should opt for a louder and more bustling study area. Sometimes a little background commotion is all you need to actually get some work done. If you're one of those people who can't handle the silence of the library or your own room, head to a coffee shop or maybe even a student union hangout. There will be tons of people around and you can opt for some breaks while you are there without having to move an inch. Other benefits of this option are that you can eat while you work. Just one piece of advice: make sure you remember to take down that Abercrombie model wallpaper you have set as your desktop background. No one wants to see it. Or maybe they do, but either way, I speak from experience when I tell you to put up a pretty picture of a beach somewhere. You never know who will walk by your computer while you're studying at the downtown coffee shop.

Studying with others

Be forewarned: study buddies are not for everyone. A study buddy or even a study group can be a great thing for you, but it can also be distracting or disastrous depending on the type of person you are. Usually, a study buddy is a friend with whom you can get work done. He or she doesn't necessarily have to be in your class or even in your major, just someone you know you can be quiet with and bounce ideas off of as needed.

Study buddies can be great, but make sure you are ready to take on the distraction and avoid the pitfalls of chatting instead of getting some studying done. Bottom line: embrace the distraction that a study buddy might bring, but don't overuse it. Make sure that both of you do some studying and help each other with anything you can.

If for some reason, you feel the need to go home or somewhere else to work on your own, don't feel obligated to stay with your friend. Finals are a stressful time and good friends understand. Studying together is not primarily a social activity, so they should not be offended if you have to leave for some quiet time.

Study groups

Study groups tend to be a little more focused than a couple of study buddies sitting around together. Usually study groups involve people from your class and not necessarily close friends. This is great because you can delegate and divide up the studying work and share it with one another, teaching and learning at the same time without the major temptation to dish on the hottest gossip. Make a list of all the topics you need to know and get ready to divvy up the work. Everyone in the group should have some work to do and report back to everyone else—you can even make a group study guide out of the combined work and give a copy to each person. If you plan to work in a study group for finals, be sure to start way before finals so each group member gets a chance to review everything, and not just his or her part of the study guide.

Dealing with the stress

If finals are around the corner, be prepared to accept the fact that it is going to be stressful. There's nothing that you can do about it besides accepting it and moving on; the worst thing you can do is stress about being stressed out.

There are many ways of dealing with finals stress, but some are better than others. The main idea is to take plenty of breaks. Try going to the gym or take the edge off with a swim. Really, any form of physical activity should do the trick. Don't think that exercise will make you tired and leave you too worn out to work. In fact, exercise does just the opposite. It releases endorphins that make you feel better and helps you be even more focused when you sit back down in front of your books.

The worst thing you can do is stress about being stressed out.

As for other stress-relieving activities, some schools organize fun events during finals that help chase the stress bug away. Last winter, my friend Hillary and I went to an on-campus event for stressed students in the student union. It was a great idea. Students were getting free massages, taking breaks to play ping-pong with their friends, and much more. Keep your eyes open for similar opportunities on your campus. And if they're not there, seek off-campus ways to pamper yourself during finals, like getting a facial or manicure. The most important thing to remember when dealing with stress is that working too hard or too much might not always be the best strategy for getting a good score on your final exam. Sometimes, all you need is a break or good night's sleep to let all of your hard work sink in. After all, there is only so much you can do.

And the rest? It's up to karma, or something like that.

Insights provided by Olga Belogolova, Boston University

U Chic Essentials—Head of the Class

Don't be shy
Never be shy about asking others, especially alumni and professors, for advice. Besides getting great advice on what major to pursue, how to do better in class, or which internship to go for, alums want to help. Bottom line: it's never too early to start networking with this all-important group of people.

Always think two steps ahead
Love the classes you're currently taking in humanities? Consider how you can turn this love into a career. By thinking two steps

ahead, you will be that much closer to figuring out what you were born to do after college.

Team up

One surefire way to get to the head of the class is to team up. Join a study group or find a study buddy. Depending on your learning style, either option will pay multiple dividends by keeping you on track, ensuring that the material makes sense, and pitching in whenever you're unable to attend. Success guaranteed.

Looking for more great advice? Head to www.UChic.com for our fave resources and websites—they come highly recommended from our guide's contributors and editors. Be sure to leave your suggestions as well!

CHAPTER 4

Getting Involved

The previous chapter focused on getting to the head of the class. Well, this chapter is about forgetting everything that was said in the previous chapter and focusing on how to have a life *outside of class*. Just kidding—don't forget *everything*! We just felt it was important to address your extracurricular life, which is equally important to your studies.

When it comes to getting involved in college, just follow your instinct. Find your niche—that special thing that you will do in college—and start it as soon as possible. By carving out time for that niche early on, you're ensuring that this will be a priority throughout your collegiate life, so when the going gets tough (like during finals), you know that you can always come back to your fave activities when the stress dies down. Also, by getting involved in extracurriculars early on, you're giving yourself additional opportunities to expand your horizons, possibly leading to great things like internships and even jobs as you get closer to graduation. Not to mention all the friends you'll make!

One word of caution: watch out for the "buffet effect." With everything that you have to choose from, you may have an urge to try everything and overindulge, so to speak. Don't. Getting involved in too many things can take you away from the main reason that you are in college in the first place—to get a great education. So get involved, but make sure not to put too much on your plate. Read on for some great insights on your life *outside of the classroom*!

ditch the dorm; get a life!

During your tenure as a dorm dweller, you will be presented with myriad opportunities to socialize with others on your floor at parties, dances, movies, and outings. All these activities are fun, a great way to meet the other people you live with, and a perfect opportunity to relax after a busy week filled with tests and papers. Taking time to have fun is an extremely necessary part of school because, let's face it, you will burn out way before you complete your four or five years in higher education if you don't take time to just chill. Having said that, another vital and rewarding aspect of college life extends beyond the confines of the dormitory—get involved with something, either on campus or beyond.

Picking Up Stories and Guys

Johannah Cornblatt, Harvard University

When I walked into the newsroom of the *Harvard Crimson* the first day of my freshman year, I noticed instructions on how to open a document for a new story taped prominently on the wall. But after I saw a cute sophomore boy sitting at the desk across from mine, I pretended not to see the directions and, sweetly, solicited his help. It was like that scene in *Mean Girls* when Cady claims to be bad at math in order to convince Aaron, the charming senior, to tutor her. I didn't play dumb for long, though. News editors quickly sent me to interview students around campus for a story on e-registration, a new feature (pretty standard these days) that allowed us to sign up for classes online. Halfway through writing my article back in the newsroom, I glanced up at the clock and realized I had missed dinner. Luckily, aforementioned cute sophomore had also lost track of the time. He asked me out to a burrito place across the street, and so began my years-long romance with my college boyfriend—and, that same night, my relationship with Harvard's daily newspaper. I'm definitely not the only *Crimson* editor guilty of what they call "Crimcest." You'd be amazed how good even the nerdiest Harvard boy looks when you're stuck laying out the paper together at 4 a.m.

While the *Crimson* can certainly spice up your love life, another big perk of working on the newspaper for me was the friends. I met two of my current roommates at the *Crimson* during the first week of our freshman year, and we've spent many a late night together in the newsroom since. One is now an executive editor like me, and the other, who writes a biweekly column, is now Harvard's Ann Coulter (although she notes that she's "not insane or anti-Semitic, only conservative and blonde"). I remember how the three of us idolized the senior girls on the *Crimson* when we were freshmen, and it's funny seeing younger girls look up to us like that now. Friendships really cross class years at organizations like the *Crimson*, and girls who have graduated still keep in touch with us, offering advice on everything from boys to careers.

Whether it's for your own pleasure or to enhance your résumé, making an effort to venture beyond the dorm can enhance both your outlook on life and your curriculum vitae. Figuring out how to get involved in a student organization can seem daunting at first. Fear not: there are many tips and tricks to help you negotiate your way into having a fulfilling life outside of class. Branching out beyond the dorm will expose you to new people and activities.

WHERE TO START

When you're first exploring your options in the extracurricular field, think of what interests you. Is it playing a particular sport? Speaking a foreign language? Film noir? Bible study? Whatever it is, chances are there is a club in honor of it on your college campus. And if there isn't, you can always start one yourself. Because there are so many options in college, the difficulty will be in narrowing down the playing field to activities that really interest you.

If you need some help brainstorming what clubs might catch your fancy, here are a few ideas to get you started:

Are grades your thing?

Does the thought of spending more time studying to achieve that latest A or honor make shivers of joy run down your spine? If this is you, consider applying to an on-campus honor society. Many departments have their own honor society or there can be one for an entire class such as Phi Eta Sigma, the honor society that academically inclined freshmen can join at the University of Washington (UW) after achieving a specific GPA and the required community service hours. The benefits of honor society membership are twofold: one, let's face it, they look great on a résumé. It shows that you aim high, achieve the goals you set, and are intelligent and disciplined. Second, your honor society peers are great study partners and the element of positive peer pressure can further your academic ambitions. Third, you may be required to devote time to community service in projects that are for good causes, which can get you out into the world and make you feel great about yourself.

Do you have a deep-seated desire to dive for a Frisbee while others give chase and tug at your jersey?

Or does soccer sound like the perfect way to bond with your fellow man or woman? If the answer is yes, it sounds like an intramural sports team or league is the way to go. These teams range from all-out competition where players vie for titles and trophies to weekend bowling leagues where teams compete for beers and bragging rights. You'll be able to find the level of play you're looking for, and if not, put up some fliers and start a team!

Do you dream in different languages?

Fantasize about traveling to foreign lands? Indulge your inner wanderlust without having to pony up for a pesky passport. Foreign language clubs and language exchange programs are a great way to get immersed in a new language, brush up on skills carried over from your high school French class, and even help an exchange student practice his or her English.

U Chic Tip!

Other options for clubs and organizations, both on and off campus, include:

On Campus:

- Student radio shows or newspapers

- Church groups or Bible study

- Student government

- Heritage-oriented clubs (Korean, Native American, African American, etc.)

- Photography

- Political clubs (Young Democrats, Young Republicans, etc.)

- On-campus magazines or journals

- Music groups (choir, jazz, a cappella, etc.)

- Spoken word, poetry slam

- Martial arts

- Lifestyle-focused clubs (vegan, cooking, etc.)

- Seasonal outdoor activities (snowboarding, wakeboarding, boating, etc.)

- Theater and improv groups

- TV show viewing club

- Nature clubs (camping, bird watching, wetlands, ocean beaches, etc.)

- Study-centric clubs (become a peer tutor in English, writing, math, or other subjects)

- Volunteer and advocacy groups (Habitat for Humanity, Voices for Planned Parenthood, PETA, etc.)

- Dance (swing, ballroom, etc.)

- Mentorship clubs (meeting with upperclassmen to talk and get their feedback and advice on the college experience)

Off Campus:

- Volunteer as a docent at a museum or art gallery

- Serve as a mentor in a local chapter of the Boys & Girls Clubs

- Join a professional networking group based on your study area; for instance, communications or public relations majors can join the Public Relations Student Society of America (PRSSA). Many of these professional organizations require membership fees but offer lower membership rates for college students.

THE COMMITMENT

Wherever you think your passion lies, it's important to ask yourself if it's something that you are, indeed, passionate about and interested in. There are things you will tell others you are passionate about because they sound noble (volunteering to help children in Third World countries, for example), and then there are the things you truly love to do. Make sure that you don't neglect getting involved in something that goes into that "truly love to do" category. It will make you happier overall, and thus better able to succeed in and enjoy the other things you are involved in. Also, those activities you sign up for just because you truly enjoy them sometimes end up being the ones that look the best on your résumé—when you do things you are truly passionate about, you will be more willing and likely to rise to a leadership position.

The caveat is to remember to take part in something that you genuinely believe you can commit time to, even if it's just for a few hours a week. If you have a busy schedule with other commitments such as sports or work, make sure that you take these activities into consideration when getting involved. Before getting committed to anything, you need to be fully aware of the expectations for group membership and whether you can meet them before getting involved.

There are things you will tell others you are passionate about because they sound noble (volunteering to help children in Third World countries, for example), and there are the things you truly love to do. Make sure that you don't neglect getting involved in something that goes into that "truly love to do" category.

Some groups are more dependent on attendance while others are more laid-back. For instance, to be part of a book club, reading the assigned book before the next meeting is required. If you didn't do the reading, you can't be a star discussion member. So when considering whether to take up a new activity, just make sure you will be able to juggle the timing in your hectic collegiate schedule. You don't want to leave anyone hanging if you're not able to make a meeting, but you also don't want to be needlessly stressed on top of your already busy days. Extracurricular activities are meant to be a fun, bonding experience, not an added stressor.

PURSUING YOUR ACADEMIC INTERESTS WITH EXTRACURRICULARS

If you're at a point in your studies where you have a good idea of what you'd like to major in, you can also check out meetings or gatherings in different academic departments. Many departments post their clubs and functions in student lounges and places within the department such as study and writing centers. You can also find out about many of these opportunities online.

Best thing about these get-togethers? You don't have to necessarily be a "declared major" to take part. Before I declared my major in English, I often took part in Castalia, a monthly gathering held by the English Department in which students and faculty listened to a group of selected graduate students read their latest works. Even before I was officially in the major, this was a fun way to get to know other undergrad and grad English majors while participating in a function held by the department that I was interested in joining.

U Chic Tip! Focus Your Efforts

Maggie Biunno, Hofstra University

Don't try to take on too much! This tip worked for me. When I started college, I focused on joining a few groups like the school newspaper. I started at the bottom as a staff writer, moved up to an assistant position, then feature editor, and finished as the managing editor—second in charge of the entire paper! The best part about being involved in the paper was the opportunity to use what I learned inside the classroom. Thanks to this experience, I discovered that I wanted to be more than just a writer. I wanted to be an editor as well. What could prepare me for the future better than that?

ORGANIZATIONS WITH A SIGNIFICANT TIME COMMITMENT

Groups like the school's dance team, choir, orchestra, and band require a large time commitment. These groups will not try to hide this from you. At the first meeting they should be able to tell you what kind of commitment they expect from their members. If you find yourself enjoying the organization's activities, then it should be worth your time. You just have to make sure that you are not letting your academics fall short and that you are managing your time wisely.

START YOUR OWN ORGANIZATION

If you've been looking at the opportunities on campus and you can't find an organization that you want to join, why not start your own? Just realize that starting an organization will be fairly time-consuming—you are going to have to find members and work to get the organization recognized (and funded) by the university. Chances are that if you are interested in an area and a club does not exist for it yet, it won't be that tough to find people who are looking for a similar organization.

Getting involved on campus may at first seem overwhelming. But if you have a good idea about activities on campus that might interest you and keep an eye out for opportunities, joining a club or volunteer group can greatly supplement your years at school. It's a great way to meet people that you might not meet in class or in the dorm and get exposed to activities that the dorm doesn't offer.

Insights provided by Anna Prestek,
University of Washington–Seattle

for the future madam president

You walk onto campus for the first time, ready to make a difference. All through high school, you demonstrated leadership potential— captain of your varsity volleyball team, president of the National Honor Society, secretary of your senior class. You want to continue working with student associations in college, and more important, you want to do this as a leader. This section is for all you natural-born leaders wanting to get up-and-running as your class leader.

So where to start? I was in your position less than a year ago. I had no idea where to even begin getting involved in the student government association at my school. Well, with a little bit of effort and seeking out the right connections, I now serve as the chair of the Freshman Class Committee at Georgetown University. Thanks to this experience, I have a little advice to share that can help you access the halls of leadership on your campus.

GETTING INVOLVED IN STUDENT GOVERNMENT

In your quest to become a student government leader, you first need to decide what level of participation you want to have within the organization. Stop by the student government office on your campus to find more information on all your options.

Many campuses offer students a wide variety of student government opportunities, requiring anywhere from a little to a lot of your time. A word of caution: do not pledge yourself to a large commitment before you know what other organizations you want to join. If given the chance, student government can become a huge part of your life, and take up a lot of your free time. I regularly spend around seven hours a week for my Freshman Class chair duties, and I see other student body leaders spending many more hours in their offices. It is an amazing experience and extremely fun, but you need to first make sure you know what kind of time commitment you are looking at before you sign on for a project or position.

Most universities offer students the opportunity to be involved in different branches of the student government, including the executive board, the senate, and spots on small committees that are dedicated to a single issue. The more public-oriented positions will require a campus-wide election. At the beginning of your first semester, you will see information on how to run for specific positions such as the senate. However, the smaller committees are generally appointed positions, especially for freshmen. If an election is required for a smaller role, it is held in the spring. Therefore, freshmen are usually appointed to these areas on an as-needed basis.

Don't be afraid to ask upperclassmen in student government at your school how they initially got involved and in what programs they would recommend that you participate. They might suggest that you join a committee dedicated to an area that you may find particularly interesting, like expanded wireless Internet access, better cafeteria food, or free newspapers on campus.

RUNNING FOR OFFICE

If you're campaigning for student government, the first thing to do is make yourself visible to everyone on campus! Go to meetings of every club that you can, and introduce yourself to its members. Tell them that you are running for a position and that you would greatly appreciate their vote. Next, make your posters and flyers memorable. The most successful candidates are the ones whose flyers catch people's eyes or make them laugh. Be creative and daring with your ideas and slogans (but remember to keep them appropriate).

WHAT IF YOU WANT TO BE THE PRESIDENT?

This is an ambition that many freshmen have when they first enter college. In order to achieve this goal, you must be heavily involved in student government from the outset. Apply for an appointed position your freshman year, within the executive board if possible. Talk to the current president and vice president and see what roles they played in the government during their early years on campus. Also, it is important to forge strong relationships with many different groups of people on campus, as well as with other members of the student government. Never underestimate the power an endorsement from another organization, or from other important student government leaders, can have on an election.

Being elected is about experience, vision, ideas, and having connections with as many different groups as you can. The entire student body elects you. That means that in order to win, people must believe that you care about all facets of the university, which can most easily be achieved by having alliances with many different clubs and organizations that stand for different issues.

Even if you don't win, the experience of campaigning is one-of-a-kind and will shape the person you become in the future. Don't get discouraged if you lose a race or aren't appointed to the position you want. There is always time to work your way up through the organization, and every step of the way is a blast!

SHY AWAY FROM THE SPOTLIGHT AT TIMES?

What if you don't like giving speeches in front of large crowds and don't want to be heavily burdened by one activity your freshman year? Luckily, there are many ways to get involved in behind-the-scenes capacities within student government. One great way not only to get involved, but also meet others in your same class, is to join a class committee. Generally appointed by the current administration, class committees are responsible for planning events for their specific class, conducting fund-raisers, and making sure that there is a strong camaraderie within their class. If your student government does not offer the option of the class committee, why not ask if you can start one? They are the perfect opportunity to meet other motivated people in your class while not taking an extremely public or time-consuming position.

AND MOST IMPORTANT

Remember to have fun! Although student government can be demanding, it is extremely rewarding. You can see the effects of your work all around campus, which is immensely gratifying. Whether you launch an initiative to beautify campus through recycling or have free movies on Friday nights, student government allows for you to see what you have accomplished. If you are anything like me, you will catch the "student government bug" and want to be involved for all four years of college.

Insights provided by Alexa Rozell, Georgetown University

make a difference

Your résumé is filled with accomplishments: internships, accolades, stellar GPA, and skills galore. But no volunteer activities? Even if you're no Mother Theresa, you should be volunteering! College is known as an arena for opportunity, a place of forward thinking and innovation, free love and revolution. Although career advancement is usually at the top of our list of reasons for volunteering (shallow, I know), there are other reasons to commit to helping others.

Making a difference in someone's life, whether in your own community or somewhere else in the world, is a great way to experience something you've never done before while promoting social welfare. Also, the things you can learn while volunteering can translate into life and job skills that improve your chances for snagging an internship or job that you really want.

The New Way to Travel: Voluntourism

Thee Gardner, Duke University

While students have always done study abroad, it seems like more and more of my friends in college choose the volunteer route. In fact, I know girls who've done work in Mozambique, volunteered in South Africa, and rebuilt homes in New Orleans. It's called "voluntourism"—when people not originally from an area do a combination of tourist activities and volunteer work.

"I would do it again in a heartbeat. In fact, I probably will do it again," says Anita, a recent college grad, who volunteered in Belize last spring break. She helped rebuild a school, fixed and varnished furniture, put up drywall, and read to small children.

Where do voluntourists travel? Everywhere, from Uganda to France to New Orleans. Volunteers can do all kinds of activities depending on the location they choose—from building schools to teaching children English to working in wildlife preserves to working in hospitals and orphanages.

And it's not just students who volunteer. There are volunteer programs targeted to people over 50, teens, families, and working professionals. So if you decide to be a voluntourist, you can take your best friend, your little sister or brother, or your mom! Choosing whether to volunteer abroad can be a very big decision. Traditional study-abroad programs can usually give you academic credits toward graduation and/or give you a transcript from a foreign university. However, voluntourism has unique perks that you can't get from a study-abroad program.

First, voluntouring is often more affordable. Study-abroad programs include tuition for classes, which can add up to thousands of dollars. It's often possible to do month-long volunteer programs for under $1,000.

Voluntouring can give you a realistic perspective on what life is like for the less fortunate in a specific country. You can do your part to help out the rest of the world. "It's too easy to point to a poor neighborhood and say, 'Oh, isn't that sad,' and then go back to the hotel and back to the States without doing anything," says Itohan, a junior who went to Belize with Anita. "I have two working hands and feet—so in essence, I have no excuse not to help!"

The great thing about voluntourism is that you never go it

alone. Programs are often coordinated by foundations that have staff members traveling with the group. If you've never volunteered abroad before, they'll tell you what to do. Also, you still get to be a tourist! Itohan and Anita both saw the Mayan ruins while they were in Belize. Volunteering doesn't mean that you don't get to have fun.

Is volunteering abroad right for you? It's an incredibly rewarding experience. However, not everyone's cut out for it, especially if you're thinking of traveling to especially rural or obscure areas. Could you go to the bathroom on the ground or in grass? Could you live without electricity, hot water, phone, or Internet? If so, great! But if you can't live without a hot shower each morning, your makeup bag, and a cup of Starbucks, you might want to think again. Each program is different. Do your research.

Also, ask yourself this question: Do you have skills or capabilities to contribute in the place you want to volunteer? For example, if you want to teach children English, are you a good teacher? Do you work well with kids? If so, go for it. If not, check out a different voluntourism program where you can make use of your special talents and skills.

Want to be a voluntourist? Check out websites like www .crossculturalsolutions.org and www.volunteerinternational.org. Or just type "international volunteering" into Google and see what pops up. Happy traveling!

MAKING A DIFFERENCE IN YOUR OWN BACKYARD

While there are many people throughout the rest of the world who are in need of help, you will also find people who need a hand in your own community. To make a difference in the world, sometimes it's as easy as getting in a car or bus to travel to a different city in the United States. Check out AmeriCorps or City Year for some domestic volunteer opportunities.

Something as simple as putting a smile on someone's face can be very contagious and truly change that person's outlook on life. Try volunteering at your local soup kitchen or spending time with the sick or elderly. These are perfect opportunities to gain insight into who you are as an individual as well as the truth about the state of American life.

I was able to witness this firsthand while delivering greetings and flowers at a hospital. The power of a balloon or a "Get Well Soon" card is immeasurable. Also, volunteering at a hospital is a great opportunity for those of you planning to go to medical or nursing school.

No matter what you end up doing, the perspective you will gain while helping others will change your outlook on life. To find these opportunities, see what your college has to offer. Most campuses have a community service office (some are even student-run) that connects students with local volunteer opportunities.

NOURISH THE FUTURE

Try being a role model for a child who needs one. You remember what it was like when you were young and had so many questions about life. Now imagine a child without access to successful and secure adults to help guide them along.

Teaching, tutoring, or mentoring a child can make a major difference in his or her life. You can help decrease dropout and teen pregnancy rates. Girls have to deal with issues of self-image and sexual discovery at younger and younger ages. Help them understand what's happening and how to make the right decisions. Believe me—if you can handle the kids of today, then you can definitely deal with difficult coworkers in the future.

Where to look? If you are looking to make a difference in a child's life, try the local chapter of Boys & Girls Clubs of America or Teach for America, a two-year opportunity after graduation. Interested in law? Look into volunteering for CASA (Court Appointed Special Advocates—www.casaforchildren.org). The organization, which has grown to a network of more than 59,000 volunteers who serve 243,000 abused and neglected children nationwide, will train you to advocate on behalf of an abused child in a courtroom setting. This is an invaluable experience for someone interested in becoming a public interest lawyer.

SAVING MOTHER EARTH

You've heard it before: if we don't take efforts today to protect our precious ecosystem, the future does not look great for our children and the plants and animals with which we share this world. As one option for volunteerism, try getting engaged in activities that help protect our planet. It can be as simple as setting up recycling in your dorm or sorority house, or even becoming an activist by canvassing for Greenpeace or urging your congressional representative to support legislation that protects the environment.

Green is definitely the new pink!

If you are more hands-on in your desire to save the planet, go out and get local businesses and organizations to plant trees. Or even try to make your next vacation environmentally safe by going to the beach and saving the turtles. Green is definitely the new pink!

SUPPORT AN IMPORTANT CAUSE

The people we meet in our lives can have a major influence on our futures and our decision to volunteer. If your mother has breast cancer or your grandfather is suffering from Alzheimer's, why not get involved in a cause that works to end these diseases? An added benefit: helping the causes that mean a lot to your family can also bring you closer together.

You can do little things like buying an awareness tag or make greater commitments, like volunteering at the March of Dimes or the local American Cancer Society office. You can share a special bond with your fellow participants through similar stories of survival and suffering. The passion and motivation it takes to pursue and uplift a cause will enhance your life in so many ways.

HAVE FUN

No matter what you do, add some fun to the mix by inviting your friends to join you. Skip the spring break trip to Panama City and instead go with friends on a trip to California to work for Save the Whales. This experience still includes lots of sun and waves, and can offer much more as far as bonding is concerned.

U Chic Tip!

Remember that volunteering doesn't have to be a drag. Going with groups can actually be loads of fun. You get to see another side of friends, and it can also be a great opportunity to make memories that will truly last a lifetime. I'll never forget shelving dented cans with friends at our local Salvation Army "Grocery Store" and getting rid of the outdated fashions in our closets.

Family members especially make great volunteer companions, so suggest it for the next family reunion or when Mom is complaining that you don't spend enough time at home.

You will also meet many new people you may have never run into otherwise when you choose to volunteer. Who knows, you may come out of a volunteer experience with an entirely new group of friends.

No matter what your background—whether you were born with a silver spoon or not—it's time to get out of your comfort zone to see how others live and think. Pushing yourself to do things you would normally shy away from will help you to gain perspective on what is really important in life.

Insights provided by Jessica Cruel,
University of North Carolina–Chapel Hill

tips for the busy
student athlete

Student athletes live very different lives from the rest of the student body. From 6 a.m. lifting sessions to six-hour bus trips, time is precious for this segment of the population. Student athletes at every level must carefully balance their sports with academics, relationships, and their careers. It requires a huge commitment, but it also generates great rewards. Here are some tips for the busy student athlete looking to stay on top.

TIP 1: KNOW YOUR PRIORITIES

Life as a student athlete is different from that of the regular student. When you leave home you might think that you are "on your own" and completely free to do anything you can imagine, but that is not necessarily the case if you're playing college sports. Many times, coaches can be just as strict as parents. Like your parents, your coach is not going to want to hear that you've been in trouble for underage drinking or public drunkenness, or that your grades are falling. This is probably one of the most important aspects of being a student athlete. You have to respect what your coach tells you to do. He or she expects your all. Your team expects your all.

Also, understand that your school expects more from you than from the majority of the student body. You represent the university and are expected to act appropriately. This includes Facebook and partying. Be responsible, or your scholarship could be at stake.

TIP 2: ACADEMICS MATTER GREATLY

One of the most important aspects of being a student athlete is your grades. If your grades slip too low, you could be held on academic probation. The easiest way to avoid this is to simply go to class. I knew a girl who always waited until the last minute to get her assignments done. Her procrastination didn't pay off: she ended up with a GPA lower than the academic standards and got kicked off the team. It can happen to anyone, so be sure to keep your grades up. And remember, just like the NCAA commercial says, "Most college athletes go pro in something other than sports."

Why I Quit

I quit playing soccer for my college team just after my junior year season had wrapped up. Every time people ask me why I quit with just one year left, I respond one of two ways: "It's not just the senior year season. It's the spring season. It's summer training. It's preseason. I just could not invest all my efforts into that single activity for one more year." Or, "There were too many opportunities I was missing out on. I just enjoy other things. I had a spring-term internship. I enjoy being active in a sorority, working on my school newspaper, and going on weekend vacations."

Do I regret playing college soccer? No: I had great teammates and I needed the structure for the majority of my college career. There are no excuses for falling behind when you're on a tight student athlete's schedule, because you just can't. But eventually, I grew out of the desire to play every day, to attend numerous athletic events, and to be held back from other things. The sport I had played since age four had turned into an obligation, not a passion.

TIP 3: VALUE YOUR HEALTH

Make sure to get adequate sleep, eat healthy, and relax. This is important for your sport, but it is also important for your general health. If you don't sleep enough, your playing will suffer, your academics will suffer, and you will probably be upset. Athletes expend a lot of calories, so make sure you eat often and eat healthy.

Relaxation is also important. Take the time to slow down and have some time to yourself.

How I Dealt With Getting Cut from the Team

Kara Apel, University of South Carolina

I felt like I was on the top of the world my freshman year.

I was on our school's football dance team and was not only keeping in shape but also doing what I loved the most: dance. Not to mention, I was getting class credits, a stipend, and the opportunity to dance in front of over 80,000 people each weekend!

I loved every single moment I was on the team. From performances to practices, it was one of the best experiences of my life.

Little did I know, everything would come crashing down the next semester.

Unfortunately, we had to try out each season to secure our spots on the team. I was nervous, but I thought I would be pretty much a shoe-in since I had already made the team once. Shortly after my audition, I found out I hadn't made the team for the next season.

I was angry, I was hurt, and most of all—I was confused. How could this have happened to me?

Luckily (or, I guess in this case, unluckily), one of my closest friends on the team didn't make the cut either. We had each other's shoulders to cry on, and I don't know what I would have done without her.

I had placed so much of my self-worth in something that wasn't tangible. I wasn't sure who I was anymore. Who was Kara, the nondancer?

Thankfully, I had been able to get involved in some other activities that semester, so I was able to stay busy. One of those activities was the school newspaper. I spent a lot of time there my spring semester writing for the news section. Since I didn't have dance practice in the spring, I had a lot more time on my hands and since I was majoring in journalism, it was a perfect fit!

Although I worked hard at the newspaper, I was shocked when I got the call from the news editor asking if I would want to come on board in the fall as the assistant news editor. This happened a few days after I was cut from the team.

It was fate! Looking back on that now, I really understand that everything happens for a reason. If I had made the team, I wouldn't have been able to accept an editor position at the newspaper. If I hadn't done that, I wouldn't have eventually become editor-in-chief.

I also wouldn't have become as close to my fellow teammate who had been cut. She and I have stayed best friends ever since that day.

I'm not trying to sugarcoat all of this—getting cut from the team sucks. It's embarrassing and disappointing. However, after I stopped feeling sorry for myself, I was able to appreciate all the great things around me.

Even though it was heartbreaking, I'm thankful I got cut from the team. Ironic, isn't it?

TIP 4: HAVE FRIENDS BOTH ON AND OFF THE TEAM

There is much to be said about expanding your circle of friends. Since you spend so much of your time dedicated to sports, it can be a great stress relief to just chill with friends that have no connection to sports whatsoever. Having trouble meeting people? Join a club or two that meshes well with your practices, but be sure not to overload your schedule. Also, there is always the option of joining a sorority. Sororities, in general, are eager to recruit women that are actively involved on campus and in sports, and are, therefore, willing to work around a busy student athlete's schedule.

Now, I am not saying that you shouldn't be close with those on your team. Your team is practically your family, and with every family comes occasional drama and issues that develop. Cliques will form. But there is good news! You can be one of those rare people that is friends with everyone. Certainly, one can't avoid all conflicts, but it is possible to stay out of most petty arguments by simply refusing to feed into it.

TIP 5: ENJOY!

As a student athlete, your life may be stressful, but sometimes it helps to remember why you play the sport in the first place. As kids, we started playing sports for fun and friends. These two things should still matter most. And if they don't, you should think about doing something else.

*Insights provided by Krista Naposki, Elon University,
and Amanda Sandlin, Rider University*

U Chic Essentials—Getting Involved

Follow your passion

Get involved in activities that come naturally to you and get you excited. You'll be more apt to stick with them, and even to aim for the all-important leadership roles in the group. Don't be swayed too much by popularity.

Beware the buffet effect

Does the following scenario sound familiar? You're at a buffet and the many delectables entice a greater appetite than you really have. Ah, if only you had enjoyed just one or two of the items that caught your eye. Getting involved on campus can lead to a similar buffet effect. Try hard to limit your activities to your favorite few, and you'll be able to dedicate more time and receive more enjoyment from them.

College is your testing ground

What you learn outside of class can often be more important than what you learn inside. So get out, and get involved! Getting involved on campus or in your community is one of your best opportunities to test the skills that are most important in the real world. And don't be afraid to take the lead early on. By getting out of your comfort zone, you're building experience and getting your name out there as a go-to person.

Looking for more great advice? Head to www.UChic.com for our fave resources and websites—they come highly recommended from our guide's contributors and editors. Be sure to leave your suggestions as well!

CHAPTER 5

Tech Etiquette for a Facebook Age

S hould I ask the hottie in history for his number or should I just friend him on Facebook?"

"Is it OK to break up with someone via text message?"

"Should I text my new love interest or is a phone call more appropriate?"

"Am I spending too much time on Facebook? Am I an addict?"

Do any of these questions sound familiar?

With iPhones, smartphones, and Facebook, socializing is a whole lot easier these days. But with this ease comes the added stress of knowing *when* is the right time to use *which* form of communication. Also, you can almost forget the importance of in-person interaction every now and then.

To provide some much-needed rules of engagement, read on for some fail-safe tech etiquette for a Facebook age.

to call or text: communication rules for dating

College life comes complete with an array of attractive, educated people at your disposal. Throw in some alcohol, coed dorms, and an ever-growing list of Facebook event invites, and you've got yourself one crazy dating scene. It seems like there are no real rules, and if there are, people sure aren't afraid to bend—or completely break—them.

Let's set the scene. You meet an adorable, delicious boy at a house party, complete with his astrological sign tattooed on his bronzed bicep (and, of course, you totally check your horoscope like every day). You engage in a heated discussion about all your other interests (finally, a guy who will admit to loving reality TV!), and find that you have a lot in common. You're really into each other, so you exchange numbers and go home happy, elated even.

However, it's the next morning and the dilemma sets in. You have his number, now what? What's a modern girl to do when she has two completely viable options for communication— to call or to text? And there is always Facebook to complicate things further.

WHEN TO CALL

If you have something serious to talk about

My number one pet peeve is when people—girlfriends and boyfriends alike—decide to initiate a fight, debate, or other meaningful discussion via text message. In the age of texting, sometimes it's easy to forget that some conversations are supposed to be long, drawn-out, and, above all else, meaningful. There are still certain situations, especially in dating, that require you to actually use your voice—and not a keyboard or cell phone keypad—to express yourself. Even if we're talking about your boyfriend of three years, he deserves the chance to actually hear what you have to say.

Also, text messages can be easily misinterpreted when trying to discuss something where emotions are involved—those little smiley faces do not tell all! Sarcasm and other voice inflections are often misread in text messages, causing a whole mess of confusion between the two parties involved. There have been numerous occasions when girls have misread text messages and caused lots of unnecessary drama with boyfriends. If you really want to ensure he understands why you freaked out the night before, discuss the events over the phone, if not in person!

If you aren't distracted

My ex-boyfriend and I attempted to carry on many a phone conversation when I lived in the dorm. Let me tell you— living around 40 girls did not make for optimum relationship communication time. If you want to chat it up with that new boy in your life or have a quality phone date with your current BF, make sure you are somewhere quiet, free of giggling girls chugging wine and/or discussing the latest celeb gossip. Devote your concentration to the conversation and really listen to what your beau is saying. You'll be surprised how much you will enjoy talking with your sweetie when you give him your full attention.

If you want to make plans

It's tempting to ask your guy to hang in a text message, but wait until you show up at one movie theater and he accidentally goes to another. Confirming when, where, and how you and your dude are going to meet up is best done through verbal communication and will help avoid confusion later. It's faster than waiting for a text message response, which as we all know can take hours—if you get one at all. Make special plans more solid over the phone.

If you want to show that you're truly interested

When you take the time out of your obviously super-busy schedule to actually dial your crush's number, it shows that you have a genuine interest in him and what he has to say. Although firing off a short "What's up?" text is quick and painless, it does not say much, literally.

If you want to break it off

Don't commit the cardinal sin of college dating—the text message breakup. Although I don't think that having a "You-were-the-best-and-worst-thing-that-ever-happened-to-me" tear-jerking conversation over the phone is much better, it at least gives the other person an opportunity to defend himself and spill his side of the story. Breakups aren't easy no matter how you have to handle them, but a phone conversation is a much more civil way to move on.

WHEN TO TEXT

If he texts first

Take the scenario where you meet at a party. We can argue that chivalry is dead, but let's be honest here—you know that any guy who is truly interested in hanging out with your fabulous self will soon send you a quick, flirty text or call you up to take you out (or at the very least, invite you to tag along to a frat party). If the cute boy texts you first, a text response is not only a way to show that you, too, are interested, but it's also polite. Manners are always classy; and classy is always attractive.

If you're super busy, duh

College students are constantly swamped with papers, 300-page readings on thrilling subjects like the principles of formal logic, 45-minute presentations, what have you. Between all your activities, it might be hard to find the time for a phone call—especially if you just want to check up. Sending a friendly "How's it going?" or "I love you!" text message—depending on the situation, of course—is totally acceptable. In fact, it might even be the perfect way to go—especially if your partner is busy, too! You can also use text messages as a way to arrange times to communicate other ways. Send a quick "Call me after six!" text message if you miss a call during class so your sweetheart knows you aren't too busy or completely ignoring him.

If you're already in a relationship

The rules change quite a bit when you're already attached. While you still shouldn't use the text message as an easy way out (like to break up) or as a way to tackle some serious drama, text messages are a good way to communicate with someone you already know and love. They know your style of speech, they know how your brain works (or at least attempt to understand it), and they will have a better idea about how to decipher your text messages than someone you just met. And when it comes to social networking sites like Facebook and MySpace? It might be OK to occasionally post on your BF's wall, or send him a cute message that you think will brighten his day—but delving into anything too serious using the Internet is an absolutely terrible idea. It's there forever, for the whole world to see.

And before you sext that text

There's flirting and then there's *flirting*, but sexting doesn't fall into either category. What seems like naughty fun now may turn into a nightmare if you're not too careful. Although nude cell phone images of stars like Pete Wentz and Vanessa Hudgens proved embarrassing for them but didn't derail their careers, you most likely won't be so lucky. One vengeful upload by an ex and you could find yourself blackballed from your career of choice (yes, employers DO Google you before an interview or job offer! More on that later). Flirty text messages are fine. But since texts live forever, steer clear of any revealing pics you might not want your mom, dad, or future boss to see.

Remember that while phone calls and text messages are great ways to communicate with the opposite sex, face-to-face encounters are ideal. In order to establish a real connection, you have to be able to see, hear, and touch the other person. No text message could ever replace a good snuggle session on your comfy couch or a romantic dinner at your favorite sushi restaurant. It's easy to stumble in the fast-paced dating world of smartphones, YouTube, Google, text messages, iPods, you name it. But with proper tech etiquette, new technologies can make your love life a whole lot easier and more interesting.

Insights provided by Erica Strauss, Kent State University

tech and social media essentials

If you didn't realize it already, technology and social media are an essential part of your college career and beyond. Master these things now, and you're well on your way to professional success, guaranteed.

DEVELOPING AND PROTECTING YOUR ONLINE REPUTATION

We put everything online—from our relationship status to our Friday night plans. But how much is too much? Here are some tips for staying on the right side of it.

When setting up your social networks in college, it's important to think of what type of image you want to have online. CNN reports that a recent Microsoft survey found that 70 percent of job recruiters and hiring managers have rejected a job applicant based on information they found online. What kind of information? "Inappropriate" comments by the candidate; "unsuitable" photos and videos; criticisms of previous employers, coworkers, or clients; and even inappropriate comments by friends and relatives, according to the survey report, titled "Online Reputation in a

Connected World." Although the real world may seem a distant concern, the online reputation you're creating in college today can come back to haunt you tomorrow. The best rule of thumb for any social networking site? If you wouldn't want your mom or your future boss to see something you're planning to post online or send as a text message, you may want to rethink your strategy.

Email Etiquette

Speaking of your online presence, when using email to communicate with your professors and classmates, it is super important to keep the tone professional. First things first, make sure your email has all the necessary information and that it is written concisely, as professors and classmates, alike, already get a ton of emails every day.

Also, don't keep resending the email if it's not answered. Professors, especially, will try to respond as quickly as possible to your inquiries, but you have to give them time. If they don't respond in a timely fashion, consider stopping by their office or leaving a voicemail on their campus phone. If after several days of patiently waiting you still get no response, follow up with a short and sweet note, asking if they received your first note and that you look forward to their response. And those tardy responses from your student peers? There are probably a couple of reasons they haven't gotten back to you—either they didn't want to answer or they couldn't help you. So you may just want to consider moving on to someone else who can help.

In all email communications, do your best to use correct

grammar and avoid slang. It's never appropriate to curse. As we all know from those horror stories in the media, inappropriate or poorly written emails can be misinterpreted and potentially prove harmful to your future hopes and aspirations. Run spell check before you send and make sure any necessary documents are attached. After all, nobody's going to take you seriously if you spell the course name wrong in the subject of your email. It's smart to practice good email etiquette for when you want to start emailing potential employers about those dream internships or jobs!

Facebook

My go-to rule for Facebook is to organize your "friends" by setting up groups for family, friends, and work contacts. Next, determine what each of these groups should be able to see, using the "privacy settings" section of your Facebook account. For instance, you probably don't want your younger cousin or aunt to see your girls' night out pics, so of course you would want to limit who can view these. We have tons of great advice in the next section on Facebook. Another great tip? Making photos and videos in which you are tagged "private" allows you to view them before sending them out into the Web. This helps you keep a handle on what others are posting about you.

Twitter

Do you tweet? To build goodwill on Twitter, as a general rule of thumb, don't share anything you wouldn't want your grandmother reading; don't use profanity; don't complain; and generally don't use this as a platform for negativity. Instead, support causes you believe in if you'd like, but don't get into a tweet-fight if someone disagrees. It's the Internet; there are millions of different opinions, and someone is bound to disagree with you. Try finding something you really like—a passion, a topic, a policy—and find people in those Twitter groups. The more people you follow and maintain a positive relationship with, the more people you will network with—the goal of online networking. Also, Twitter's privacy settings are different from Facebook's. For instance, if you make the tweets protected, only your friends can see them and that really limits your ability to network online, which is your primary reason for being on Twitter.

LinkedIn

Another website worth looking into while in college is LinkedIn, a social networking site for professionals. If you start building connections—both off- and online—you'll have no problem transitioning those connections into professional ones after graduation, when you're looking to land your first job. How best to build your network in school? Whenever you attend a career fair or other networking event or meet an alum, exchange a business card and connect with your new contact as soon as possible on LinkedIn. The sooner you do it the better, as your new contact is more likely to remember you and be impressed with your most excellent networking skills. Who knows? It may just land you an internship or even a job sometime in the future!

When you're hard at work building positive and meaningful online relationships, do not neglect to build positive personal and professional relationships offline as well. And, last but not least, if there is one thing for you to take away—never forget that everything said online is permanent, so think twice before you say or do anything that you might come to regret in the future.

Before moving on, let's address some tech essentials that will come into play at some point during your college career.

COLLEGE COURSES GO HI-TECH

Taking an online course is something many students consider while in college. And why not? The length of the course is usually shorter, and it's generally cheaper than regular courses. However, it can be hard for some students to learn online. In my experience, the most important thing to do with online courses is to plan ahead of time—use some sort of online calendar or written calendar and plan out the hours you will spend on classes and homework each week. If you schedule the course time into your life like a regular class, you will be able to maintain the somewhat hectic schedule of an online course.

BUY, RENT, OR DOWNLOAD COLLEGE TEXTBOOKS?

Between the costs of tuition, room and board, books, a computer, and the ever-essential daily Starbucks run, it's expensive to be a college student these days. And we're in a recession. (Good timing, right?) Now more than ever, it's important for students to watch their wallets and look for ways to save (ideally without sacrificing your morning Venti). Enter online book rental services. Everyone complains about trips to the crowded bookstore for overpriced textbooks, but now there's an easy alternative: you can rent all the textbooks you need online for much less than the cost of buying them. Online rental companies, like Chegg.com and CampusBookRentals.com, provide a variety of rental options and prices. Renting textbooks is a great way to save money. In fact, during my last semester of college, I saved $300 on textbooks alone by renting them online. I was able to return them quickly and efficiently with a prepaid label and box.

THE E-BOOK READER REVOLUTION

Textbooks are expensive, heavy, and not very useful (or worth much) after the semester is over. Unfortunately, when it comes to college, they're just another fact of life. But what if you could lighten your load and save money at the same time? Try e-book readers or e-readers. Working with an e-reader is definitely one way to save money, as books cost less. Why else are they a great option? They are yours to keep forever and can be altered in any way you like. You can highlight, add a note, get a definition, or bookmark a page. Kindle, Nook, or the iPad—which one is right for you? It's a question of personal preference, but my favorite is the iPad—it has every single e-reader feature built into it, and you can use Barnes and Noble books, Amazon books, and, of course, download books from Apple. The only downside to some e-readers is that the pages sometimes don't correspond with the exact pages of the print version. A way around this? If you're going to use an e-reader for all your books this year, be sure to ask your professor for a chapter-by-chapter breakdown of assignments.

That covers most of the tech basics that come up in college. Keep in mind that when it comes to any of these social media platforms and technologies, it's all about personal preference— whatever feels right for you is right for you, no matter what.

Insights provided by Amanda Cross, University of Central Arkansas, and Victoria Reitano, Quinnipiac University

when it's time to unplug

You see it everywhere you go on campus: people texting and talking on their cellies, taking pics with their iPhones, and updating their Facebook accounts with their latest FourSquare destinations. It's like a whole generation of kids are so wired into social media that they can't go through a day without it. But is it an addiction?

According to a study conducted at the University of Maryland, a majority of subjects admitted that they were functionally *unable* to go without their tech toys for a period of 24 hours. The study, "24 Hours: Unplugged," challenged 200 students at the College Park campus to abstain from their phones, laptops, TVs, iPods, and all other media for 24 hours. After their 24 hours were up, students were asked to write about their experiences on a private class blog.

"I clearly am addicted and the dependency is sickening," admitted one person in the study. Many students reported withdrawal symptoms similar to those of alcohol or drug addiction, including anxiety, nervousness, and a feeling of helplessness. An overall analysis of students' responses determined that the biggest issue was an overwhelming sense of disconnection from friends and family.

"What they spoke about in the strongest terms was how their lack of access to text messaging, phone calling, instant messaging, email, and Facebook meant that they couldn't connect with friends who lived close by, much less those far away," explains project director Susan D. Moeller, a journalism professor at the University of Maryland and the head of the International Center for Media and the Public Agenda, which conducted the study on campus.

What can we glean from all of this? Today's college students rely heavily on social media and the Internet to provide them constant contact with friends and family, while at the same time filling them in on breaking news, gossip, etc. Certainly this in itself isn't a good or bad thing. But when reliance on your iPod or smartphone turns into a situation where you can't even spend an hour not texting or checking the latest Facebook updates, it's time to take a step back and try living life instead of reading about it.

facebook's dark side

No longer exclusive to college students, Facebook.com is one of the fastest-growing social networking websites today. It's just how college students communicate. In fact, the Facebook epidemic has reached the point that it is strange when you meet someone in college who *doesn't* have a Facebook profile; one wonders why they would choose not to partake in the Facebook fun.

Did You Know?

In 2006, about 3 in 4 college students had a Facebook account.

Not long ago, many experts felt that spending large amounts of time using the Internet for social interaction was a sign of a personal deficiency in social skills. In other words, people who spent a lot of time socially networking online were doing it because they felt socially awkward face-to-face. However, in the rapidly evolving world of online communications, such generalizations are no longer accurate. Today's students have integrated online communication like Facebook and other social networking sites into their daily lives to enrich, rather than replace, their already existing relationships. But like anything else, it has its drawbacks as well.

YOUR PROFILE SAYS IT ALL

The average college student logs into their Facebook account nearly every day, spending anywhere from 10 minutes to 3 hours a day checking out the latest details on their friends' profiles. There are even categories of Facebook users determined by the number of "friends" that one has prominently displayed on the front page of one's profile. If you've got under 200, then consider yourself a casual Facebook user, one who thinks it is fun but doesn't quite see its full potential so doesn't waste too much time on it. Have 200–300 friends? You're the average Facebook user, one who probably checks his or her account and exchanges wall posts with friends at least once a day. For those entertaining 300–400+ friends, congrats. You're popular, one who makes a lot of friends and acquaintances and uses Facebook to keep in touch with all of them. But 500+? You've entered new territory—desperate. Let me guess: you are one of those people who Facebooks everyone, even when you haven't met the person yet!

For all of the benefits that Facebook provides, however—like keeping in touch with friends (especially when you're wanting to procrastinate)—Facebook does have its dark side as well.

WHO CAN SEE YOUR PROFILE?

By now, you've surely heard the stories on how potential employers search for you on social-networking websites like Facebook and have made hiring decisions based on what they find. These stories are true. Those fun party pics with you and your drunk friends might not work for future employers. However, college students are entitled to partake in a little fun with their friends, and there's no reason you shouldn't have pictures to document the memories. But you should always take precautions with *what* you post on Facebook.

U Chic Tip! Don't Post It All

With the variety of individuals on Facebook today—parents, employers, university faculty members, and even police officers—it is important to censor what you post. A safe rule of thumb is to not post anything you wouldn't want your parents or boss to see.

If—for whatever reason—you must post the pictures, exercise caution. Use the "limited profile" feature, and use it liberally. If you must be Facebook friends with someone who you'd rather not have viewing your entire profile—say a parent, younger sibling, boss, etc.—be careful here. I, for one, am Facebook friends with my company's executive director. I immediately put her on "limited" to make sure she cannot see any pictures or anything else she could possibly deem inappropriate for a member of her staff.

Also, make sure to use other privacy restrictions like only allowing your friends to view your profile. Many students are now even making their Facebook profiles completely "unsearchable" so that employers cannot check their Facebook profile during the recruitment season. Last important tip: you can also block specific individuals from seeing your profile. Certainly, the technology will continue to change while you're in college. Be sure to keep up on these changes to make sure that you are not jeopardizing any future opportunities with a little bit of totally normal college debauchery.

DOES FACEBOOK CONTROL YOU?

A recent poll by Sophos (an IT firm) of 500 full-time employees who are recent college graduates found that 14.8 percent of them admitted to being logged onto Facebook virtually all day during work, and another 8 percent admitted to checking their Facebook up to 10 times a day at work!

If you worry that you might qualify as a Facebook addict, then you most likely have a problem. Interested in changing? Try documenting for a couple days how often you go on Facebook and how much time you spend on the site during each visit. You might be shocked to learn how much time you waste each day reading up on the details of the lives of your friends and acquaintances. Once you have a good feel for the average amount of time you waste on Facebook, substitute this time with something more positive like going to the gym, meditation, yoga, or spending time with your good friends *in person*. I'm not saying that the solution is to give Facebook up entirely. We all know that's an impossible suggestion. But just try finding some balance in your life and you'll feel a lot better for it.

Facing Facebook Addiction

Updates. Friend requests. Fun photos you can't help commenting on. While social media has proven to be indispensable when it comes to keeping up with everyone and his or her brother, sometimes there is such a thing as too much of a good thing. While psychologists have yet to classify Facebook obsession as an actual addiction, a recent article on CNN.com reveals that a growing number of doctors are seeing new patients with compulsion issues. How can you determine if you have a serious problem? See if any of these statements sound familiar:

- You've put off going out with friends and doing schoolwork on more than one occasion to play around with your profile.

- You're constantly checking updates on your phone, even when you're in class, hanging out with your pals, or on a date.

- You obsessively keep track of the guys you once dated and the ones you secretly have a crush on.

- If given the choice, you'd choose an hour online over an hour of sleep.

- Your grades are starting to take a hit. Why? With all your free time going to Facebook, there's little time to study!

If more than one of these applies to you (especially the one on bad grades!), it's time to unplug your profile, take a step back, and assess the situation. Can't stand not knowing what's going on with your friends 24/7? Consult your school's mental health services center for advice or counseling on how to combat compulsive behavior.

FACEBOOK AND DATING

Facebook has changed the way our generation perceives relationships and interpersonal communication, and that's not necessarily always a good thing. What happens when you're going on a first date with someone, and are only pretending to learn new things about them from your conversations, since you've already memorized their favorite movies and TV shows from their Facebook profile? What you can learn about someone from staring at a computer does not, and should not, in any way, replace interacting with them "IRL."

In the age of the emoticon, people claim that online communication makes dating and friendships easier, but actually, when you look deeper, it can be an obstacle to our ability to interact with people in person. It's easy to come up with witty one-liners online, but more important to be able to improvise in person. Facebook is fun, but can take a lot away from the process of getting to know another person one-on-one. Don't let this happen to you.

Friending and Un-friending: The Rules of the Game
Victoria Reitano, Quinnipiac University

When you connect with someone on Facebook or elsewhere on the Web, you are publicly proclaiming your association with that person. But let's face it: your name is all you have when you communicate online, and the related associations you build are vitally important. That's something you need to remember every time you choose to friend or un-friend someone on Facebook, for instance. In my opinion, un-friending someone is an important thing to think about ahead of time. You're always going to have those people you used to talk to, but no longer do, so you need to determine a policy for how you'll deal with these contacts. I generally un-friend anyone I don't speak with in real life—if we're only friends online or I can't remember why we're friends online, then we shouldn't be "friends" on Facebook. Same with ignoring friend requests. The only time I would do this is if I didn't know someone or knew them but never associated with them offline. In the end, it's up to you to decide how you want to deal with these relationships.

MAINTAINING STRONG FRIENDSHIPS

A blog once claimed that social-networking sites like Facebook are perpetuating weak ties and fewer strong relationships. Why? Essentially, the problem lies in how easy it is to become "friends" with someone. Within one meeting and a couple clicks of a mouse, you can be listed as someone's "friend," but does this really translate to a friendship? Does writing a happy birthday message on someone's wall once a year really mean you're buddies in the real world? I don't think so. Maintaining a friendship with someone requires a lot more effort than a once-a-year wall post lost among hundreds of others.

On the flip side, according to Wikipedia, social networks are great because they help us create lots of ties and get access to new information that we wouldn't otherwise have access to while allowing us to keep in touch with our closer friends.

But never forget that it's also easy for those who were once close friends to be relegated to weak online acquaintances. Make sure not to let networking sites like Facebook overtake your social life, and don't forget to maintain your friendships offline as well! When you no longer see someone in class every day or are too busy to hang out with them, it's easy to substitute the occasional wall post or message saying hello, but this is not a good replacement for spending time together in person and won't help build your relationships.

PARTING WORDS OF ADVICE

Facebook is a fun and extremely useful tool—there are plenty of people you might otherwise lose touch with in life that Facebook will allow you to keep in touch with—but like anything else, use it in moderation. Because I know how addictive Facebook can be, during finals week each year I usually let a friend log into my account and change my password so that I don't log back into Facebook until after exams are over. It's just one extra way of making sure Facebook doesn't interfere with what is important to me…like doing well on an exam! Don't let it take over—if you find yourself spending large amounts of time memorizing people's profiles or commenting on photos the night before you have a major history paper due, don't forget your priorities and log off of that site!

Insights provided by Nisha Chittal, University of Illinois

U Chic Essentials—Tech Etiquette for a Facebook Age

Build the relationship in person

In order to establish a real connection with someone, you have to spend time with them in person. No text message could ever replace those fabulous in-person moments like a good snuggle session on your comfy couch or romantic dinner at your favorite sushi restaurant.

Don't post it all

With the variety of individuals on Facebook today, it's important to use good judgment about what you do and do not post online.

Save the important stuff for in-person

In the age of texting, sometimes it's easy to forget that some conversations are supposed to be face-to-face and meaningful. Dating in particular calls for real conversations.

Looking for more great advice? Head to www.UChic.com for our fave resources and websites—they come highly recommended from our guide's contributors and editors. Be sure to leave your suggestions as well!

CHAPTER 6

Love Life

I t's rare to find a woman in college these days whose primary goal is to get hitched. But it wasn't too long ago that some women went to college solely for their Mrs. degree. Of course serious relationships still exist in college these days. It's just the way we approach and view dating has radically changed.

So what to expect? From short-term relationships to long-term relationships to an occasional hookup, be prepared for *anything* when it comes to dating in college. To give you a crash course on the college dating scene, we've pulled together some essential dating advice from college women nationwide. Having been there and pretty much done everything you can imagine when it comes to dating, these women have much to share!

the scoop on the college dating scene

Let's face it. After you've said good-bye to your parents and finished unpacking, what you're really excited to check out is *not* the campus or your classes.

But as much as I wanted to meet a cute guy and establish a long-term and stable relationship in college, that was not my sole motivation for going to school. After all, this is the age of the independent woman. As an independent woman, you're here to make your dreams your reality, and finding a man should not be your first goal in mind. It's just an added bonus, icing on the cake, when you meet that special someone in college.

Since the rules of dating have changed drastically (even since your older sister was in college), I wanted to share a little advice on how to enjoy the college dating scene without losing sight of yourself, your goals, or your future.

STAY TRUE TO YOURSELF
Let's start with the don'ts: *don't date just to be like your friends.* Before you start dating, make sure you do it for the right reasons.

I'm sure your parents have told you time and time again to always act for the right reasons, and now being on your own, it's time to test out your ability to stay true to yourself. Don't make decisions about your own love life based on what your friends are doing. Even if all of them are dating, this does not mean that you have to enter the dating pool. Also, having a boyfriend will not prove anything to yourself or your friends about your maturity or self-worth.

Don't set out looking for a boyfriend. It's so easy to get caught up in a relationship and have your social life revolve around him rather than to make your own friends. And if it doesn't work out, you'll regret not taking the time to make connections with others when you're sitting at home alone in your dorm room trying to recover from a breakup. In college, especially, there are so many new people to meet and interesting opportunities that it can be a bit overwhelming at first. But what should be first and foremost on your new agenda are your friendships. Take the time to get to know your girlfriends before you call anyone your boyfriend. After all, guys come and go. Some may even break your heart, but after all is said and done, your girlfriends will stand by your side through it all.

A friend of mine and her boyfriend broke up after a two-year relationship. They met right when they came to campus, hit it off, and jumped right into a relationship. For two years, her life revolved around him, and she lost touch with many of her friends. When her relationship fell apart, it was hard for a lot of her friends to be there for her since she had cast them aside in favor of her boyfriend. It took some time, but eventually she earned back the trust of all her friends. Her breakup was hard to deal with, but it opened her eyes to the fact that there is always more than one important person in your life.

> But what should be first and foremost on your new agenda are your friendships. Take the time to get to know your girlfriends before you call anyone your boyfriend. After all, guys come and go. Some may even break your heart, but after all is said and done, your girlfriends will stand by your side through it all.

GETTING STARTED
OK, I'm done with the don'ts. Once you've made your friends and you are ready to take the plunge into the dating pool, who can you date and where do you meet them?

BOYFRIEND MATERIAL
When starting to date someone, ideally, you want to start with a clean slate. You shouldn't have to pick up the pieces from a previous dating disaster. Guys without girlfriends—meaning they are single but also over any previous girlfriends—are your prime dating material. While everyone comes with their own baggage, fresh baggage is not fun to deal with. It takes time to get over any relationship and the solution is not to jump right into the next.

On the flip side, sometimes guys are just not ready for dating.

Not everyone comes to college with the maturity level it takes to be in a meaningful relationship, and the unfortunate truth is that girls mature faster than guys, and some guys still have not caught up even by college.

Another problem you may come across is that some guys are, at times, only looking to hook up. They aren't looking to get into anything serious right away since they are still trying to figure out exactly what they want out of a relationship—almost like window-shopping. But hooking up with someone—with the hope of eventually dating—never really works out the way you want. While there is nothing wrong with wanting to date or wanting a commitment from a guy, you have to be up-front about your needs from the very beginning. Otherwise, you may soon discover that you've been wasting your time on the wrong person, and no one likes feeling that she's wasted time.

WHERE *NOT* TO MEET

At this point, classes can seem like the perfect place to meet someone, but mixing business and pleasure can be a difficult duo. Dating someone you share a class with could work against you— if you break up, you'll still see each other every day. Even dating someone with the same major can be dangerous. My school is by no means a large one, so every year I have the same drama majors in my classes. It's not like you can stop going to classes or really avoid seeing them. I have friends who have dated people with the same major and when it doesn't work out, it can get ugly. The choice is yours to make, but be sure there is a solid connection between you and your fellow cutie of a classmate before you start dating.

BEING A GROUPIE IS NOT THE WAY TO GO

At all cost, avoid becoming a groupie. Let me describe the typical scene: hanging around at the same place every single weekend with the same group of guys and girls. During my freshman year, my friends and I hung out at one of the sports houses (like a fraternity house for a sports team) every night. We pigeonholed ourselves into the category of girls who only date jocks, which couldn't be further from the truth. Only one of my friends was actually dating a jock; the rest of us just considered ourselves friends with the guys. But not everyone seemed to believe that, including nonjocks whom we were interested in. Once we realized that everyone looked at us as groupies, we got smart and quickly switched up our hangouts. It was too soon in our college career to be affiliated with only one group and, besides, jocks don't have the greatest reputations when it comes to dating. Fortunately, we only spent one semester as "groupies" and no long-term damage was done to our reputations.

MORE ON THE SUBJECT OF REPUTATIONS

If there is one piece of advice I could give that you should take to heart, it's that your reputation is extremely important in college, especially at a smaller school. While your college may be bigger than your high school, people still gossip and word does travel. Now, you know that there will always be petty gossip that you just brush off, but when even your closest friends show concern for you, it may be time to take a step back and reflect on what you're doing. Some of us can go a little crazy with our newfound sense of independence and make decisions that we eventually regret. If you come to college fresh out of a breakup and start sleeping around, it can definitely damage your reputation. But don't worry; nothing is permanent. As soon as you realize that you aren't happy with choices you're making, start making better ones. Your reputation may stick for a little while, but once you start making changes, your reputation will change as well.

Dormcest: Pros and Cons

Kristyna Serdock, Stony Brook University

So you just can't help it. The guy who lives just two doors down from you is just so hot, and you want to get to know him better—a lot better. The dormcest (a.k.a., dating around the dorm) temptation happens to every incoming freshman, because there are so many guys just outside your doorstep day and night. From the occasional hookup to the very serious, engaging in dormcest has its good points and its bad. But you have to play your cards right to avoid as many of these awkward situations as you can (because trust me, they will arise). Weigh this list of pros and cons carefully before getting involved with the boy next door.

Pros

- He is always around. If you want to grab some food or need a study buddy or a study break, you know exactly where to find him.

- You get to meet his friends from the get-go. It's always better to get comfortable with his friends early on. That way, you avoid any surprises.

- You have the perfect way to de-stress when it's time for finals and when all those tough papers are due. College gets demanding with the finals workload, and now you have a backrub resource at your beck and call.

- He can look after you. You never know what can happen on campus, especially with everyone living so close to each other. If a weird situation happens at a party, he'll be sure to keep an eye out for you.

- You have a reason to stay in. On busy nights it's so tempting to get pressured into going to all these events after class, but if you don't have the energy after a long day, blame it on him. You have someone to stop by and bug for a bit before you relax for the night.

- You have the perfect excuse to dress up. If you know you'll be seeing this guy all the time, then you get a chance to wear all that stuff you'd otherwise end up saving for Friday night.

Cons

- He is always around. If you're not as into the hookup as he is, you're going to be bugged a lot—especially if it's just a physical thing. When a guy knows that someone will give him what he wants, he will try to get it. A lot. It's easy access (I am not calling us easy, but we are just easy to find). If he knows he can walk up the stairs and crawl into your bed, he'll quickly take over your space in an all-consuming way.

- If you don't like his friends, you can't avoid them. They will always be around his dorm or where he chills. There is no changing that.

- It can harm your reputation. There's a 100 percent chance that other guys know what you and your dorm boy have done together, and once things end with you two (or haven't even ended yet) they might think you do that sort of thing all the time, and will try to get with you as well. However, this sometimes has a strange attraction and positive side to it. If you're cool with it, it's like your relationship résumé is being handed out all over the building.

- Roommates might not like him or you. There's always the chance that whoever you're staying with or whoever he's staying with will not like the idea of the two of you always taking up space together. You have to consider their privacy as well, so once this relationship turns into more than just a one-time deal you should have a talk with your roommate to at least let her know where you stand. Maybe you can set up some sort of schedule, or code, but make sure you're not just kicking her out to have some alone time without any warning.

- The fights will draw a lot of attention. There are so many people close to your situation who have seen more of your dirty laundry than they should, so when you fight it's probably going to be a spectacle where everyone drops what they're doing and listens in. Bottom line: public fights are embarrassing.

- Someone might want more and the other doesn't. You might not have been expecting anything serious when you first got involved with this guy, but at some point one of you might start feeling something more. When this happens, handle it as soon as possible. If you're the one who wants more, don't get too clingy. If it happens the other way around, and he's the one who wants to be with you, then you need to be honest and let him down gently.

WHERE TO MEET THE RIGHT GUYS

At this point I'm sure you are wondering where you will meet someone to date. For the most part, many of the guys that my friends and I have dated we met through our friends. Classes *outside* your major area of interest can be a safe place to meet guys as well.

Maybe you could take an interesting elective class to see who else is in it. Extracurricular activities afford another opportunity—just beware if it is an activity where you spend a lot of time together. Don't be afraid to put yourself out there. Sporting events and off-campus bars or local cafes are good as well. Make an effort to search out a place that fits your style.

Ever heard of dormcest? Perhaps the most overlooked location for dating is your own housing building. We've all heard about the girl-next-door, but what about the guy-next-door? It certainly is convenient to hook up with someone who lives in the same dorm. You don't have to worry about what to bring over, it's a short walk, especially if the weather is bad, and the walk of shame is minimized. On the other hand, once it's over it can be hard to avoid that person. Chances are you will still bump into him, and even worse, he could be with someone new when you see him next. So before you become friendly with the guy-next-door, make sure you can handle seeing him with someone else.

In college, the only real dating rules are those that you make for yourself. There are no parents to check up on you and enforce a curfew. What you choose to do is completely up to you, so set some rules for yourself and be picky about whom you decide to date. When I say picky, I am not talking about only dating blondes or athletes. I am talking about setting standards for yourself.

U Chic Tip!

Don't date someone if you have to justify your relationship to all your friends. It's not a good sign when you have to give your friends a fair warning before they meet him.

WHAT YOU CAN EXPECT TO RUN INTO

Predicting what you'll experience in the world of college dating is just as tricky as predicting the weather. There are times when you'll bask in the sunlight of a new relationship. Other times you'll muddle your way through murky waters of ambiguity. And don't forget about the storms. You have to prepare for the unexpected.

Open relationships

Perhaps it's human nature, but we usually want what we can't have. You know the "grass is always greener on the other side" phenomenon. This is especially true when dealing with guys with girlfriends. For your own sake, stay away from the guy with the girlfriend back home. Even if he is in an "open relationship," getting involved with him is just asking for trouble. First of all, the term "open relationship" is a bit of an oxymoron. "Relationship" implies monogamy while "open" does not. If you want to avoid any future drama, be sure to stay away from these guys.

If you do decide to date a person in an open relationship, try not to get too attached. Chances are that if it comes down to choosing between you and his girlfriend, he will choose his girlfriend. No matter how fun or pretty you are, you have to admit that it makes sense; he has more history with her and is more comfortable. I have been in this situation once before, and the best advice I can give is to run away if a guy mentions that his relationships aren't monogamous.

What happens when you want more? Here's a little tale to illustrate. I wasn't looking for any kind of relationship, but one night while out with friends I met a really great guy, or so I thought. We had similar interests and hit it off right away. Unfortunately, he and his girlfriend, who was at school in a different state, were having problems. They decided to be in an open relationship. This is the point where I should have walked away, but I thought I had a chance at something with this guy. To make matters worse, he pursued me as if there were no one else in the picture, randomly surprising me, having dinner with me, and basically all the stuff you do when you like someone. Ultimately, he and his girlfriend worked things out and I was crushed. He even had the audacity to tell me that if things didn't work out this time with her, maybe we could give it a shot. As much as I hoped that would happen, I had to make the decision to not date someone who would always consider me second-best.

Rebounders

Like I said earlier, be careful or even steer clear of anyone who has recently gotten out of a relationship. They are on the rebound, and it might be at your expense. There is no set amount of time that it takes a person to get over someone. Depending on the individual, it can range anywhere from one week to three months or even more. Some guys never get over their ex-girlfriends! Make sure whomever you start to date is still not hung up on his ex—if he's constantly talking about her or comparing you to her, it's best to let him be. To be fair, sometimes he may not even know he's constantly talking about her. Speak up and make him aware of it. When it comes down to it, he shouldn't have to choose his memories over you. But, if he seems to wish his past memories were his present life, it is best to move on.

Fraternity guys and athletes

To set the record straight, frat boys, athletes, and the like are sometimes at a disadvantage. It seems that they are always portrayed in a bad light. A close friend of mine is dating a guy in a fraternity, and true, at times, it can be frustrating. When there is drama between her and her boyfriend, it seems the whole frat knows about it and she becomes "the bitch." On the other hand, there is something to be said for stereotypes; they don't come out of nowhere. My motto is to give everyone a chance. More often than not, guys will surprise you.

In all honesty, when it comes to dating in college, you will most likely meet someone when you least expect it. Maybe he lives next door to your best friend or maybe you will meet him at a party. No matter what the situation, just be yourself and live up to your own expectations. The rest will follow suit!

Insights provided by Jillian E. Sorgini, Hofstra University

long-distance love

I fell in love for the first time when I was sixteen. His name was Ryan and he was everything I wanted at that age: passionate, dark, addicted to punk music and cigarettes.

We were high school sweethearts, the couple that made everyone sick with incessant hand-holding and kissing in the hallways. We were inseparable for five years to be exact. And when the day came that I had to squeeze all my belongings into my parents' minivan and head across the state, I knew that it meant leaving him, and completely changing the dynamics of our once perfect romance. I had to face up to a harsh reality after I started to call Kent State University home. Long-distance relationships take some serious effort, and sometimes it isn't worth it. I had to learn firsthand the ins and outs of what makes a long-distance relationship work—and what can cause it to crumble.

Whether you're trying to make the transition from high school sweethearts to committed college lovers, or you met someone from another university or even another country, having your sweetie miles away is never easy. So, what can you do to make it work? And if it's not working, how do you decide to move on?

REALIZE THAT IT WILL BE HARD WORK

First and foremost, realize that in a long-distance relationship, you will experience challenges that new couples in college don't. Sure, you will have to tackle issues of trust, jealousy, and intimacy—just like any couple—but you can't just make it all better with a good-night kiss. However, all is not lost; your relationship can survive. Just make sure from the very beginning of the separation that both you and your partner are ready to expend the extra energy that comes with making a long-distance commitment.

ESTABLISH BOUNDARIES

An important word of advice: your lover might see a long-distance relationship as the perfect way to have his cake and eat it, too. Don't let this happen to you unless you are OK with sharing your guy. Make sure that both of you are clear about the way the relationship is supposed to work. Are you going to remain exclusive or will you be allowed to date other people? If you meet someone you feel you might have a better connection with, will you remain friends? These are just a few of the many issues you'll want to address before the separation. If you take the time to be up-front about the relationship from the get-go, this prevents confusion and possible heartbreak later.

TRUST YOUR PARTNER

Once the boundaries are set, you then have to let go—not of your guy but of your tendency to worry or not trust your partner. Yes, this one seems obvious, but when distance becomes a factor in an otherwise super-sweet relationship, the equation changes quite a bit. In order for your LDR to work, there has to be a very high level of trust.

DON'T BUG YOUR BEAU WITH ENDLESS PHONE CALLS

Demanding that he tell you where he is every second of every day will do nothing but tear you, and your relationship, apart. You both are in a new place and an exciting time of your life. Let him—and yourself—grow, learn, and have fun without a cell phone glued to the ear. Besides, no one really likes the girl who sits in the corner on the phone with her boy all night. Plus, you'll have much more to say when you can finally talk with your guy without distractions.

BE HONEST ABOUT YOUR WEEKEND PLANS

Don't tell your partner you plan to sit at home on a Friday night if you're ready to waltz your way to the local hangouts in your brand-new Manolos. Even though my BF and I were miles apart, I couldn't bring myself to tell him what I was really doing, and sometimes I'd ignore his phone calls on Friday night just to avoid a fight. I found out the hard way that this breeds mistrust in a relationship; every time I didn't answer, he assumed I was doing something I shouldn't be. He never cared if I hung out with other guys—he cared about me and wanted me to enjoy college—but by me not being honest, I created a pretty sticky situation. By avoiding his phone calls, I created an issue that was hard to resolve.

LEARN TO TRUST YOURSELF

Do you think you can resist the temptation of going home with the cute boy at the bar after a few Jäegerbombs? Don't put yourself, or your partner, in the position to get hurt. It's always OK to go out, in fact that's one of the amazing qualities about an LDR: you can still maintain your freedom. But if you're constantly tempted to go home with someone else, or always want to go out "just in case" you meet Mr. Right, you need to reevaluate your current relationship. It's natural to miss the closeness that comes with a regular relationship, and you might be eyeballing that hottie just because you miss your own. But if you go out with the sole intention of meeting someone new, you probably just need to break it off with your current beau.

AND IF YOU DO MEET SOMEONE ELSE OR FEEL TEMPTED TO CHEAT—DON'T!

Break it off with your partner before you start romancing another student. My LDR came to an end toward the end of my sophomore year. I had finally started to feel comfortable around a certain group of people—I found my niche, if you will. I also started to get a little too comfortable with a boy in this group of friends. I noticed that I would get more excited when he called or sent me a cute text than when my own boyfriend did. I knew that this was a sign that I needed to talk to my BF and decide what to do about it. It was crazy—I called him to talk about my feelings for the other boy and he had a very similar situation for him at home. So we decided, very mutually, to leave the relationship behind. This communication between us at the time of our breakup has made it possible for us to become friends (after a good nine months of no communication whatsoever!). Honesty really is the best policy, and I'm so glad that I was honest with my boy at the time.

COMMUNICATE

Communication is key in every relationship—but people in LDRs have to be a little more creative in their approach to keeping in touch. My long-distance boyfriend was a little short on cash, so even though we were only 2½ hours apart, weekend visits were not always an option. I missed his forehead kisses, his calloused hands; I even missed riding around in his disgusting car while he blasted music I absolutely hated. So, I knew I had to do something to keep us connected.

Because you can't see each other every day, you have to form a strong emotional connection in other ways. Buy a webcam and schedule online "dates." Send each other handwritten letters (doodles of hearts and flowers optional). Decide to read the same books, watch the same movies, or do other activities "together"— like stargazing on the phone with each other. These shared moments will help you to remember that even though he is far away, he is still breathing the same air.

BE THOUGHTFUL

Basically, anything you do to enhance communication in your relationship will help you to feel more connected. Make sure you put thought into every little thing you do. Make him a mix CD of the latest metal songs (even if you detest them!), send him tickets to that concert he mentioned wanting to see, or that basketball game he wanted to watch, etc. Take note of every little thing he says and be creative when it comes to letters, gifts, etc.

KNOW WHAT TO DO WHEN YOU DO SEE EACH OTHER

OK, it's been several weeks or even months since you've seen your significant other. Winter break is around the corner or one of you has decided to visit the other in his or her new environment. Will it be awkward?

When you first see your partner again, remember that it might be a little different from the last time you saw him. It's a lot easier to notice changes in people we don't see every day than in the ones we do. Some couples will find that they feel the exact same way about each other, and that their partner hasn't changed much since their last visit. Other couples, who sometimes have to spend months apart, can notice big differences the first time they see each other. Be prepared—you never know which situation you will find yourself in! I had been dating my guy for three years before I even left for college, so I figured that as soon as I did see him, of course, everything would go back to normal. Everything was the same for a while—a few months, actually. But as I became less of a presence in his life at home, he started to fill his time with other things, and other people, as did I. I noticed that we related differently—we were both growing up! The distance gave our relationship some renewed excitement.

Also, remember that just like you wouldn't spend every waking moment with your sweetie if he lived close, make sure to give each other some space during visits. You don't get to see each other often, so when you do finally meet up, make the time memorable without suffocating each other.

LET YOUR SWEETIE DO HIS OWN THING

If he comes to visit you and has other friends in the area, encourage him to go out and reconnect with others who are important to him. Just like you'd want to catch up with all your old pals, watch *Gossip Girl*, and drink cheap wine, boyfriends will have their own rituals they want to take part in when they come to visit. If you go to visit him, do the same. Go see some friends or even get up early one morning to grab coffee and explore your beau's new environment. Besides enjoying the opportunity to sleep in, he will appreciate your independence and probably will end up missing you and anxiously waiting for you to return. It's always better to keep him wanting more than for him to feel suffocated by your affection.

DO SOMETHING EXCITING

The best way to keep any relationship exciting is to experience new things together. You should make an effort to split your visit between "downtime" with your partner—like lounging on the sofa watching *Nip/Tuck*, nestled in each other's arms—and going out. Even if you simply go out for sushi, attend a lecture on campus, or get drinks at a few bars together, you will have shared a piece of your everyday life with each other and have a new experience together.

MAKE A POINT NOT TO "SURPRISE" EACH OTHER WITH UNPLANNED VISITS

If you live close enough that you could make the trip to see your sweetie on a whim, make sure you clear it with him first. You wouldn't want your beau to intrude on any important plans you may have with your friends, so make sure that you do not do the same. Besides, would you really want to stumble in on a study session that may make you jealous because it happens to be with a few other ladies? Save yourself the drama and call ahead.

ENJOY THE BENEFITS

Don't get me wrong. Long-distance love is difficult, but there are benefits to it as well. Unlike other college couples, who can feel smothered when their lover lives down the hall or in the same apartment complex, long-distance lovers can experience the best of both worlds. Not only can you cultivate your own interests and do your own thing most of the time, you also can enjoy the comfort and satisfaction of being in a committed relationship. You can do all the things you love and you will become a much more interesting person to be with.

ACCEPT CHANGES

The reality is this: people change. This means that the person you started dating six months ago will not be the same person six months from now. In a long-distance relationship this is especially hard to deal with, because you are not around to watch the changes occur. Instead, you might wake up one morning to realize your once super-shy man has turned into a social butterfly. This could come as a major shock, but one important aspect of a long-distance relationship is learning to deal with those feelings and accepting the changes both in yourselves and in your relationship.

FREEDOM OR COMMITMENT: WHICH TO CHOOSE?

If there is one thing that college is universally known for it's freedom. You are finally away from your parents, your boring hometown, and any restricting rules from the past. You don't need to check in with Mom or Dad before going out with the girls, and there is nobody to make sure that you get to bed on time (or go to bed at all!). Relationships, on the other hand, are all about commitment and, yes, restriction. Relationships in college—especially those long-distance romances—can seem downright ridiculous to some people. Why shun the very freedom that you've been so longing to have? There is some truth to this assertion. You and your LDR both want to fully enjoy your college lives, but that can seem like a near-impossible task when you're committed to someone halfway across the country. And not every relationship—long-distance or not—is meant to be. So how can you tell if it's time to call it quits?

You have your eye on someone else

This is exactly why long-distance relationships tend not to be satisfying in college. College is the time to explore yourself and your options. You shouldn't feel guilty when you find yourself staring at that cute boy in sociology class with the shaggy hair and Johnny Depp–esque eyes. Being in college gives you an all-access pass to plenty of educated, attractive, and ambitious potential lovers. These lovers can teach you a lot about the world, other people, and even yourself. If you feel even a little inkling that you might want to see other people, it's probably time to wave buh-bye to your cross-country boyfriend and try to connect with someone a little more accessible. As I mentioned earlier, I decided I needed to call it quits with my high school long-distance lover when I started to find myself attracted to a guy in my new group of friends.

Lack of proximity = lack of touch

Any relationship, whether sexual intercourse is involved or not, thrives on the ability to touch one another. Not only is touch essential for humans to develop normally, it is also essential in relationships. Basically, when your lover is hours away, you can't call him up for a late-night cuddle sesh. He can't walk with you hand-in-hand to class, take you out for a quick bite to eat, and you can't drag him to see the newest Angelina Jolie flick. This lack of physical closeness can put a damper on even the steamiest of relationships. If you find yourself craving a little smooch-fest too often, it may be time to ditch the long-distance romance.

BUT WHY DO WE HAVE TO PART? WE'RE PERFECT TOGETHER

Basically, you think that you and your lover are a match made in heaven. You both adore Kurt Vonnegut, playing the guitar, and don't ever get bored when you're together. So why would you want to part ways with someone who seems perfect for you?

This is an all-too-common problem when deciding to continue a relationship or not. There seems to be no real reason to end the relationship besides the distance factor. Sure, your sweetie resides miles away, but your relationship is peachy. This nonchalance would be fine if you weren't in college—a crucial time for discovering yourself and your interests. Is it really possible that this kind of relationship isn't putting any kind of restriction on you, or hindering your development as an individual in college? Take an honest look at your current situation and you could be surprised. When I was involved in my LDR, I would try to hang out with new friends in my hall, but I'd always be on the phone with, or waiting for a phone call from, my then-boy. I also made frequent trips home, and even though I'd feel left out when the girls would all talk about their weekend plans for frat parties and trips to surrounding cities, I gave that all up for my boy back home. Eventually, my new friends told me that all my "Baby-I-miss-you" phone calls were annoying—and I tried to cut back. But I know now that I'll never get back those adventures I missed out on with those girls—and I can't say I'm happy with my decision to choose a boy over new friends.

So what can you do if you find yourself in a similar situation?

TRY TAKING SOME TIME OFF

Rather than completely ending a seemingly great relationship, try taking a break. Give him—and yourself—some space. Completely cut off communication for a trial period, say a week or so. You will probably be tempted to call your boy, but don't. Do you notice any differences in your relationships with other people? Do you feel more connected to your school—more willing to get involved in activities and spend your time doing things that don't involve waiting for phone calls or planning visits? After the trial period is over, call your BF and discuss how you both felt during your time apart.

But no matter what dating obstacles you encounter during your college years, remember to enjoy every moment and make a conscious decision to learn from each and every one of those stupid mistakes. Really, college is the time to explore who you are, so make sure that your relationship does not restrict this exploration in any way. I cherish the time I spent with my long-distance boyfriend, but we eventually decided to call it quits. I'm happy for that decision—I'm much happier in my current situation. And even though my long-distance relationship was a ton of work, I think, in the end, it was totally worth it…just like all good things in life.

Insights provided by Erica Strauss, Kent State University

the dos and don'ts of the online dating world

How many of you do everything, from paying your bills to making a doctor's appointment, online? Going after the guy of your dreams (via a singles site) seems pretty straightforward when all it takes is a cute headshot, some flirty replies, and a click of a mouse. But sometimes it's easy to get lost in the vast and unending complexities of the World Wide Web. Individuals on the Internet aren't always who they say they are, and young women looking for significant others on dating sites should be careful to protect themselves when sharing private information. After all, just because someone says they have a UPenn Wharton degree and a slick investment banking job doesn't mean it's actually true, right?

According to a recent HuffingtonPost.com article, 40 million people in the United States have used online dating sites. Of those, one out of ten users on online dating sites are scammers. But wait—it gets even worse: one out of ten sex offenders reportedly use online dating sites to meet people. And the number one things most guys lie about? Age, height, *and* income!

On Making a Relationship "Facebook Official"

Megan O'Connell, University of Wisconsin–Platteville

Max and I met through mutual friends but didn't really take the time to get to know one another until we were partnered for a grueling 50-page research paper for a writing class we shared. (I bet you can guess where this is going!)

We spent countless hours with each other, diligently working on this paper. Or at least I was. Half of the time, I wanted to wring his neck, but the other half, I was finding myself laughing at his jokes (and maybe even finding him somewhat kind of cute). After working on this huge paper with him for two months, I did learn one thing about him—he was smart.

When we finally turned the paper in, he surprised me with a request for a date. I declined because I didn't want to ruin the great friendship we had built during the past several months.

And so the budding friendship continued. Over the next year and a half, Max became my best friend. We ate together, studied together, partied together, and basically did everything together. We even lived right across the street from each other for a year.

By spending all this time with him as a friend, I also discovered, in addition to his intelligence and great sense of humor, that he was one of the kindest people I had ever met. So after a year and a half of

Max patiently waiting, he finally persuaded me to date him and the next day we were "Facebook Official."

I made this leap because I knew Max very well at that point, and trusted him to be as courteous on my Facebook Wall as he was to me. I knew he would not post inappropriate things on my wall, and I knew it was a relationship that would last a long time.

When becoming "Facebook Official" with someone, make sure that the person will represent you in a positive manner and make sure it's a relationship you plan on committing to for a long time. Also, follow your gut instinct, because you'll know when the time is right. That's what I chose to do and couldn't be happier!

While these stats sound pretty depressing, it doesn't mean you can't be one of the few lucky ones who meets your match via an Internet personal. If you're definitely ready to take the plunge into the online dating world, just keep these safety tips in mind:

- Don't share your address or phone number on a publicly viewed page. Be discreet about who you do give this information to—even in private emails.

- Don't rush into anything. If you think you've met your match, set some ground rules before you meet, like two weeks of emails or texting so you can feel each other out.

- Do provide a close friend or family member with all his information before you go out on a first date together. Things like his name, phone number, email address, where he lives and works, and what he looks like can be valuable information if something bad should happen to you.

- Do suggest grabbing a quick cup of coffee during your lunch break or right after dinner. Picking a crowded safe zone and setting time limits are both good measures to protect yourself against someone with not-so-nice intentions.

- Do avoid alcoholic beverages. Alcohol lowers both your inhibitions and defenses.

- Don't let him pick you up or drive you home. He doesn't need to know where you live or if you live alone. Make sure you park somewhere brightly lit and heavily trafficked, in case he decides to walk you to your car. This may seem overly paranoid, but better to be safe than sorry.

Follow these tips, and your online dating life—if you choose to engage in one—will go off without a hitch!

Insights provided by Erica Strauss, Kent State University

is love possible in an age of hookups?

My mom is pretty cool, all things considered. She texts, she has a Gmail account, and she even knows the difference between an iPhone and an iPad. Unfortunately, the definition of this term "hooking up" remains elusive to her, often resulting in hilariously awkward conversations that start something like, "Oh honey, since you're working in New York this summer, maybe you and Jane Morris's son can hook up one evening for dinner." Or, "Honey, here's Benjamin's phone number—you go to school in the same place, and I've been waiting for you two to hook up forever!"

I understand my mom is from a different generation in which courtship and serious dating were the norm, so I can see why she might be a little confused. But how to explain this to my own friends who seem a wee bit hazy on the definition as well? Some refer to a dance-floor make-out as a hookup. Others say hooking up is an appropriate term to describe any action up to third base, while still others refer to it as the whole (naked) nine yards. Despite the various definitions swirling around out there, the main implication of a statement like "I hooked up last night" is noncommitted, sexual action with a friend, acquaintance, or stranger.

The fact that the phrase "hooking up" has become such a common term says something about today's teens and young adults. The changing nature of college dating and sexual relationships has dramatically altered the way women view their own sexuality. While the sexual revolution in the 1950s and '60s brought the advent of the birth control pill and women's lib, the twenty-first century has ushered in a whole new crop of coeds who have casually declared their bodies open for business.

WHAT EXACTLY IS A HOOKUP?

Before diving any deeper into this important discussion, let's first set the record straight on the exact definition of a hookup. A hookup ranges from kissing to intercourse and anything in between. It can involve multiple partners or one partner, and can be as consistent or inconsistent as you choose. The word "hookup" can refer to the actual person that you hooked up with or the act of hooking up. Other than that, there are no rules involved.

One of my friends says she has many ex-hookups but few ex-boyfriends. Her hookups (we're talking about actual people this time, not just the act), which are always monogamous, last anywhere from three months to over a year. If that sounds to you like something more than a hookup, you're not alone. It qualifies as "boyfriend" to me. But to her and her hookups, they were not comfortable using the term boyfriend or girlfriend. Maybe it signified too much of an emotional commitment. As she would always say when questioned about it, "If something isn't broken, why try to fix it?"

Did You Know?

Believe it or not, some college campuses have sex toy workshops, erotica weekend conferences, and full-blown "Sex Weeks" (even in the formerly stuffy Ivy League). According to the media, 75 percent of college students admit to engaging in a hookup, and even if they haven't, they know somebody who has. Not exactly shocking when you force a bunch of hormonally charged young adults under one roof together.

As many of us can attest, it's difficult not to get attached to someone after you are physically intimate with him. After all, your brain is wired that way. Touching, hugging, and any other sort of physical contact creates a mental and physical bond with that person. Even if you don't necessarily want a relationship with the person, your body craves that sense of attachment. But here is where the problem lies: when your body is telling you one thing and society tells you another, it's enough to leave anyone confused.

THE STAGES OF A HOOKUP

Like long-term relationships, there are several distinct stages of a typical hookup that may be helpful to know. So, I'll try to explain.

The attraction

Hookups typically don't happen out of the blue. Chances are, if you are hooking up with someone, he has certain alluring qualities that appeal to you. Sometimes it is simply the chase and once you've had your fun, you are done and move on. But sometimes, the hookup can be everything you thought it would be and the thrill of the chase and the unexpected keeps you coming back for more. So you move on to the next stage.

The pseudo-relationship stage

There is a fine line between detachment and attachment. What can start out as an unattached hookup can quickly morph into a pseudo-relationship with real feelings. This is when it gets really confusing. When engaging in any sort of hookup, many of us forget the emotional ramifications.

Is a long-term relationship possible?

Now, I am not saying that all hookups are wrong and always end badly. In some instances, a hookup can turn into something more, but it can take some time. What I've learned from experience and through friends is that if you gradually ease into hooking up with someone you like, you have more of a chance at having an actual relationship. Easing your way into a hookup gives you and your partner time to establish more than just a physical connection. However, this also means that from the beginning there is some sort of emotional investment before you hook up, so make sure you acknowledge your own feelings and be up-front about them with yourself and your partner.

Taking a Stand on One-Night Stands

So what do you do when you're over hooking up and ready to look for something a little deeper? The Love Fidelity Network (LFN) has experienced steady growth all over the country as it continues to spread its message and provide students with an alternative to casual sex. The nonprofit organization has gained a presence on multiple campuses through the promotion of marriage, abstinence, and the ever-elusive true love amongst college students. Though this may appear like a tough crowd to conquer, the tides seem to be changing. LFN and other organizations like True Love Revolution are attracting followers in droves, as more and more students start to examine the value of conventional dating and long-term relationships.

Celebrities are also speaking out about the dangers of hooking up and what it can do to your self-esteem. Kelly Clarkson's feminine anthem "I Do Not Hook Up" says it all, while Lady Gaga has taken a more direct approach. In a recent interview, the singer stated that she was embracing abstinence after experiencing some serious hookup action during her college years. "It's not really cool anymore to have sex all the time. It's cooler to be strong and independent," she insists.

While the rate of sexually transmitted diseases on college campuses is rising, and the number of men and women who actively perpetuate hooking up seems overwhelming, conservative forces are gaining ground as they continue to encourage the search for true love and meaningful relationships. Some say it is empowering to own and wager one's sexuality; others argue that reserving your sexuality for one person is the end all, be all. Only time will tell if my mom's version of the term will ever become a reality again.

THE PROBLEM WITH RANDOM HOOKUPS AND YOUR REPUTATION

The truth of the matter is that there is a definite double standard when it comes to hooking up. No one really cares about how many girls a guy has hooked up with. If it's a high number, in fact, he's viewed as a player—not a bad thing. For us girls, the more guys we hook up with, the more negatively we are viewed. It's sad to say, but even in today's society there is still not sexual equality.

However, hooking up can be empowering for a woman. Rather than settling down or being obsessed with finding a boyfriend, the new hookup culture encourages girls to explore their options.

For those women who can hook up and walk away feeling empowered and unattached, all the more power to you. In certain instances, I completely agree with the fact that sometimes a hookup is all you need. Sometimes feelings and emotions can complicate things, and a hookup can be the perfect solution. With the stress of school and other social activities, it can be hard to find time for dating. Sometimes a hookup is a nice release.

SO IS TRUE LOVE POSSIBLE?

As for finding love in this age of the hookup, it is definitely harder—the hookup culture brings a whole new level of complication to the game of love. However, since the rules are yours to make, do what you feel comfortable with doing. If hooking up is not for you, then wait until you meet someone you care about and prove your friends wrong. Love is out there; you just have to be patient enough to wait for it. While you're waiting, though, never forget the wise words of Janis Joplin: "Don't compromise yourself. You're all you've got."

Insights provided by Jillian E. Sorgini, Hofstra University,
and Kylie Thompson, Harvard University

U Chic Essentials—Love Life

Focus on you, first

College is the time to focus on you first and your love life second. You're going places, and nothing should hold you back from your dreams. If a relationship isn't working out or is even affecting your ability to do your thing, stand strong and make a decision—the relationship either has to change or you have to end it.

Don't fall into the "I Need a Boyfriend Now!" trap

Take your time getting to know yourself before you start stressing about finding someone. It will happen when it's meant to happen, so don't stress yourself out.

Honesty is everything with long-distance love

If your eye is starting to wander and you're trying to maintain a long-distance relationship, don't worry because that's natural. But if you are unhappy or you've taken a serious interest in someone else, then it's time to make up your mind. You'll feel better making a clean, honest break than sneaking around and having to lie.

Looking for more great advice? Head to www.UChic.com for our fave resources and websites—they come highly recommended from our guide's contributors and editors. Be sure to leave your suggestions as well!

CHAPTER 7

Sorority Chic

*I*s the thought of not knowing many people in college completely stressing you out? Or maybe you're trying to figure out how to get to know more people on campus. The important thing to remember is that you're not alone… pretty much everyone—at some point—is experiencing the same feelings. We've already covered several ways to break the ice and get to know people at your new home. One option we haven't covered in detail—and you're probably curious about!—is sorority membership. Known as "recruitment" or "rush," the formal process of joining a sorority is a great way to get to know a lot of people fast, even if you don't end up committing. From the recruitment process to knowing how to find a sorority that's right for you to dating frat boys to the secrets of sisterhood—everything sorority—we've got you covered!

going greek 101

I never planned to join a sorority. As soon as I entered Kean University as a curious freshman, a sorority began recruiting me, but I didn't take the bite because it didn't feel like it was for me. I spent my next two years of college without even thinking about Greek life. And then one day I realized I wanted to be more involved in my university, but I wanted something more than joining a club or a group. I suddenly decided that I wanted to go Greek.

Greek Speak

A list of definitions that may come in handy if you are considering Greek membership.

Alumna/Alumnus—Sister or brother of an organization who has graduated.

Bid—An exclusive invitation given to individuals who are asked to join the sorority.

Big Sister/Big Brother—A member of an organization who guides/ directs a new member through and/or after the new-member process.

Executive Board—Commonly referred to as both the E-Board or Leader's Council. Typically, this board includes a sorority or fraternity's president, vice president, rush and social chairs, etc.

Greeks—The name given to members of sororities and fraternities, which they use to identify themselves by combinations of Greek letters.

Initiation—A special event or ceremony for new pledges that officially kicks off their membership in the sorority.

Legacy—A Potential New Member who is closely related to a woman with membership in a national Panhellenic member sorority. The definition of a legacy varies from sorority to sorority, but it almost always includes a woman whose mother, sister, or grandmother was a member of a particular sorority. Legacies are usually given special consideration for membership, but sororities are not required to invite them to membership.

Mutual Selection—The process during membership recruitment when the sorority members seek the women who will best enhance their sisterhood and the Potential New Members determine which sorority will be the best fit for them.

Panhellenic Council—The governing body that controls all sororities and fraternities on campus. Panhellenic officers make all the rules and take action when a sorority or fraternity steps out of line. Members are often made up of executive officers from the many Greek organizations that reside at a specific college or university.

Pin—New sorority members are given a pin to wear that designates them as a member of the sorority. Typically, you receive this pin during an official ceremony.

Pledges—New members who have accepted their bids, but have not yet been initiated into the sorority.

Pretty Playbook—The rules or guidelines on what to wear during rush. Usually sororities will hand out fliers or post instructions on their websites or Facebook pages to help guide you on what is appropriate for each event.

Quota—The number of women to which a sorority can offer a bid during Recruitment. This number is defined by the Panhellenic Council.

Recruitment Counselor (RC or Rho Chi)—Formerly known as Rush Counselors, these are sorority women who disaffiliate with their own chapters during Recruitment in order to help the Potential New Members with the selection process. They offer impartial support and answer questions during Membership Recruitment.

Recruitment Week—Also known as "rush week." This is when potential members attend parties and meet the sisters of each sorority.

Rushee or Potential New Member—A term used to designate potential members.

Sisterhood/Brotherhood—The act of behaving as a family of sisters/brothers.

Socials—Also known as Mixers, these are themed parties held by various Greek chapters.

Symbols—A sorority or fraternity's symbol is unique to each organization and has significant meaning to the organization. Often the meaning behind the symbol is kept confidential and known only by the members of that sorority or fraternity.

THE RECRUITMENT PROCESS

Joining a sorority can be beneficial for those who want to become more involved on campus. During my junior year, I was in two classes with a girl who was a member of Lambda Chi Rho, a local sorority founded in 1962 at Kean University. I'd spent my first two years at Kean maintaining a 3.0 GPA for my scholarship while having fun socially, but as my years dwindled down I wanted to get more socially involved. After realizing that not all sororities were obsessed with drinking and partying nonstop (the stereotype we all know) and were actually very diverse, I started attending Lambda Chi Rho recruitment events.

During my rush process, they had open teas or "interest meetings," where we did things like make collages from magazine clippings, throw a Halloween party, make ornaments for a nursing home, and have a mixer with a fraternity. These events helped me see that a sorority could be well-rounded and that I could have fun doing even the simplest things with my potential sisters.

At the end of each interest meeting, the sorority members would ask us recruits if we had any questions about the sorority or Greek life, providing us a platform to express any concerns or raise any questions we had. Having an open forum to ask questions made me feel comfortable about getting involved with my sorority.

Sorority Recruitment Step-by-Step

First round—open house: The first round is an "open house" where you, the Potential New Member (PNM), get to visit all of the sorority houses on campus. This is an informal opportunity to meet women from all of the sororities, and it can sometimes take two days if there are a large number of sororities on campus. At the end of the round, you get to select a number of sororities you would like to visit again. The sororities also select the PNMs they would like to visit their home again. The Panhellenic Council (Panhel) brings all this information together and generates a list of invitations for each PNM for the next round. Feel free to wear jeans, but make sure you look your best!

Second round—skits: The second round usually features skits that each sorority prepares to show the PNMs what life is like at their chapter. After you visit all of the sororities to which you were invited back, you again narrow down the list to your favorite ones. The sororities also narrow down their list of their favorite PNMs. Panhel once again tabulates the information and generates the invitation lists for the next round.

Third round—philanthropy: Whew! You're almost done. Each sorority has a national philanthropy in which they actively participate. During the third round, you will spend time doing something that is related to their philanthropy. It usually involves crafts or making something and is a casual activity. It is also a great time to get to know more of the sisters in each house while talking informally. Once complete, you will go through another round of narrowing down your list to your faves and the sororities will do the same. Panhel tabulates the information, generating an invitation to the last round of recruitment.

Fourth round—preference: Now that you've visited all of the houses and narrowed down your list, you're ready for the fourth and final round—"preference." This is a more formal and ceremonial round, and everyone will be dressed up. This round usually involves a ritual-like ceremony that speaks more meaningfully about the sorority, sisterhood, and the sorority's symbols. After attending all of the preference parties, the PNMs and sororities once again must make their decisions. The mutual selection process ends when Panhel matches the PNMs and sororities according to the lists provided by each. But you're not done yet!

Bid day: The day has arrived when you finally get to find out which sorority has selected you! Typically, the PNMs will all gather in one location and receive an envelope which includes the name of the sorority to which you've been matched. Once you open your bid and know the results, you are then dismissed to find your new sisters. Afterwards, you will participate in a pledging ceremony, and an initiation period will soon follow, during which you will be educated in the history and background of the group and become integrated into the sorority. During this period, you will most likely become very close to members of your pledge class, as you work through the steps towards becoming an initiated member of the house.

WHAT TO WEAR

So now you know the recruitment process, but what should you wear? Rush is vastly different depending on what school you go to, where you attend school, and how large a Greek system exists on your campus. While there is no universal fast and hard rule as to what you should wear, here are some general guidelines on how to look your prettiest without giving off the wrong impression.

You're rushing a sorority

I know what you're thinking. "Duh. That's why I'm reading this section." But honestly, I can't emphasize this enough—you're not going to a frat party, or a club, or even looking to snag a hot guy. There's no need to show off a ton of cleavage or wear a short skirt that makes your butt look amazing. Just remember, you're trying to impress girls with style—not the male ego. Think pretty, *not* sexy. Also, the little details *do* count. Guys don't care about manis, pedis, or if you bothered to get your eyebrows waxed this week. But we of the opposite sex do notice those sorts of things, so make sure you're primped, plucked, and presentable before you sign up.

Yes, there are levels of fashion formality to follow

Again, this changes depending on which school you go to, but typically rush starts out more casual and gets more formal as the events progress. When I rushed (and this seems fairly standard for the most part), there was an event where jeans or shorts were worn and T-shirts were provided. The first invite is typically slightly less formal, so opt for a nice skirt and sandals. Second invites usually require casual sundresses, while the third invite is typically the most dressy (a cocktail-type number might be required).

Trust us, money isn't everything

If you're in love with your oh-so-expensive True Religion jeans and feel the need to wear them for rush, go for it. If you feel more confident and comfortable in your favorite pair of Levi 501's, that's totally fine too. Choose what you think best represents your style and personality—not the most expensive item in your wardrobe. This obviously doesn't mean that you can just show up wearing an old pair of sweats and a T-shirt (again, these are girls, and frankly, we live in a world where style and fashion *do* matter), but, overall, if you really get along and connect with a house, it shouldn't matter if you're sporting Bebe or Betsy Johnson.

Accessorize, accessorize, accessorize!

The members who are rushing you (i.e., the active sisters of the sorority chapter who you'll be meeting and chatting with) see a ton (like *hundreds*) of girls each day. Outfits start to blend together, and in a time when retail stores are everywhere, not everyone can have an original ensemble. That's why it's absolutely *critical* to accessorize with pieces to highlight your unique look and show off your personality and style. Plus, if someone ends up wearing the same dress or fancy top, you'll still be able to rock your outfit without feeling one ounce of insecurity.

Warning: Don't plan on accessorizing with purses or clutches. These are typically left outside during rush and some schools even provide everyone with one large identical tote bag to decrease the possibility of someone's expensive purse getting jacked by a frat boy (true story—it's happened).

Choose clothes that make you look and feel good

So much of what goes into being chic isn't about having the "right" pair of jeans or even the cutest dress—it's about wearing something that makes you look your best. Don't try to squeeze into a size 2 skirt if a size 4 or 6 actually fits you better. Just pick out something that makes you feel good about yourself. That alone should make other people want to know where you got all that confidence (and style!).

U Chic Tip! Keeping Your Facebook "Sorority Recruitment Ready"

Madeline Greene, Minnesota State University

Preparing for sorority recruitment? As technology continues to evolve, there are a few more online platforms you'll want to consider before recruitment is in full swing.

Whether you are a current member preparing for recruitment or you are a potential new member searching for a group to belong to, ensuring that your social media presence best portrays your ideas, beliefs, and plans for the future is important.

Why is this even important? It's not uncommon for sorority members to check out the potential new members' Facebook profiles. While they may get a feel for how you look on paper (GPA, extracurriculars, etc.) and how you act in person, they want to know how you represent yourself when you think nobody's looking as a test for how you will represent their sorority, if you're asked to join. First impressions mean everything, so you don't want to blow it before you even meet someone.

Be sure to look at your posts, photographs, and what you liked in the past, and make sure they align with how you perceive yourself and want to be perceived. Any photographs with alcohol or statuses relating to partying may change the way the sorority chapter feels about you as a potential member or the way you feel about a chapter.

A good rule of thumb is that if your mom and grandma were looking at your profile, would they be proud of the way you represented yourself? Social media profiles are becoming a large part of recruitment these days, so be sure to look yours over with a fine-tooth comb before rush begins!

FINDING THE RIGHT FIT

Before diving into any formal or informal recruitment process, it's worth putting some thought into what type of sorority you'd like to join. During this process, be sure to seek an organization that focuses on your desires. Do you want a more academic-oriented sorority or one that is more focused on social life? All organizations must maintain a balance among social, academic, and service in order to survive on campus. Some sororities focus on one aspect more than another.

Go to different events of sororities and feel out the girls. Although they, too, will be deciding if you fit, in the end, you want to make sure you like your potential future sisters. It's not enough to join because you know a few people in the house; make sure you can deal with the company of the rest.

FACTORS TO CONSIDER WHEN CHOOSING A SORORITY

How social am I?

You will discover that some sororities have more of a reputation for partying than for hitting the books. Now, of course, not every member will fit these stereotypes. But in most cases, the reputation for the house, overall, proves true...they either meet or exceed their reputation. If you're the honor-roll type and need to go out just once a week to be satisfied, you may find yourself the lone advocate for moderation. And the same goes for the more social gals. Joining an "honor-roll house" may not be the perfect fit for someone needing friends who have an active social calendar.

Perfectionistas?

Some houses aspire to be at the top of everything: top grades, top number of charity hours, top intramural teams, top awards at the annual Greek Award ceremony (almost every university has these), etc. If you're the perfectionist type, then these houses are probably a good fit for you. Just remember that you may be asked to commit a little more time than usual to sorority activities, and the expectations on you may be higher.

Are all the members from the same high school or city?

It's not unusual for a particular sorority to have several members from the same city or high school—friends recruit friends. If you are in the minority—let's say that you're from a public school in Chicago while the rest of the house is from a top private school in St. Louis—you may feel a little out of the loop. But it all depends. A go-with-the-flow personality will have no trouble fitting in while others may be happier with a little more diversity.

A popular house?

If you're leaning toward membership in a particular house for no other apparent reason than it's known for being a good one at your school, fugettaboutit! There is no such thing as a good vs. bad house. A sorority will be "good" as long as it's a good fit for you. Focus first on where you feel most comfortable (after all, you'll be spending a lot of time with these ladies). If you're paying attention during the recruitment process, you'll know which houses feel like a comfortable fit, and you'll be less likely to be taken with the "popularity factor" when making this important decision.

Bottom line: if you want to join a sorority, do so for the right reasons—*your* reasons. Don't join something because it sounds good or your friends think you should do so. If you don't follow your gut instinct, you'll end up unhappy with your decision, maybe even dropping out. Don't let this be you. There is almost always a place for everyone who wants to join.

HOW TO JOIN

Organizations vary in requirements for membership, but usually you must take part in a recruitment process or "rush" first, which consists of events organized by the sorority to help you get to know them better and vice versa. Each college and university has a timetable for the official recruitment process. Check your school's website or Greek life directory to get this information. Also, be aware that some chapters have an informal process as well that occurs at a different time of the year.

The formal recruitment process

Formal recruitment is different at every school and in some cases every sorority. Some schools have a week set aside—sometimes before school begins in the fall—where all Greeks get to recruit new members. Other schools may extend the process over a two- to three-week time period. Large universities will require everyone who is interested in joining a fraternity or sorority to sign up with the interfraternity council at the university. Once the recruitment process begins, each potential recruit is required to visit every sorority at least once to talk to them and find out what they're about. Schools require this in order to make the process more fair; the hope is that by seeing each sorority and witnessing the diversity among the houses, you, as a potential recruit, will choose a house based on personal preferences rather than joining a house because someone told you to.

As for what to expect each day during the process, you will attend multiple events while you are narrowing down your list of sororities that you're interested in joining. Remember that sororities will be doing the same thing to you. You will then revisit the houses where there is mutual interest. You may not get an invitation back to a particular house. If this happens to you, do not take this as a rejection and get down about it. They're not rejecting "you"; they don't even know you. There is a lot of randomness to the process, and the decision to invite someone back is often based on factors out of her control—sororities may give preferences to girls simply because they know someone in the house or come from a particular high school. And then there are the preferences that go to "legacies." A legacy in a sorority is a woman whose mother, aunt, sister, or sometimes grandmother was a member of a sorority; this increases the chances of a girl getting a bid to pledge. Not all organizations do not accept the concept of a legacy, but most do. Formal recruitment ends when bids are given out.

What if I go through the entire recruitment process and don't receive a bid? Is there something wrong with me?

Not at all! There are many reasons why someone may not receive a bid at the end of the process, including

- not meeting a sorority's minimum GPA requirements

- inability to attend recruitment events due to involvement in other activities

- poor judicial standing with the college or university

- showing a lack of interest in the chapter

- not treating chapter members politely or with respect

- not completing the formal recruitment process

Some of these potential issues can be circumvented with preparation. Unfortunately, others cannot. If it happens to you, for whatever reason, you should not feel embarrassed or bad about the outcome. There are plenty of other fulfilling opportunities for you to get involved with on campus, and you should not spend a minute longer dwelling on this. Move onward and upward, as we like to say!

If you do not receive a bid to join a sorority, here are some other options you can consider:

Informal or open recruitment (more on that below)
Often after formal recruitment, some chapters will still have open spots and can extend bids. Also, some sororities may "snap bid" the women they want and will not announce that they are still recruiting new members. Other sororities will hold informal recruitment activities in the following days or weeks in order to meet potential new members, even those who didn't go through formal recruitment. It's important to note that not all sororities will be able to participate in open recruitment, as they've already met their quotas, leaving you with fewer chapters from which

to choose. But for women who want to join a sorority and are willing to be open-minded about their options, open and informal recruitment can provide another opportunity to join a sorority that year.

Try again

You can also choose to wait another year and try again at the next formal recruitment. This can work well for women who had a low high school GPA, which hurt them with sororities that had to cut based on higher GPA requirements. If you get better grades your freshman year, you will greatly increase your chances of being able to join a sorority. Another bonus of waiting another year: you get the opportunity to network on campus, potentially meeting and making friends with current sorority members. This can be an asset when going through recruitment next year, since being known (in a good way, of course!) can make a potential new member more attractive to sorority members. One word of caution: if the sororities on your campus are known for extending bids primarily to freshmen, being a sophomore can make it almost impossible to get a bid. As this varies widely from campus to campus, it's important to do your research and know what the options are for rushing as a sophomore or junior.

Start a new sorority on campus

Avoid going through the recruitment process altogether by starting your own sorority! But as you can imagine, starting a sorority is a lot of work and takes a tremendous amount of time and commitment. Also, there are no guarantees it will be a success or that the group will be able to eventually affiliate with a national group. But it is always an option and one to consider if you're a natural born leader.

Embrace the independent life
While there are benefits to sorority membership, there are also many other ways to be involved on campus, as you read about earlier in this book. The last option is to choose to be a proud and happy independent. Although failing to receive a bid from a favorite sorority can feel like the ultimate rejection, we can guarantee that if you talk with anyone who didn't receive a bid, they'll tell you that it was the best thing that could have happened. And as they say: things always happen for a reason.

The informal recruitment process
Unlike the formal recruitment process, which is typically organized by the university, informal recruitment happens when you befriend members of a sorority outside of the formal period of recruitment. Usually, girls going through informal recruitment were interested in a sorority but did not have the time to pledge that semester, or changed their mind on membership and have expressed an interest in Greek life.

My "Informal" Greek Experience

Kara Apel, University of South Carolina

When I got my Greek Life brochure in the mail the summer before my freshman year, I barely glanced at it for more than five minutes. All I could see was fake. Fake hair. Fake tans. Fake smiles. "Fake" was definitely a word I thought described sororities to a tee.

But even without this negative impression, "rushing" in the fall would have been really hard for me to do. I was lucky to have made the Carolina Coquettes (the University of South Carolina's football dance team) for my freshman year. Sorority rush week was the same week as "hell week" for Coquettes, when we had three practices each day. Even if I had wanted to go through the sorority recruitment process, it would have been practically impossible to do. With this in mind, I closed my brochure and basically closed my mind to joining a sorority.

The summer flew by, and the start of school came, along with rush. That first week of school, I watched the girls on my dorm floor running around like chickens with their heads cut off trying to figure out what to wear for each day of the recruitment process. As I watched them do this, I couldn't help but wonder why these girls would put themselves through all this stress during an already stressful first week of school. However, as the semester crept by, I started to understand why. The sorority girls who lived in my dorm were constantly going to mixers, participating in Greek-life events, and having a blast hanging out with their "sisters." I had already made friends on my own without the help of a sorority, but somehow I couldn't help but feel like I was missing out on what seemed to be a fun aspect of college life. Surprisingly enough, I was starting to become a little jealous of the girls whom I had brushed aside as fake earlier in the year. In the end, I decided to go through informal rush that next spring semester, and ended up pledging Gamma Phi Beta, a national sorority. I am so glad that I gave sorority life a second chance.

My journey to becoming a member of a sorority was not the normal ride. Not everyone gets the luxury of rushing in the spring, but if you can, I would definitely recommend it. Looking back, I'm glad I didn't rush my first semester in college because it really allowed me to settle in and figure out who I was before I joined a sorority.

Typically if you are hanging out with members of a sorority—like going to the movies or hanging out at their house—you are participating in the informal recruitment process. There are no time constraints on informal recruitment. The goal with informal recruitment is simply to provide another opportunity for girls who did not participate in formal recruitment, whatever the reason.

U Chic Tip!

Be careful about looking like you're "shopping" too much for the right sorority. Sometimes your indecisiveness, if witnessed by members of a house that you've expressed interest in, can make them second-guess your true interest in their sorority and may affect your chances of getting a bid from them later.

WORK ANY LEGACY TIES YOU HAVE

If you have a family member who is an alumna of a sorority that has a chapter at the school you're attending, call her up! Usually she will still be involved or have connections with her sorority and can give you more details on what it is like to be a member. Also, she may be able to help you through the rush process by sending a letter to the chapter on your behalf in advance of the process. Many sororities will take alumnae connections (especially if your mom belonged) into consideration when making bids to potential future members of their chapter. If you don't have these legacy ties, no worries. These ties will not make or break your chance to be a member of a particular house, since there are usually only a few members a year at most who are legacies.

PLEDGING

After rush, the members of the sorority that you've expressed an interest in will decide whether they believe you would fit in as a member. If their decision is yes, they will extend an invitation or bid to join. It is then up to you to decide which sorority or house fits you best, and then accept one of the offers of membership.

Once you accept a bid, there will be a new member education process, also known as pledging. Pledging differs from organization to organization, and unfortunately some sororities and fraternities have taken the pledging process to a negative extreme by occasionally making the news for hazing, although today there are much fewer bad incidents than in the past. That's why you might want to be on the lookout during recruitment for each house's pledging process to make sure that it's worth the time and commitment in order to become a member.

BECOMING A SISTER

It can get frustrating going through the pledge process since it can go on for several weeks, and may take some of your time away from school. Annoyances aside, pledging is important because it bonds you with the other women who are in your pledge class, helping you learn the values, history, and traditions of the sorority. I had two pledge sisters whom I became very close with during the process and they are still good friends today. A pledge sister or brother is the term used most often for mainstream sororities and fraternities, while traditionally African-American, Hispanic, and multicultural organizations refer to the people they go through the process with as a "line sister" or "line brother."

Many sororities have a more educational approach to pledging than making you do silly or harmful things. When I pledged my sorority, there was a lot of tradition, history, and education that I had to learn during the pledging process. I was never forced to drink, walk around in the woods blindfolded, or do anything else that caused me mental or physical harm. And you, too, should be able to have the same positive experience. If not, then it's time to say something to the house leadership or even take your complaint to school administrators. In some cases, you may have to speak up for a friend who is being mistreated. Also don't be afraid to drop out of a house that is involved in hazing. No one should have to put up with mistreatment of any kind in order to join any organization.

Finally, don't let the uncertainties of the entire recruitment and pledging process prevent you from considering sorority membership. Remember, everyone else is in the same boat. Until you are a member you will not be able to completely understand the entire system and truly appreciate it for what it is.

> Don't be afraid to drop out of a house that is involved in hazing. No one should have to put up with mistreatment of any kind in order to join any organization.

MONEY, MONEY, MONEY!
So, are you really just paying for friends?

For years one of my friends would say that she'd never join a sorority because she wouldn't "pay for friends." Back then, I agreed with her, although I never put down any of my roommates or acquaintances who were in a sorority. However, after joining, I came to realize that the money you pay is not "for friends" but for financial expenses the sorority will incur for the year.

Where does the money go?

Sororities have a treasury and treasurer (who is usually on the executive board) who oversees finances. Money from the treasury is usually applied to fund-raisers, recruitment events and T-shirts, "Meet the Greeks"-type campus activities, or other important events. Also, chapters of national sororities pay dues to their national headquarters. National organizations have hundreds of chapters nation- and worldwide, and are basically run like a business at the headquarters level.

Other expenses you can expect

Budgeting is very important to maintaining a sorority membership. My sorority has payment plans for girls who cannot afford the dues in total, as we all understand that other school expenses can make it difficult to pay at times.

In fact, sometimes we will even pay for another sister's dues when she cannot afford it for whatever reason, because, after all, we are a sisterhood and really do feel like family.

Budgeting is very important in maintaining a sorority membership. My sorority has payment plans for girls who cannot afford the dues in total, as we all understand that other school expenses can make it difficult to pay at times.

LIVING ARRANGEMENTS

Many of you may have heard of sorority houses. A sorority or fraternity house is the house of the organization and is usually located somewhere near the university. Some of these houses are merely for meetings and administrative purposes; other houses are actual homes where members are expected to live at some point in their college careers (usually sophomore and junior year). Some houses can only hold 20 members while some go up to 100! At big colleges and universities, recruitment events and bid day are held at the sorority house. However, some schools don't have sorority houses, so the members will instead take up a couple of floors in a dormitory building or apartment complex. The reason for the closeness is because members benefit when they can interact with one another on issues pertaining to the sorority and have meetings and access to one another.

Keep in mind that just because you've joined a sorority does not mean that you have to live in the same house or floor as your sisters. Usually, you will have options for where you live. At most larger universities you will live in a sorority house near campus with 50–100 other girls during your sophomore and junior years, but you will have options for where you live during your freshman and senior years. At my college, there isn't a frat row (an area typical of some colleges where the entire street is lined with sorority and fraternity houses) or an area specifically for Greek housing. However, I know many members of different Greek organizations who have rented or bought their own houses around the college, and it serves as their unofficial "house."

FINAL WORD

So after it's all said and done, is a sorority for you? Even if you're not sure about it but are still curious, go through the recruitment process to try it out. And don't feel pressured to rush a sorority when you first arrive on campus. You're in college to learn, grow, and explore. If joining a sorority is an important part of the collegiate experience for you, then great! If not, then great as well! Seize the moment when you feel it is right. If you don't meet the sorority of your dreams your freshman year, you may discover it later on in college like I did. Best advice I can give: always keep your options open.

Insights provided by Donyel L. Griffin, Kean University

life as a greek

As an incoming college student, you probably have had minimal to no experience with sororities, and may be wondering what exactly they do. Is there anything more to it than partying? Yep. Here's a quick summary.

CHARITABLE PURPOSES

Charity is a big part of any Greek organization, and for my organization, certain events are mandatory. It doesn't mean you get scolded if you cannot attend an event. These events are something we recognize as important to the survival and mission of the sorority. First, you'll most likely be expected to attend community service events. Usually, the sorority will host a philanthropic event like a walk or run, while some events are sponsored by the college. At my school, for example, the Kean University Greek Senate hosts the "Somerset Hills Holiday Party," where we do crafts with kids from a school. The senate also hosts "Up Til Dawn," which raises money for St. Jude's Children's Hospital. All Kean University organizations are required to have representatives attend these events whether it's the entire organization or just two people. A lot of Greeks always show up to these events. And why not? They're fun!

SOCIAL TIME

You've probably been curious about the social aspect. Being in a sorority does encourage you to be social not only within your own house but with other Greeks and students at your university as well.

Most sororities have "mixers" with fraternities, which are parties exclusively for that sorority and fraternity. Mixers are usually big events, and for the most part, you'll probably be expected to go (especially those during the recruitment season). In addition to these mixers and meetings, there are other functions as well, like sisterhood outings, cocktail parties, and formals that bring back memories of high school prom. For the most part, these events are not mandatory.

Most colleges have Greek Week to encourage unity among Greeks with events, outings, games, and on-campus activities. At my school, our version is Greek Olympics. During Greek Olympics, organizations compete against one another for points in events like softball, pool, basketball, tug of war, volleyball, and dodgeball. My sorority ended up winning third place. It's not all about winning, but it did feel good for us to get a Greek Olympics trophy for one of the first times in recent years!

THE FRATS

As previously mentioned, there will be several opportunities to "mix" with fraternity guys either through parties or some type of cohosted charity event. Some houses may even have a brother/sister relationship with one another where they "mix" often, team up for service projects, and support one another with recruitment and pledging.

As for the dating scene, as a Greek I've never dated a fraternity guy so cannot speak from personal experience, but I have plenty of friends or sorority sisters who have. Based on what I've heard about my friends' experiences, there are some definite pros and cons to dating a fraternity guy.

If you're dating a guy from a particular fraternity, this gives you an opportunity to set some of your single sisters up with his brothers. Also, you will both understand where each other is coming from in terms of what it means to be a Greek member. Some non-Greeks don't understand the reasoning behind all the weekly meetings and events, making it hard to have a relationship during the busy times.

Sometimes dating a frat guy can be overkill on Greek life when Greek-related stuff is all you ever seem to talk about. Another con is no matter how close your sorority is with your boyfriend's fraternity, keep in mind that they will have to mingle and sometimes network with other sororities. For some girls, this may be difficult as jealousy sometimes comes into play. You might want to also think about the future. For example, if you break up with the guy, what happens? As one sorority sister put it, "It can be as simple as a hookup with a guy from a fraternity to make it feel weird to mix or hang out with the entire fraternity."

Many girls feel like dating a frat guy goes hand in hand with being in a sorority, but it doesn't. If it works for you, great! But don't feel pressured to date or hook up with a frat guy if you think it's not for you or may cause problems in the long run.

GPA AND OTHER REQUIREMENTS

Other sorority responsibilities include weekly chapter meetings and having to keep up certain grade requirements. Yes, surprise! Most sororities do have grade requirements for their members. Your Greek system may have a minimum GPA of 2.3 or more to join a house! Some houses may even consider your high school record when deciding to offer an invitation for membership. It makes sense: students who can't obtain satisfactory grades usually won't be able to balance the requirements of belonging to a Greek organization with their school activities. If your grades do meet the requirements to join, but for some reason you fall behind after pledging, your chapter may require that you complete a certain number of study hours per week. But every campus and house is different. It all depends. Most sororities have required weekly meetings to discuss upcoming events, fund-raisers, new ideas, or other important issues. These meetings are ones that cannot be missed.

A Lifelong Commitment

Miryam Chico, Kean University

I believe my sorority's motto truly encompasses what sisterhood means to me: "Unity and Sisterhood, Now and Forever, One and Inseparable." A sisterhood is a lifelong commitment and experience. It doesn't end when you graduate college. It's something you work at throughout your life, and gain immeasurable memories and relationships from. Sisterhood has allowed me to not only learn about a different group of women, but also to grow and learn from them. I've gained lifelong friendships that I would not have found elsewhere. Sisterhood has provided me with a network of people who share my joys and sorrows and also act as a source of encouragement and support, especially as an undergraduate since I was an out-of-state student who didn't know anyone on my campus.

Besides the mandatory activities, it's entirely up to you how involved you want to be in your sorority. Some members are highly active while others may be less active for personal or financial reasons. When I first joined my sorority, I never imagined that I'd become vice president, later president, and then chosen as Greek Senate Sorority Sister of the Year! It all depends on how much you want to be involved and—like everything in life—your sorority experience will be what you make of it.

SISTERS FOREVER

Being in a sorority is not like joining the softball team or choir or student government. While all of those activities are great, your strong attachment to them usually ends once you graduate college. Whereas, in a sorority, you're a sister forever, long after your responsibilities as a student end.

The bond forms as soon as you join

Many sororities and fraternities adopt the terms "big sister" and "little sister," or in my sorority we refer to it as just "big" and "little." And while the process for choosing little sisters differs from organization to organization, it has the same goal: ensuring that someone is there to guide a new member into the organization and beyond. In my house, everyone has a "big" who picked them when they were "little." And then once you are eligible for a "little," it's your turn to start the process again.

No matter what terminology you use, when picking a "little," you want someone you think you will get along with or have something in common with. When I picked my little, I liked that she was very motivated academically and she seemed to have an easygoing personality while being strong-minded. With time and a little effort, many big/little relationships have transcended college. Of course, not all big/little relationships will be close, but for many they are. In fact, for some girls, it's like having the older or younger sister they never had.

Networking beyond college

Many girls benefit from alumni interaction. Even in a local sorority like mine, networking is extremely important. One of my alumni sisters was able to get an internship at a magazine, and later a job, through an affiliation with another alumni sister who worked at Time, Inc. Although alumni move on and develop careers and families and other obligations throughout life, a part of them feels a sense of loyalty to the sorority and even to sisters they may have never met. This most likely will be the same case for your sorority. So, don't hesitate to reach out to those who have come before you. They are there to lend a hand.

For me, sisterhood means a support system, a family away from home, and a group of girls who share common goals. Everyone is not the same and never will be, and in any organization, you are bound to be closer with some more than others. But if you stick it out through the good and the bad, your dedication will most likely result in an experience that will provide benefits to you throughout your lifetime.

Insights provided by Donyel L. Griffin, Kean University

U Chic Essentials—Sorority Chic

Forget the stereotypes

Leave the stereotypes at the door. Within each sorority, you'll find a diverse group of women from a variety of backgrounds and with different interests. Really, there is no such thing as a cookie-cutter sorority.

Consider informal recruitment for a less-intense process

Informal recruitment is a great option, as it lasts a little longer, is more casual, and provides you a better opportunity to have more one-on-one time with the sorority members of a prospective house. However, as sororities use informal recruitment to fill their quotas, not all sororities will offer an informal process, one of the main differences from formal recruitment.

Greek life is not for everyone

If after speaking with friends who are sorority members or even going through recruitment you still are questioning whether you should join a house, it may not be the right thing for you. And guess what: that's OK! There are plenty of other things for you to get involved with in college.

Looking for more great advice? Head to www.UChic.com for our fave resources and websites—they come highly recommended from our guide's contributors and editors. Be sure to leave your suggestions as well!

CHAPTER 8

Healthy, Safe, and Happy

⚬⚬⚬

Midterms, papers, friendships, boyfriends, all-nighters, pub crawls. All of these activities and interactions—some more fun than others—can take a toll on your health in college. And it probably comes as no surprise that your health and happiness are important components of the fabulous college life. This chapter covers health issues you may face in college, but is by no means comprehensive. To completely be up to speed on all health matters, visit your school's student health center or their website for a more complete picture. But to get you started, we've tackled the common issues and concerns that you may face, giving you a crash course on staying healthy and happy in college.

dealing with the blues

Your dorm room has become a refuge where you retreat from feelings of doubt, anger, and hopelessness. You can't remember the last time you had enough energy to make it to a coffee date with your friends or your weekly art class at the YMCA. And most of all, there's a lingering haze of despair that seems to follow you everywhere. You've tried to push it aside, hoping it would dissolve in the midst of homework, club meetings, and finals, but it hasn't. And now you're at your wit's end. It's starting to take a toll on your productivity and you're not eating well, or hardly eating at all. If this scenario paints a reality that is all too similar to your own, stop. Understand that what you're going through isn't just a bout of homesickness or the blues. You may be dealing with depression.

THE BLUES OR SOMETHING ELSE

We all face periods of sadness. From the "winter blues," which can be caused by a lack of sunshine during the winter, to a period of sadness after a breakup with a boyfriend, it's common to have times when you just don't feel like your normal, more positive self.

But these moments usually last for no more than a few weeks or even a month or two.

So how do you know if it's merely a fleeting case of the blues or something more serious? Feeling blue poses a serious problem when your sad feelings linger, according to Dr. Kala Annambhotla, staff psychologist of the Counseling and Testing Center at the University of North Carolina–Greensboro.

"It's normal for people to feel sad, anxious, or discouraged from time to time," Annambhotla said. "These feelings usually lift within a few days to a week, as people find solutions and support from friends," she continued. "Students should seek professional help when they notice that their low mood lasts too long or occurs frequently, when symptoms feel severe, when they notice that their mood is causing academic, social, or other problems, and/or when they feel stuck and can't seem to solve the problems causing the depression."

If your feelings do not subside and they are starting to affect your work and everyday life, you may be suffering from clinical depression and should consider seeking professional help. Now, before you start freaking out that there is something horribly wrong with you, take heart! Though it may seem as though you're alone in your struggle with a depressed mood and constant sadness, you're not. According to HalfofUs.com, an online portal for college students coping with mental health issues, "nearly half of all college students reported feeling so depressed that they couldn't function during the last school year." That's a lot of people!

Even more surprising is a World Health Organization (WHO) statistic that depression affects 121 million people around the world. According to the website of the nonprofit medical practice Mayo Clinic, depression can manifest itself in a variety of forms, ranging from "mild" to "severe." Mayo Clinic describes clinical depression as being a "severe persistent form of depression."

U Chic Tip! What to Do if You or a Friend Is Suicidal

Amanda Ferrara, New York University

Do you know what you would do if a friend was suicidal? What if you were? What would be your next step toward getting help? If a situation arises where you or someone you know needs to get help, do not let yourself be unprepared. Take 10 minutes to visit www.suicidepreventionlifeline.org to read about the warning signs of suicide and to find crisis centers in your area.

If you ever encounter someone, perhaps even yourself, displaying the warning signs, there is also a number you can call for assistance: 800-273-TALK. And don't forget about resources on campus like mental health centers which are there to help in situations like these. Remember: when it comes to someone contemplating suicide, every second counts.

Common causes of depression

The stresses of college, if unmanaged, can lead to depression. Take Maria Pascucci, for example. Her self-imposed pressure to succeed led to high levels of stress and ultimately depression during high school and college.

"My biggest stressors during college were balancing academics with outside employment and a constant worry about the future. Uncertainty about the future scared me to death, and not living up to the high expectations I'd placed on myself," Pascucci said. The pressure to succeed raised her stress quotient and took a toll on her well-being. "I was battling stomachaches, insomnia, and depression. During my last semester of my senior year, I had a panic attack after finding myself unprepared for a final exam in Women's History and bolted out of the classroom," Pascucci said.

For Pascucci, counseling and yoga were vehicles that helped propel her toward recovery. She recounts her story below in an excerpt from the article "New Year's Resolutions: Love, Me."

For a while I wallowed in self-pity. Then I was simply tired of being angry and chose to move on. I started working through my rigid expectations through journaling and with the help of a counselor. We talked about how I was really failing no one but myself by never trying new things for fear of making mistakes. My counselor suggested that I try yoga to soothe my anxiety. She said that I needed to practice mindfulness. I shrugged my shoulders and said, "Whatever, my mind is working all the time." What my counselor meant was that I was spending so much time always thinking that I never stopped to look around and appreciate what was right in front of me.

Now Pascucci is the president and founder of CampusCalm .com, a Web portal and company dedicated to helping students deal with the stresses of high school and college life. She is proof that depression is an obstacle that can be overcome.

HOW TO BEAT IT

Your depression may seem like an impossible obstacle to get around. But like all things in life, there is definitely a light at the end of the tunnel. Statistics say that most people respond positively to treatment. WHO reports that treatment such as psychotherapy and antidepressant medication proved to be helpful for between 60 and 80 percent of people suffering from depression.

Talk with loved ones

As the nonprofit group Mental Health America notes, depression can happen to anyone, at any age, at any time, so you shouldn't get down on yourself for feeling the way you do. Depression isn't something you should keep hidden or feel ashamed of. The best way to deal is to be open about what you're going through, like

Maria Pascucci who, for example, opened up to a counselor about her feelings.

Annambhotla's advice to depressed students echoes Pascucci's story: "I advise depressed students to talk with supportive friends and professionals and be patient with themselves as they recover. They may want to simplify their life while still pursuing goals that are important to them. Learning to accept yourself and taking pride in your accomplishments is so important."

Quit being so hard on yourself

Annambhotla also said that antidepressant medication may also be an option for students who are experiencing decreased levels of energy and disrupted eating and sleeping patterns. By taking the steps to get the help you need, you can help put yourself on the road to recovery and the reclaiming of your sense of self-worth.

Tools for dealing with depression

1. **Your Campus Health Center**—Your campus health center is staffed with knowledgeable and understanding professionals who have experience helping students deal with depression. You can call ahead to make your appointment and stop over on your way to bio lab.

2. **HalfofUs.com**—This website is dedicated to helping college students deal with a range of mental and emotional health issues, touching on topics like depression, cutting, and

drug and alcohol abuse. The website includes information about depression, testimonials from celebrities and college students about their struggles with depression, and an online assessment called "Check Yourself," that allows you to screen yourself or a friend for a mental health disorder.

3. **CampusCalm.com**—This website is geared toward college and high school students and offers tips and articles for dealing with academics, self-esteem, and self-worth. The site offers a free online "Stress Less" kit, and has other valuable information.

4. **MayoClinic.com**—The website of this nonprofit medical practice has detailed information on depression. It outlines the signs and symptoms to look for, the possible causes of depression, and the different methods for treating depression.

Insights provided by Janine Camara,
University of North Carolina–Greensboro

sex ed 101

While many of you will be signing up for calculus or political science, there don't seem to be many open sections for talk about the birds and bees. When I told my friend I was writing this section, she laughed, "What's there to know about sex? Use a condom and get in there!" But that's the problem! Everyone assumes they know everything they already need to know about sex, and if not, they always have their latest issue of *Cosmo*.

Although you may think you're the sex guru, even you can benefit from a no-nonsense guide on sex in college to keep all the facts straight. Now, by no means do I purport to be the definitive expert in this field. Heck, people spend years in medical school and residency learning about the more complicated aspects surrounding sex. But thanks to several years in college and having to face the variety of sex-related issues that can come up, I have some real-world advice that can help you prepare. So sit down, strap in, and get your number 2 pencils ready, for you have just enrolled in Sex Ed 101.

FOR THE FIRST-TIMERS

Breathe. Having sex is not as daunting as it seems. First, you must realize what your own expectations are about sex. Even if this isn't your first trip to the rodeo, your feelings toward sex can fluctuate and it's important to be honest about your expectations. These expectations can be physical (*to the left, no right, yeah that's it*) or they can be emotional (*not yet…let's wait…OK, NOW, NOW, NOW I'm Ready!*). Each sexual experience you have may not be the same—even if you're doing it with the same partner! So while that McDreamy fantasy is great to keep on standby, don't freak out if it doesn't happen your first time.

Once you've made the decision that you're ready to have sex, it's best to schedule an appointment with your gynecologist just so you know what you're working with. Your doctor can also talk to you about pregnancy and diseases. This includes prevention and detection. The only surefire way to prevent pregnancy or disease is via abstinence. There are also other options you can consider to limit the risks. There's birth control, which if used properly, is over 99 percent effective in preventing pregnancy. Birth control can come in the form of a pill, shot, or an external device being implanted in your body. It's best to talk to your doctor about these options and what may be the best one for you.

If you've already had sex and haven't seen a doctor, you should get yourself checked out. Sex can breed a bunch of baddies that, if ignored, can become a big nasty problem. If you don't have your own doctor, talk to your general practitioner and see if he or she has any information on how to find a gynecologist. You can also check out your health center on campus to see if they have a women's health services center. My school has a full-service women's health department (with on-call gynecologists). If they can't do it in-house, they'll be able to direct you to the proper place that can.

> While a friend is a great resource, it's better to discuss these matters with a physician. It's like cutting your hair—would you trust your best bud or your stylist with a pair of scissors? Think of it that way, but with your vagina, which is a tad more important than a new 'do.

When you're in your doctor's office, feel free to ask questions, questions, and more questions! Talk about discharge! Talk about pain! If something seems off, bring it up. Don't feel embarrassed; they've heard it all. Your sexual health is one of the most important things to protect. Being uneducated can lead to risky behavior, resulting in problems that you'll have to deal with for the rest of your life. This is the time you can address STDs (sexually transmitted diseases), vaccines, birth control, even a change of diet or ask about that thing you saw on TV (*can I really twist my body like that?*). In addition to any health concerns, this is also a great place to learn about your body and libido. While a friend is a great resource, it's better to discuss these matters with a physician. It's like cutting your hair—would you trust your best bud or your stylist with a pair of scissors? Think of it that way, but with your vagina, which is a tad more important than a new 'do.

HOW TO PROTECT YOURSELF

The numbers are staggering. According to a 2007 Stanford University Sexual Health Peer Resource study, one in four college students has a sexually-transmitted disease, with Human Papilloma Virus (HPV) or genital warts being the most prevalent. Sure, you think it can't happen to you, but it can and it just might. So how can you make sure you don't become a statistic?

The surefire way to protect yourself is through abstinence. The next best way to prevent diseases is to use the barrier method. What I'm referring to here is the use of condoms when engaging in both vaginal and anal intercourse. There are different types of condoms, which include male condoms that create a barrier around the penis and female condoms that create a barrier inside the vagina. It's best to try different condoms and brands to see what works best for you. Latex is most popular (they prevent pregnancy about 97 percent of the time if used properly), but for those with an aversion to latex, try polyurethane condoms. (All other condoms—sheepskin, lambskin, etc.—don't perform as well, and you will be doing yourself a disservice by playing with them.) Condoms also come in a variety of sizes, and while there are XXLs, believe me when I say it's all fluff. If you've sat in a sexual-health presentation, you may remember the part when they stretch the condom over their forearm. Snag a free condom from your health center, and try it out yourself.

Condoms can serve as a barrier when performing oral sex on a male. There are even flavored and specialty condoms, for more flair. When performing oral sex on a female, it's best to use a dental dam. Dental dams stretch across the vulva, and create a barrier between the mouth and genitals to prevent disease. Most dental dams can be found via sexual health centers, or at special sex shops. Unfortunately, some infections spread to areas not covered by condoms. Therefore it's best to talk to your partner about their sexual history.

WHAT TO DO WHEN YOUR PROTECTION FAILS

Now that you know how to protect yourself if things go right, what do you do if things go wrong? Although condoms are a medically proven method of protection, there are times when they could slip off, break, or even get stuck inside your vagina. While these things don't happen often, it's important to be careful and make sure you're using it the right way, as incorrect usage leads to faulty results. When using condoms, always make sure you leave space at the tip to allow for shifting during ejaculation. Also, always check the expiration date, as expired condoms can be more brittle and ineffective.

So what do you do when your protection fails? Don't freak! You can engage in a backup method, such as emergency contraception. Emergency contraception pills (Plan B is approved for use in the

United States) contain a heightened dose of progestin that acts almost like a supercharged birth control pill. Just as the label says, it should only be used in an emergency, and is only effective up to 120 hours after sex. Just so you're aware, some colleges do offer Plan B at their campus pharmacy. Cost varies, though a lot of schools will allow female students to secure the pill for free. You can consult your campus health services website to see if the pill is offered. If it isn't, look for a drugstore nearby and speak with an on-site pharmacist. Just remember, the pill must be taken within 72 hours, and the sooner you take it, the more effective it is. Keep in mind, it does have some unpleasant side effects like nausea, dizziness, irregularities in your period, and lower abdominal pain. Remember, it is not 100 percent effective against pregnancy, and is not at all effective against STDs. It would also be best to get yourself checked out by a doctor, because it has happened that remnants of the condom are left inside.

PREGNANCY AND STDS

The best way to find out if you're pregnant is to track your cycle and mark it in a place that you regularly update, like your planner. Once you notice your period is out of whack, make an appointment with your doctor for a follow-up and grab an over-the-counter pregnancy test while you're waiting for the appointment. But it's important to not solely rely on these tests as they can end up being wrong.

Detection for STDs is a little more difficult than just looking at your calendar, especially since most STDs show few to no symptoms. Regular checkups with your doctor will help detect STDs. When you're being examined, make sure that they are testing you for *everything*—that includes the standard group of STDs, including herpes and HPV. In between checkups, do your own inspection. Prop yourself up in your bathroom, prep yourself with a mirror, and make sure that there is good lighting. Don't worry about feeling silly. It's yours—why not check out the goods?

If something feels or looks wrong, check in with your doctor. If it's nothing, mazel tov. It's just best to be sure. If you do find out that you have an STD, make sure you talk to your partner(s) and tell them to get tested. Awkward, of course, but it has to be done. Otherwise, they can't protect themselves or others.

Don't worry about feeling silly. It's yours—why not check out the goods?

TAKE ADVANTAGE OF THE RESOURCES AROUND YOU

No matter what situation you're facing sexually, there are a *ton* of resources on campus. Some schools may offer more services on campus than others, but most provide students with the information they need. Your best bet is to look to your campus health center. These centers are such a huge resource because they cater specifically to the college demographic. As a result, they focus on issues that impact college kids the most, such as pregnancy,

STDs, and diseases that may begin to show up in a young adult. They offer all sorts of resources, and usually provide pamphlets, health guides, free condoms, and peer-education programming.

If you find that your health center on campus does not carry information on sexual health, there are still other resources you can try. First, ask your health coordinator if they work with any particular hospitals or clinics in the area. If they don't have any ties to any local centers, hit the Web and look for local hospitals and health centers. Or go to your local government's resource page, or nationally recognized organizations, such as Planned Parenthood. There's plenty of information out there—you just have to find it!

CHOOSING ABSTINENCE

Before we end this class, it's worth mentioning abstinence. When it comes to sex, the first question you must address is whether or not you plan to have sex in the first place. Since sex is such an individualized experience, you need to make sure that you're having it or not having it for the right reasons. It may be helpful to weigh out your feelings and see how that corresponds with your values, beliefs, and your life plan. If you find that remaining abstinent is important to you, choose it and embrace it. While the decision to abstain is a personal one, sometimes it becomes difficult when you're surrounded by people who may not relate to you and your decision. But just because they may not share the same ideas doesn't mean that they won't understand. So, don't be afraid to stand your ground in a challenging discussion or situation.

Why I Chose Abstinence in College

Madeline Greene, Minnesota State University

College is a roller coaster of emotions. Choosing your major, meeting lifelong friends, learning about yourself and others, making mistakes, exploring the world, and preparing for life after college can feel like a whirlwind of change.

During my four years, I went through all of those growing pains and still, right after graduation, I continue to find myself looking back on that roller-coaster time, thankful for the lessons it taught me. One lesson, in particular, profoundly impacted my life—the choice to be abstinent in college.

I made a decision in my teen years that I was going to wait until I found the right person to have sex. It wasn't about what my parents wanted or what my religion taught me. It was a personal decision that I made for myself. For me, it was something that I wanted to give to someone I really cared about, and I wanted to make sure that I wouldn't regret my decision down the road.

In college, this decision was tested many times. I thought that I would find Mr. Right and that I would be married (or at least engaged) by the time I walked across the stage to get my diploma. Let me tell you, I couldn't have been more wrong.

Dating in college is difficult because there are two competing things at play. On one hand, you're trying to commit to another person while, on the other, college is really one of the most selfish times of your life (in a good way). The entire focus of being there is about *you* and finding out what you want for the future. It's important to take this time for yourself. Add in the pressure of explaining your choices—like my choice of abstinence—to that other person, and you can imagine how difficult it was to date at times.

I struggled with this issue in many of my college relationships, and let me tell you, it was not easy to navigate. While some of the guys I dated were understanding and even respected my decision, others found it hard to believe that I hadn't done what everyone else was doing. I found myself questioning my decision, and, at some points, even regretting that I had decided this was what was right for me. Many times, I thought about just getting it over with. But every time the opportunity came forth, something stopped me.

I learned many life lessons in college but this one, above all, means the most to me. I learned that sometimes you have to go your own way, blaze your own trail, and navigate through hard times by following your heart. I am glad that I have waited until the right person comes along. I am proud that I didn't cave when I was questioned and stayed true to myself. I stayed abstinent in college because that was what was right for me. It caused some heartache and turmoil, but it also allowed be to be confident in my choices and do what was right for me.

As you begin your collegiate journey, I challenge you to sit down and find what is right for you. Don't allow others to weigh in on your decisions if you already know what is best in your case. Above all, follow your heart. My choice was to wait for the right person to come along and, while I'm still waiting, I have faith that Mr. Right is out there somewhere.

Most times, your friends will be supportive, but intimate relationships are a whole other matter. What's most important is to be up-front about your needs with your partner, and to express your desire to abstain. Sure, there might be some jerks out there who will tease you or even get angry or pushy; don't back down. But by and large, if you're honest and up-front with your partner from the beginning, he'll understand that it's a decision that's important to you and will respect you for it.

And don't forget that there are many other ways to be intimate without having sex. Touching and kissing can be just as intense as going all the way. Also, don't underestimate the power of words. Some couples I know who practice abstinence undergo these intense dream sequences where they describe their sexual fantasies in a safe and personal environment. This creates a feeling of physical intimacy without actually having to be physical.

There's so much to say about safe sex that there are not enough pages in this book to cover it, but I hope this crash course has provided a good overview for all you potential sex goddesses out there.

Insights provided by Aja Johnson,
University of Maryland–College Park

staying safe on campus

A few months after I moved into the dorms, a young woman was sexually assaulted in my housing complex. My friend Hailey and I were concerned that the word was not getting out to the rest of the campus, and decided to try to do something about it on our own. We spent a whole day running around campus, and were sent from office to office trying to talk to the right person that would help us get the word out. Luckily, we were able to convince campus police to make us hundreds of copies of the crime report. Hailey and I proceeded to post them in every housing building, on every door. This was an unfortunate crash course introduction on the importance of being safe on campus.

WHY SAFETY MATTERS

College students, especially female college students, need to learn how to be safe on their campus. Why? We can simply flip open the *LA Times* to find an article about a woman being shot outside a party in East LA. Or the story of a woman being shot and then pushed out a window. From the headlines to music videos, physical violence—especially against women—is just a part of everyday life in our culture. The result of this is that the college campus is not always a safe place for female students. In the face of this, we need to take control of our lives and our safety, and learn how to be as safe as possible. Now this does not mean that women have to walk around scared or survive in a state of fear. I believe women are capable of living their lives fully and being safe at the same time.

Ditching the Victim Label

Did you know that one in six women will be sexually assaulted during her lifetime? It's almost too hard to believe. Even more startling? College women are four times more likely to suffer sexual assault. Why? The college coed environment of easily accessible alcohol and casual campus hookups places many young women at risk and makes them more likely to be victims of unwanted sexual encounters. Unfortunately, it often goes unreported because the victim was under the influence at the time of the attack, sometimes blames herself, and is unclear as to whether the situation can truly be classified as a crime.

You can significantly decrease your chances of becoming a victim of rape or sexual assault at your school by following a few simple guidelines:

- Don't engage in binge drinking. This is one of the easiest ways to find yourself in a scary situation and not be able to do anything about it.

- Never put your drink down at parties. It's very easy for someone to slip a date rape drug like GHB or Rohypnol into your beer when you're not looking. The same holds true at the bar. Never accept a drink from a stranger unless it's directly brought to you by a bartender or server.

- Use the buddy system when out with your friends. Don't ever let a pal go someplace alone with a stranger or walk back to the dorms by herself.

- If you feel uncomfortable in a situation, don't ignore your gut instinct. Who cares if your friends or that hot guy in your Lit class thinks you're crazy? If you get a bad vibe from someone, leave immediately. It's always better to be smart and play it safe than to find yourself hurt or abused.

DO WE BRING IT ON?

Before I dive into the practical areas of campus safety, let me say that although there are ways to ensure one's safety on campus, any type of violence against women is *never*, in any circumstance, their fault. Women don't deserve assault or anything else because they left a window open or walked home late at night or wore an extra tiny skirt. Violence against a woman is never her fault. With that noted, here's how you can make your college experience safer.

U Chic Tip! What to Do When Your Friend Is a Victim of Rape

Ashley Tripp, University of Alabama

According to *Rape in America: A Report to the Nation, National Victim Center*, college students are at a higher risk for sexual assault and more than 80 percent of rape victims are under 25 years old. An *FBI Uniform Crime Report* from 2000 found that rape is reported about once every five minutes in the United States. These are sobering statistics for college women.

If the worst happens and you or a friend ends up a victim of rape or attempted rape, it is important to seek medical help immediately, even if you think you don't need it. According to UCLA's Rape Treatment Center, this is crucial, as you can discuss the possibility of exposure to an STI and the possibility of pregnancy with the health care provider.

By having a medical exam immediately following the assault, it is also a way to preserve physical evidence. And one important point here. According to UCLA's Rape Treatment Center, you should "not shower, bathe, douche, eat, drink, wash your hands, or brush your teeth until after you have had a medical examination. Save all of the clothing you were wearing at the time of the assault, placing each item of clothing in a separate paper bag."

Rape survivors experience different reactions and responses, so you or your friend may want to also consider counseling.

Seeking counseling from a trusted source is an important first step in the process of recovery. You or your friend can decide whether to notify the local and campus police or contact a campus-based resource center such as a Women's Center, Student Counseling Center, Student Affairs Office, Student Health Center, or a local or national rape hotline like 800-656-HOPE. The Rape Crisis Center also offers a 24-hour hotline at 210-349-7273. Websites like www.rainn.org and www.911rape.org are additional resources for support.

The best thing you can do for your friend is to offer words of encouragement, respect their decisions, and be a good listener. And for yourself, do not hesitate to reach out to friends and family. They are there to provide the love and support you need.

ONCE YOU'RE ON CAMPUS

When you arrive on campus, one of the first things you should do is familiarize yourself with your campus' safety system. It's there for you, should you ever need it. A good thing to keep in mind is that every college campus has campus safety system in place and campus police.

In addition to the safety system, the "buddy system" is another way to stay safe and prevent theft. Always walk with a friend, classmate, or a roommate at night, whether it's to the library or to a late-night class. Most campuses also offer shuttle systems at night in case you find yourself without a buddy. And if—for whatever reason—you have missed the shuttle and/or need to walk to your car alone, don't hesitate to call campus security and have them walk you to wherever you need to go.

UTILIZE YOUR CAMPUS RESOURCES

An important first step in keeping yourself safe on campus is to familiarize yourself with your campus' safety system. Most campuses have escort services—use them. If you get out of class late in the evening or stay a little later to talk with your professor, you can call a number and have someone walk you wherever you're going. Don't be concerned that you might be wasting anyone's time to walk you even a few blocks to your car. The campus security officer's job is to be there for you at all times.

> One time, I was on campus after eleven working on a project. I didn't even bother considering how I could walk home safely alone. Instead, I called campus police for an escort, and they actually sent an officer in a police car to drive me down to my dorm. Program the number for the escort services on campus into your cell phone, so you are never stuck walking alone at night.

There are several other things to be aware of when considering your safety on campus. Be aware of the lighting on your campus. Are all areas of the campus and your dorms well-lit? Are there large dark areas? You want to be in lighted areas at all times of the night. And if there are major areas lacking sufficient lighting, make a stink about it. It will take persistence to get these things fixed, but you deserve safety. Your campus should additionally provide emergency phones. They should be sporadically placed around the campus for you to grab and call in case of any emergency. Know where they are. Finally, be aware of any large bushes. Are there large bushes and shrubbery that would make the perfect hiding place for someone? Knowing where these bushes are and the potentially dangerous situations they may present is important to keeping yourself safe. Bottom line: Trust your gut and don't place yourself into a dicey situation that you didn't have to be in the first place.

DORM ROOM SAFETY

Now, regarding the dorms, keep windows and doors locked. End of story. This is probably tricky to do, as people are always going in and out of other people's rooms and whatnot, but it's essential to keeping yourself safe. And don't be afraid to ask your roommate(s) to do the same. Roomies should look out for one another. My last bit of advice on keeping yourself safe on campus: have your campus police number programmed into your cell and if you have a landline, on the speed dial. My speed dial number seven says "Campus Popo." This way the police are always at your fingertips in case of emergency.

Nothing Says Crazy Like Your Very Own Stalker

While it may seem like only celebrities deal with freaky overeager fans, real people can and do encounter stalkers. In many cases, the stalker will start out as a friend, boyfriend, coworker, or familiar face from class. In fact, 77 percent of female victims and 64 percent of male victims know their stalkers.

How do you know if you're dealing with a stalker? Someone is likely stalking you if

- he or she repeatedly follows or spies on you

- he or she repeatedly calls you at home or work

- he or she repeatedly sends unwanted letters, texts, emails, etc.

- he or she leaves unexpected gifts for you to find

- he or she threatens you or someone close to you

- he or she vandalizes or damages your property

- he or she repeatedly shows up for no legitimate reason at the same places you do

It's important to communicate a clear "NO" to your stalker from the moment his or her behavior becomes suspicious. Don't encourage his or her behavior by responding to phone calls, texts, Facebook messages, emails, etc. Change up your routine if you notice that somebody is closely following you. If the stalking continues and you start to feel unsafe, notify campus security or the local police department right away. Whatever you do, don't make the mistake of trying to handle the situation on your own. Take immediate action to keep safe.

TAKE A SELF-DEFENSE COURSE

If you have not already done so, sign up for a self-defense class as soon as you arrive on campus. Now, I'm not claiming that if you take one of these classes that you will have the ability to beat the crap out of every person who steps in your path. However, it does equip you with the tools to defend yourself, to fight back, to get away from an assailant. Also, it isn't just about the physical aspect of defense—like how to use a man's strength against him so you can get away—but there is also a psychological component. After taking the course, I feel stronger and more confident in my ability to defend myself. It's not just how to drop and elbow some guy in the cajones when he bear hugs you from the back. It's empowerment. My campus offered Rape Aggression Defense classes in the dorms, and also a Women's Self-Defense class through the kinesiology department. Look into your resources on campus. See what's offered and take advantage.

By preparing and knowing what it takes to be safe, you are increasing the chances that you will not have to experience one of those shocking stories. You deserve to feel safe on your campus. Be aware, know what resources are available, and take those self-defense classes—every last one of them! Safety is a major issue on college campuses that women have to deal with in a way that men don't. So educate yourself, and be empowered. We college women are completely capable of being safe, fun, young, adventurous, and wise all at the same time.

Insights provided by Monica Taylor,
California State University–Los Angeles

preventing theft on campus

No college student wants to be a victim of a crime. Safety is one of the many reasons why we pick our college. However, theft is not just in the movies, and it's not just in dramas on TV. The truth is that it does happen to normal people like you and me, and it is a real concern at campuses nationwide.

First, the good news. All campuses are required by the Clery Act to report crimes that have happened on campus, so you should be able to find this information pretty easily. The United States Department of Education has set up a website where you can check crime that has happened on your college campus for the past three years. It's called "The Campus Safety and Security Data Analysis Cutting Tool" (www.ope.ed.gov/security), and it's pretty simple to use. You just type in your college campus name, city, and state, and the public records show up. This is important to check because it can be helpful to see what the potential risks and threats are—which crimes were committed and where on campus. Having this information in your back pocket will help you avoid obvious safety missteps.

U Chic Tip! Ten Targeted Items on Campus

According to Collegestudentsafety.com, there are ten items that are typically stolen from students on campus:

1. Cellphones

2. iPods

3. Laptops

4. Cash

5. Jewelry

6. Bicycles

7. Credit/debit cards

8. Identification cards (i.e. licenses, library cards, student IDs, etc.)

9. TVs

10. Books

These items can be securely locked up or locked away which may be enough to ward off petty crime!

IN YOUR DORM ROOM

Whether you're a freshman or a senior, your dorm or off-campus apartment is home. It's where you spend most of your time as a college student sleeping, studying, hanging out with friends, and, of course, partying. The following tips are essential to keeping you and your possessions safe.

Always keep your door locked

Keeping your door locked is such an important factor in preventing theft. The only people who have keys to your room should be residence life staff members, your roommate(s), and you. That's it. It's extremely important to talk to your roommates about the importance of locking your door at all times, no matter how much your roommates "trust your floor mates" or how safe your campus may be. Theft can happen anywhere, anytime.

Invest in a personal safe

When bringing personal items to campus, it's always smart to keep a minimum on keepsakes that you bring. Instead of bringing all of your expensive jewelry, I would invest in bringing costume jewelry and only one or two of your favorite items that you can store away in your safe when not in use. Costume jewelry is a lot easier to replace than a family heirloom. As for those must-have tech items, you can put your iPod, wallet, or laptop in the safe when you're not using them. If you don't want to invest in a safe, there are other alternatives, such as a door alarm or hide-away items, which are household items that have storage for personal belongings. If you do end up investing in a personal safe, make sure you are the only person who knows the combination or has the key to the lock.

Buy a laptop lock

Buying a laptop lock is essential for dorm life. A laptop is easily the most expensive and most important item you bring to college, and having a lock on it can prevent any unwanted visitors from taking it. A laptop lock is another item that's fairly easy to use, is inexpensive, and can be found at an electronics store. Again, when getting a lock, make sure you're the only one who knows the combination!

Choose combinations and passwords that are tough to crack

Keep in mind that whether you're in your dorm or at a library, your combination has to be a set of numbers that isn't easily guessed. Combinations like "1111" or "0000" are too easy to crack. Also, it's better not to use your birthday or any personal information in your passwords and/or combinations. One nifty trick I use: Choose a password that serves a dual purpose of locking your device *and* setting a goal for yourself like "runamarathon2013" or something that you want to achieve. That way, you'll be constantly reminded of your goal, and you'll remember the password!

U Chic Tip! Protecting Yourself from Identity Theft

Megan O'Connell, University of Wisconsin–Platteville

College is a time in your life where you will be giving out a lot of important information to a lot of different sources from banks to schools to loan companies. Giving out sensitive information can lead to future trouble if you don't take precautions when giving it out. For instance, if this information falls into the wrong hands, thieves can use it to steal your identity, leading to debt you're unaware of, benefits taken using your health insurance, money stolen from your bank accounts, and many other devastating possibilities.

Whether you're shopping online, setting up an online bank account, or paying bills online, companies will request sensitive information from you. They usually will ask for your name, address, or Social Security number. Before handing out this information, verify that it is a legitimate request from a reputable business. Do some research before handing it out to just anyone.

Here's what you need to look into:

- If a company you have already given information to emails you and asks you to confirm that information, call them and ask whether they need a confirmation on your information.

- When calling companies to confirm information, be sure to call the phone number you have for them on your records, not the phone number that's listed in the email.

- Never send sensitive information over email; legitimate companies will not ask you to do so.

- Never enter your information in a pop-up or advertisement that wants secure information.

Another thing to bear in mind is the importance of shredding documents. People who commit identity theft will go to great lengths to put back together documents you simply tear apart. Investing in a paper shredder is a very smart thing to do. You should use your paper shredder to shred bank statements, loan payments, bills, and any other documents containing sensitive information.

Also, if you have any IDs or credit cards stolen from you, do not delay in reporting them stolen and/or cancelling them. If you suspect you are a victim of identity theft, reach out to the appropriate government agencies to begin an inquiry. The Federal Trade Commission's website has a ton of information on how to handle this situation for consumers and specifically college students. It even has an identity theft helpline at 877-438-4338. For more advice and information, head to www.fraud.org.

Unfortunately, college students are easy identity theft targets thanks to numerous school payments, loan payments, new bank accounts, and frequent address changes that leave a nice paper trail for would-be thieves. So don't make it easy for them! By being smart, cautious, and careful when providing sensitive information, you are lessening the risk of becoming a victim of identity theft.

PREVENTING THEFT IN THE LIBRARY

The library is a popular place for students who need to get work done and don't want distractions. So chances are there's going to be tons of students every time you go there.

Perform a bag check

Before you go to the library, take an inventory of things that you have in your bag before you go. It's important to know every item that you have with so you don't forget anything, and you'll know if anything is stolen. This is also a good exercise because you have an opportunity to leave something at home that doesn't need to be with you anyway. It's also important to check your bag before you leave the library to make sure you're leaving with everything you brought in. If you find you're missing something, check everywhere you spent time studying to make sure you didn't misplace it, and if you find that's not the case, notify campus security immediately.

Keep your things with you at all times

Even though the library is generally a quiet area with lots of people studying, theft still does happen. It's important that when you bring study materials and a laptop, that you bring a laptop lock (as mentioned before) and always take your belongings—purse, backpack or wallet—with you even if you're going to search for a book or making a quick trip to the bathroom. Keep in mind that although it might feel like a pain to have to carry all of these items with you, you can take comfort in knowing that no one can take any of your personal items because they're already with you! Now, you can ask a study neighbor or friend to watch your stuff, but do realize they are not ultimately responsible if anything goes missing.

If you're walking back from the library alone

Try to avoid walking home alone at night from the library at all costs, but if you have to, there are a few ways to stay safe. Experts say to avoid being on your cellphone while you're walking alone. This way, you're more alert and are paying more attention to your surroundings. You can also call a friend or a family member when you are leaving the library and tell them you will call them back when you are safely back to your dorm, apartment, or car. Give them an estimate on how long it will take you to get back, and ask them to call you back if they don't hear from you within that time period. Having your pepper spray or mace on hand can also help in this situation. Avoid unlit areas, even if there are shortcuts. It's better to take the long way if it helps you stay safer! And don't hesitate to call campus security for an escort. They are there for this very purpose, and are more than willing to help.

U Chic Tip! Avoid Providing TMI

Ashley Tripp, University of Alabama

Imagine that someone is able to track you no matter where you are and at all times by you just merely using your mobile phone. But wait, this is no dream. Thanks to mobile apps like Foursquare and others, they may already be tracking you. Even if you're not smartphone savvy, there's still a chance for someone to track you through other popular social media outlets, such as Facebook and Twitter. These sites allow your friends to track you when you add a location to your Facebook statuses or through photos or tweets.

As you likely already know, Foursquare enables you to "check in" to particular locations like stores and restaurants, and in exchange, you receive points, badges, and even discounts to your favorite spots. Great perks, right? Even though Foursquare says only your select friends can see your activity, creepers such as hackers, stalkers, burglars, and potential sexual predators have a way to track down your location via Twitter and Facebook. When you link your Twitter or Facebook accounts to Foursquare, you're broadcasting your location to a larger network of people. For example, one Foursquare user blogged about receiving a phone call while at dinner. The user did not recognize the person on the other line. The caller then said, "I saw that you checked in there on Foursquare." Creepy.

When using Foursquare or other similar apps, remember to

take caution about what you post so you can avoid privacy issues and potential crimes. Don't share your phone number, email, hometown, or any other personal information on your Foursquare profile page. Also, NEVER check in to where you live—that is just TMI (too much information). Still want to rack up those points at your favorite bar? Try "checking in" to your location after leaving the site instead of beforehand. And don't add anyone you don't know or don't feel comfortable having see your profile. Add people that you trust. Last but not least, while on vacation, avoid "vacation shout-outs," which puts you at risk for burglary and other safety issues. Limit your posts.

Remember, the best way to ensure you're staying safe on Foursquare and other similar apps is to keep your profiles private while applying these helpful tips.

PREVENTING CAFETERIA THEFT

Whether you have a small or a large cafeteria, it is also a place where theft occurs. Going back to the tip about the library, if you're alone at the cafeteria, get your food first with all of your belongings and then put your stuff down when you choose a spot at a table. If you're with a group of friends, ask a friend to watch your stuff. You can always take turns and when you come back, your friend can go up and get her meal. Also if you don't have a backpack or anything, hold on to your ID/wallet. I always wear an item of clothing with pockets so I can put my school ID and my room key away. Don't ever leave anything else unattended when you're at the cafeteria, because just like the library and your dorm room or apartment, it is a place where things can go missing for good.

PREVENTING CAR THEFT ON CAMPUS

If you have a car on campus, you're lucky. If you're a freshman, you're extremely lucky. Many students in their first or second year are not allowed to have a car on campus, and have to go through a number of hoops to get a car on campus. Keeping your car on campus is great, and it's always awesome to get away from campus for a while, whether it's shopping with friends, going out to dinner, or taking a weekend trip home. But it's also essential to keep your car safe while you're there.

Always, always, always keep your doors locked

Always. I don't think I can stress it enough. This tip is obviously important because if your car is locked and alarmed, there's less of a chance of it being broken into, or worse, stolen. Even if your friends borrow your car, make sure that they alarm it and that the doors and windows are left properly closed and locked.

Leave all belongings in your dorm or apartment

Don't leave any valuables in your car like a laptop, GPS device, or an iPod. If it is fairly visible, chances are someone will be tempted to try to break into your car if they see it. It's better to just leave all of your belongings in your dorm safely locked away or at home. If you do have something valuable on you, store it in your trunk. Out of view, out of mind.

Remember where you park your car

Always remember where you park your car. If you go to a big university, you might have a huge parking lot where the entire student body parks. It's important to know where you park, so you can keep track of your car. If you have a long chunk of time where you don't use your car, check on it every couple of days to make sure everything is OK. It seems silly, but you'll be able to make sure everything is intact. I would also suggest moving your car to a different spot every now and then if you can. That way, even if you're not using it for a few days, a thief won't be able to tell the difference.

We've covered a lot of ground in this chapter. But don't get us wrong. College is an incredibly fun and fabulous time in your life. These tips are merely to ensure that you don't find yourself victim of a crime that didn't need to happen. If you want more information on campus safety, check out Collegestudentsafety.com for more tips and advice.

Insights provided by Ashley Yenick, Merrimack College

a self-confidence boost

When I first went away to school, it was like an experience I never could have dreamed up. It was four hours away from my old stomping grounds, and my first time away from home. As a girl with such a strong social circle, it was weird being light-years away from everything that was familiar to me. Don't get me wrong; I was no wallflower. I was busy buzzing around campus, meeting new people, staying out late, getting in trouble, and doing all of the great things that could only go on in a college setting (where else can you get delivered fresh brownies at the drop of a dime, or partake in a midnight round of freeze tag?). Though, between the food and the fun, I noticed something missing. While I was doing things that were fun, new, and exciting, there was a part of me that felt I was drifting into the background…that somehow my self-confidence was losing out.

One of the best things about college life is the ability to get caught up in anything. It's spontaneous, it's crazy, and can be completely out of your element and comfort zone. Although fun, it can also be a bad thing for your self-confidence.

A CULTURE SHOCK

As I drifted from party to party, running into girls from my hall and guys from my classes, I found myself bending to complement each situation. I was paranoid that I wasn't smart, pretty, or cool enough. I thought I was talking too much, saying too little, and was afraid they would find out about me. I was afraid they would know I was cheating, applying a smile with each swipe of my lip gloss. I wasn't being fake, but I was stretched too thin. I began blending into the background and found myself not knowing who I was anymore.

Over time this tore at me, since I didn't realize what was happening. The littlest things brought me down; I overanalyzed, and because of it, my self-confidence all but disappeared. I began doubting myself and my individual shine became lackluster. How could this happen to the girl who once made everyone laugh? This wasn't just because I wanted to fit in; it was so much more than that. It was more like culture shock, and I wasn't prepared for it. I thought I could seamlessly be the same me as I was in high school. Yet in retrospect, it sounds ridiculous. How could I be the same me when everything was different? Even through this angst, I was growing. I was getting out there and challenging myself. It was simply ridiculous to cling to the past. I wasn't that version of "me" anymore.

When I finally looked past the self-sabotage and realized what I was doing, I felt so embarrassed by my behavior. I thought I was so much stronger than that. Yet, I was completely worn out. My spirit was silenced (as corny as that sounds). So what did I do? What could I do? I pulled back. I asked myself what I needed to eight: healthy, safe, and happy   291

do to get back to smiling, back to laughing, back to just breathing easy. I figured out this was much larger than what I could handle and looked to every resource I could find. I found out that I was struggling with my self-confidence and needed an extreme boost to my self-esteem. The more information I read, the more I found out that so many girls go through the same thing—and they were just like me. Suddenly, I didn't feel alone.

A SELF-CONFIDENCE OVERHAUL

First step, get outside your head. Reach out to your campus health center and see if they offer some form of mental health service. If they don't, ask if there are organizations on campus that do. Therapy is one of life's greatest untapped resources. It's great to have an outside element that you can spill your guts to. Plus, let's face it: you may not be hiding the world's greatest secret, but you still may not want your friends to know exactly what's going on. Heck, you may not even know what's really going on! Working with a therapist will allow for your anxieties to become tangible so they can be worked on, instead of just a mess of emotions trapped inside your head.

Therapists can suggest ways to work with your issues and provide strategies to overcome difficult situations. They also help you focus on what's really troubling you, and will troubleshoot based on particular problems instead of giving a general diagnosis that would otherwise just mute the problem instead of making it go away. If you're unsure if you "need" therapy, chances are you do. Therapy isn't for the "crazy," the weak, or the otherwise helpless. It's for the everyday girl who may be punishing herself for things she can't control. A friend of mine explained, "I feel as if my problems aren't big enough" to seek outside help. But they are! There are no silly questions, and I think the important thing to recognize is that they are there to help you. They provide an extra hand when you feel as if you're juggling a basket load of issues.

Many experts say to try out one session. And keep in mind that choosing a therapist is like choosing a great pair of sunglasses— not all will fit. Sometimes you have to try several pairs but when it works, it works. Some therapists just don't click with your personality and that's OK. Some people like their therapist to be very strict and straitlaced; others like to feel as if they're talking to a friend. Try out a session with someone you like, and if you still leave uneasy, at least you can say you tried.

What worked for me was a kind of conditioning that is both a mix of Kimora Lee Simmons's fabulousness and a tad of weepy Dr. Phil. There needs to be some concrete work to build up your mind and your self-esteem, but there also needs to be something to speak to your spirit. Remind yourself that you are fabulous and carry your own set of idiosyncrasies that make you who you are. Embrace them! These are the things people love about you. When you're feeling down, try to find something positive to affirm about yourself. Finding something positive will remind you that there are things that you love about yourself, which will combat the hate-speak you may say on a daily basis.

Believe it or not, the more times you say that you're a screw-up, the more likely you will end up believing it. At the very least, ask yourself, "Would you talk to a friend the same way you talk to yourself?" Chances are if you did, you wouldn't have any friends. People who suffer from low self-esteem issues judge themselves to such a higher degree that they don't realize that they are their own worst enemy.

TYPICAL ROADBLOCKS

Once you have seemed to hammer out a system that works for you, it's time to apply it and see how it holds up in the real world. A lot of work goes into recognizing the damage we put on ourselves, and then figuring out the best way to repair the damage. However, the work doesn't stop once you've worked out the equation—now it's time to apply the system and test its effectiveness.

While we discussed major self-confidence overhaul, most of the time it's the little things that can have even the most confident chicas checking their self-esteem at the door. There are moments when you just sort of hit an emotional snag, and need some extra support to get you through it.

Post-breakup

We've all been there. The sniffling, the Facebook stalking, the masochistic viewing of *The Notebook*. Breaking up sucks and it often gives your self-esteem a beating. After a breakup, the most common things women look for are answers. We try to categorize blame, we scrutinize our faults, harp on our shortcomings, and it really does a number on us. During this time, try to celebrate your newfound single status. Make a list of all the qualities you love about yourself. Sure, it's easy to list all the bad qualities of your ex, but it isn't about him, it's about you. Take the time to get to know yourself better, and enjoy the spontaneity of being single.

BFF no more (breakup with a girlfriend)

Breaking up sucks, but what happens when you break up with a friend? I'd rather sit through a million sappy romantic comedies with a best friend than watch my favorite movie alone. Breaking it off with a BFF can be really rough, especially since we rely on them when things aren't going right. During these years, relationships will be tested, and if it comes to a point when you and your true blue aren't working out, you may drift apart. Just like any relationship, take the time to mourn the loss of your bond and get it out of your system, but also start reaching out to the other friends in your circle. Then try to reach out to people you may not have talked to before. Ask the girl down the hall about the song she plays that you totally love, or hang out with your lab partner after class. Get involved in your student government or your campus paper. While it sucks to lose the Paris to your Nicole, it doesn't mean you've lost all the cool things that make you who you are.

Change in physical appearance

College is a time where you'll be testing your mind and your body, and you may notice your body changing as you spend more time away from home. If you see yourself losing or gaining an alarming amount of weight, try to reflect on your routine and your eating habits, as stress eating may pinpoint an underlying issue. If you're concerned, talk to a nutritionist or a doctor about a healthy diet, but remember nobody's perfect, and no one is expecting you to be either.

Failed an exam/class

Remember that all-nighter? The one last week, where you had to miss your best friend's band and the midnight waffle sale to spend the entire night cramming for that bio exam? The one you were studying for about a week? Yeah, it just came back, and you totally bombed. So, not only did you miss the killer encore but it was all for nothing. Yikes! Nothing is worse than putting your all into an assignment and finding out you failed. The first thing you should do is find out why you bombed so you can put it to rest. Look over your paper or your exam and really review your work—learn what mistakes you made so you don't make them again. If you feel shortchanged, schedule a time to talk with your professor to discuss your performance. The most important thing here is to make the progress tangible. In most cases a make-up test isn't an option, but the work you put into understanding your mistakes will help you with other assignments down the line. Reviewing your test or paper and learning from it helps channel your stress into something productive, which is way better than just throwing in the towel.

FINDING AN EQUILIBRIUM

When I finally pieced myself back together, I was able to see the person I was truly becoming. It's easy to get over a cold, but not so easy to recover from being emotionally under the weather. You can't just snap back to "normal"—and really, why would you want to? You've been through the hard part so try to think of ways of how it can work for you. We mess up, we goof off, and it's all just part of the game. Half the fun in making mistakes is the laughs that are brought on along the way.

Insights provided by Aja Johnson,
University of Maryland–College Park

staying fit in college

Everyone fears those evil, infamous "freshman fifteen," but are they really fact or just fiction? Leading a healthy lifestyle can be hard in college when you are always on the run and Mom isn't there with all three of your daily meals prepared. Classes, jobs, extracurricular activities, and your social life can cause your eating habits to go haywire.

Last semester when I was an intern, I'd come back from my internship and feel the urge to devour something easy and quick. I'd rarely eat lunch during the day, as I was busy on my feet, working on projects and helping editors into the early evening. When I arrived back on campus, I was tired and hungry. My solution? I would grab the easiest food, like a greasy Hot Pocket or fries for dinner. Sometimes I'd try to be healthy with a sandwich or salad or something sensible. But most of the time I used my crazy workload as an excuse to eat certain "bad" foods a little too much. As an incoming college student, you too will be busy. However, if you take control early on, you can develop great habits that can last a lifetime. If you want to win the "Freshman Fitness Test," here are a few tips to help you stay fit by eating better meals and staying healthier overall.

The Freshman 15: Fact or Fiction?

Talk about an urban legend—the idea that you'll automatically balloon up as soon as you arrive on campus is so ingrained into our culture, MTV is currently planning a whole reality program dedicated to this exact topic! The truth of the matter is The Freshman 15 *is* a myth. Indeed, research studies on this supposed phenomenon have proven that the average female college coed only gains two to three pounds during her first year of school; it's actually her male counterparts who are more likely to pack on the weight! If you want to ensure that you don't add a few extra pounds to your course schedule, cut down on carbs and fatty foods, amp up your fruit and vegetable intake, and make sure you set aside at least two to three days a week for an hour of cardio or strength training.

YOUR FIRST YEAR

As a new college student, it's only normal that you will have a million questions. Simple things like where to get food, where to work out, how much to spend, and how to stay on top of things can seem overwhelming when you first arrive at your new home. So let's get started.

Eating right

Most likely, you will have a university cafeteria, and the majority of you who live on campus will have meal plans. As a freshman at my school, I was required to have a meal plan of $1,200 per semester because freshmen dorms did not have kitchens. Meal plans are usually required for freshmen and have been included in your tuition bill. These days, college students access their meal plans through their University Identification Card, which swipes almost like a credit card in cafeterias and dining halls. Some universities have dining halls that are like cafeterias but are buffet-style and have an all-you-can-eat theme. Proceed with caution with buffets! Sometimes too many food options are not a good thing; overabundance can lead to overeating. But rest assured that you can eat healthy with minimal effort. These places almost always have vegetarian dishes, salads, and fruits for health-conscious students.

Some colleges have meal cards where you can go off campus to local restaurants and they will deduct money from your meal card, while others have student discounts at nearby restaurants. Here's a healthy tip: instead of going crazy at the nearby McDonald's, or KFC, look for other options like Salad Works, Subway, or alternative restaurants like sushi bars and Thai food, which offer healthier meal choices and place less of an emphasis on fried, fattening foods. But watch out for that shrimp tempura at the sushi restaurant! Check to see if the restaurant has nutritional guidelines where you can find out just exactly how many calories are in that delectable item you're getting ready to order.

Meal Plan Basics

Do you need a meal plan? Well, meal plan options generally vary from school to school, so it's hard to give one hard and fast rule when it comes to dining. However, there are definitely some pluses to buying one freshman year.

A meal card makes things easy
The dining hall may be your diet's worst enemy, but it can also be an overachiever's best friend. Many are open all day long and

are minutes away from the freshman dorms, so it's pretty easy to grab something quick before class, between afternoon breaks, or to snack on after-hours while you're studying. (Bonus: some larger schools like Duke or Boston University also have "points" options that allow you some flexibility with on-campus dining—*especially* if the school student union or campus center houses favorite chains like Subway or Jamba Juice that accept dining points.)

The dining hall is the place to be

When you're a freshman, having a meal plan can be akin to sitting at the cool kids' table in high school—you're smack-dab in the center of all the action. Many colleges and universities require first-year students to have a meal plan for this very reason—it's a great equalizer and forces you out of your comfort zone and into a social environment.

Getting busted for having a hot plate is lame

It's not unusual for some schools to put restrictions on what cooking appliances freshmen can have in the dorms, so eating healthy and staying on budget can be pretty tough if you've only got a microwave to work with. Check your school's website before you start raiding your parents' kitchen, and if you're still concerned about meeting any specific dietary restrictions, call or email your college and ask about vegetarian, vegan, or gluten-free options. Also, make sure to check and see if your dorm's dining hall operating hours work with your schedule.

Working out

During your first week, find your school's gym. Recreation hall or gym facility fees are usually included in your tuition bill, so you might as well use them! I cannot tell you how excited I was my junior year when my university finally completed our new gym. It was closer to the dorms than the previous gym, and the new state-of-the-art treadmills with TVs were definitely an upgrade!

Did you know that you can even get school credit for working out? At most schools, you can. Have you always been curious about Tae Kwon Do or would like to become a better swimmer? Check out your school's course offerings and sign up for an easy A and better body next semester.

What if you don't live on campus? Sorry, no excuse. You still have access to the gym before and after class or on the weekends. Even though you may not have the opportunity to work out several times a week, a regular routine of two or three times per week will help you see results. One year, my roommate and I did weekly Tae Bo workouts in our dorm room. Sure, we were lucky to have a spacious area that year. But no matter how big or small your dorm room is, make use of what you've got, whether it's your school's running track, the gym, or your own dorm room. Bottom line: find a routine that works with you and your schedule and stick with it!

DON'T FREAK OUT

So you've been at school for a few months, and really haven't gotten into a healthy routine yet. If you look in the mirror and don't like what you see, stop the negative feelings! Don't freak out if you're not at the same weight you were when you first started high school. What many women fail to realize is when you first enter college at 17 or 18, your body is still developing physically. So you can't compare your body to how it was a few years ago or sometimes even a few months ago!

Take a deep breath, and refocus your efforts on starting a healthy routine of exercising and eating right. Also, being healthy isn't just about the numbers on your scale; there are several other tests that are used to determine how fit you really are. Body mass index, or BMI, is a guideline used to judge whether you are at risk for health problems associated with your weight. Rather than relying on the bathroom scale, experts say that you should also know your BMI, a figure that takes into account not just weight but height to indicate body fat. In general, experts say that you should aim for a BMI that's over 18 and under 25. (To check your BMI try the online calculator at www.healthcentral.com/diet-exercise/index-1688-143.html.) You may be surprised to find that you are underweight when you consider your height and body frame.

STOP BEING LAZY

OK, so you've made the decision to get healthy. Now the question is how to do it.

Staying healthy is more about choosing not to be lazy than anything else. Lazy is having the time and means to go work out but choosing not to because you'd rather watch *America's Next Top Model*. If that's the case, pick a different time to work out or record your favorite show. I'm not saying become a gym fanatic or anything, but if you have the time, why not go? The hardest part of working out is getting yourself to the gym. I promise that you'll feel fantastic afterward.

Some of you may end up living off campus or in apartment-style dorms. If you have a kitchen with a stove, jump for joy! Your options are endless. All you need to do is visit your supermarket right away and start cooking your own meals. Cooking your own meals has two benefits: it's generally healthier *and* it's cheaper. Sometimes it will be tempting to go to Applebee's or the local diner for a quick bite, but don't cave in to a quick and unhealthy fix. And don't forget that ordering Chinese food and pizza can become really pricey on a student's limited budget.

Dating Someone?

Some of you can become unhealthy by association. One of my close friends started dating her boyfriend over a year ago, and since then, she's noticed she gained a few pounds from eating out more often.

> The problem? She feels the need to clean her plate just as he does, and most restaurants are notorious for their extra-large servings. It's not a myth that men can eat more than women and still maintain a reasonable weight.
>
> It's cool to dine out with your boyfriend or even a bunch of your guy friends, but realize that while he can scarf down 8 slices of pizza and seem not to gain a pound, it's definitely not a habit to acquire. However, don't be too afraid or shy to eat around your guy. Most likely, he'd rather see you actually enjoy food and eat well than pretend you hate food. In fact, your good habits might inspire him to make a few positive changes for himself!

Make cooking at home fun! Invite your friends to your place for a low-cost and healthy dinner. One of my former roommates and I used to occasionally cook dinner together and make a recipe of baked chicken with breadcrumbs and usually a vegetable like green beans or broccoli to go with it. It was filling, full of flavor, and more health-friendly than eating pizza and french fries. For other recipes, a great book to pick up is *The Complete Idiot's Guide to the College Diet Cookbook* by Shelly Vaughan James, which also includes recipes tested by students at four major universities.

FIND A SYSTEM THAT WORKS FOR YOU

The best way to get healthy is to establish a routine and stick with it. Take your daily planner or even a blank piece of paper and write down your schedule. Include class, work, and any other obligations you have. Next, find spots where you could fit in a workout; it doesn't have to be every day. You'll probably have some Monday/Wednesday/Friday classes with breaks in between. Just pencil in an hour at the gym at the same time for each of these days, and treat it like a class. When you set a routine, you'll be more likely to stick to your workout plan. Also, don't worry if you go off track. Maybe that's an indication that you need to rethink your schedule, and you shouldn't be afraid to readjust.

Since I hate the word "diet" (and you'll find out why later on), think about a program that doesn't tell you what to eat, but encourages you to make better decisions. My friend currently is on the Weight Watchers plan and says it works for her because she can eat all the foods she likes but just in moderation.

Working out with friends is a great way to stay motivated. You will be much more likely to go to the gym when someone is depending on you to be there. But just make sure you first discuss your goals and what type of workouts you are going to do. For example, I had a friend who inherited her workout routine from her boyfriend who was involved in track. Needless to say, her complete routine was difficult! It consisted of a long warm up, and then a lot of running on the track. Now, I had no qualms about warm-ups and doing exercises, but I have always despised running. This is an important thing to remember. Having friends to help you exercise or eat healthier can be a huge motivator, but you have to make sure not to lose track of your *own* goals. A friend may want to lose a few pounds while you'd like to lose 20. That's a *big* difference. Or maybe your roommate can eat whatever she wants and still maintain her hourglass figure with just exercise while you have to exercise and eat better to stay in shape. Everyone's body type is different, so before you try to mirror your friends' habits, find the system that works the best for you!

BE REALISTIC

Finally, the trick to being healthy and fit in college is getting rid of the word "diet" and substituting the words "moderation" and "exercise." I know that the latest diet crazes are everywhere—in gossip magazines, the news, and commercials. I don't care how often you read about it because dieting is not a healthy way to eat long-term. You may lose a few pounds initially, but they always come back unless you change your lifestyle. UCLA researchers recently found that one year after starting a diet, people were no better off than before—in fact, about half of them ended up gaining weight. Get rid of the word "diet" because restricting your eating is not healthy in the long term!

Make realistic changes to your lifestyle that can be made over time and do everything in moderation. Only you know what you can handle. For instance, if you entirely abandon a food that you love because it's unhealthy, your supposedly healthy change may not last long. It's very difficult to give up favorite foods. It might make you more likely to binge or go overboard later.

I'll give you a quick example of what I mean by moderation.

You're going to make a sandwich. Instead of a glob of mayo to top it off, use something healthier like mustard or even fat-free mayo. Or try eating only half the sandwich. And when it comes to snacking, instead of having a candy bar every day after class, cut down to giving yourself this treat once a week while filling yourself up with tasty fruits and vegetables on the other days. If you find yourself eating out every week, cut it down to maybe once or twice a month.

Be safe

Being healthy is great, but don't go to the extreme and acquire an eating disorder. Eating disorders such as bulimia, anorexia, binge eating, and overeating can happen to anyone. Actually, 5–7 percent of women in the United States will suffer from some type of eating disorder during their lifetime. Also, something else to watch out for is over-exercising. Some warning signs of a compulsive exerciser are the following: exercising even when you don't feel well, basing your daily diet on how much you exercise, constantly worrying you'll gain weight if you don't exercise every day, forcing yourself to do multiple workouts during the day, or becoming depressed if you miss a workout. If you think you've acquired any of these unhealthy eating or lifestyle habits, seek out professional help. This is something you do not want to ignore, because it may become worse over time, negatively affecting your collegiate experience and your health.

LAST BIT OF ADVICE

Remember that you're in college, so expect late-night pizza orders or times when you'll pig out on ice cream and cookies. Food is not to be feared. Your best bet to ensuring a successful college experience is to enjoy your faves in moderation and exercise throughout the week. With this approach, you will be the best you can be academically, socially, and physically.

Insights provided by Donyel L. Griffin, Kean University,
and Kylie Thompson, Harvard University

the dangers of
eating disorders

Eating is an important part of your health while in college. Unlike being at home in high school when there is a strict time for breakfast, lunch, and dinner, in college you can pig out at lunch and then have brownies for dinner. Nothing about college life is regulated in a way to mark which behaviors are normal, odd, or bordering on disordered. That is why it is so difficult to know when it's time to seek help for what may be an eating disorder.

The concept of eating disorders may not be entirely new, as you might have learned about them through a high school health class or even during a "very special" episode of your favorite teen sitcom. While we might know what eating disorders are, it's important to understand how they function on a college campus and what to do if you or someone you know suffers from disordered eating.

WHAT IS DISORDERED EATING?

In such a weight-conscious society, it's hard to distinguish what's harmless and what's dangerous. Eating disorders are extreme eating patterns that have a psychological dependency on control.

There are three main types: anorexia nervosa, bulimia nervosa, and binge-eating disorder. Anorexia nervosa is the excessive starving or limiting of food. This can be aided with the use of medication or extreme dieting, with girls losing weight at rapid speed. Bulimia nervosa follows a routine of bingeing and purging. Bingeing consists of eating a large amount of food in one sitting, followed by purging, which is ridding the body of this food in an extreme manner (via vomiting or through the use of laxatives). Binge-eating is simply using food as a means of comfort, consuming large amounts of food rapidly in one sitting. Unlike bulimia, there is no purging process.

It may be hard to spot someone who is suffering from disordered eating, as they don't always look extremely skinny.

Sufferers of bulimia especially may look overweight, and may view bulimia as a "weight maintenance" practice. Girls can develop a combination of these disorders, jumping from one to another at any given time.

THE LESSER-KNOWN DISORDERS

While these disorders are often seen on college campuses, there are also new forms of these behaviors that are attacking young women. Exercise-bulimia, where exercising takes the place of traditional purging, is silently afflicting college students and no one really knows how to treat it. Since exercising is seen as a healthy activity, one wouldn't assume that it could act as a disease. However, this follows the same pattern of overdoing it, where the length of exercise becomes excessive, with a woman (or man!) working out for hours and hours on end. In this case, exercising works just as any other traditional form of purging, with the intent to work away any food the individual consumed.

There are also more dangerous forms of disordered eating that feed off of the use of drugs or binge drinking. In this type, controlled substances are used as a way to numb the body for its need for food, blurring the individual's perception of self. While exercise-bulimia revamps the way we look at bulimia, drugs and alcohol respond to the depressive state the individual is in. The drug and alcohol use compounds the effects of the lack of eating, and can destroy the body at a much quicker speed. In these cases, it's important to refer to the motive of action. Disordered eating is not just about starving yourself, or vomiting, but about the reasons behind these actions. Experiencing extreme feelings of guilt, sadness, anger, or remorse follows these actions, and can signal disordered eating.

These retooled versions of traditional eating disorders become almost more dangerous than the former, as they take away the focus of the behavior. While it's easy to spot individuals following unorthodox patterns of behavior, it becomes difficult when the behavior appears "normal." This makes it harder for the abuser to identify exactly what the behavior is doing. Over-exercising and facilitating disordered eating habits with controlled substances are problems, but when paired with low self-esteem, and a crippling body image, these actions become part of a much larger problem. Eating disorders arise from depression, anxiety, and overwhelming feelings of being out of control. The food is representative of something larger than just raw material. Although there are issues of self-esteem, weight-management, and self-worth, the disorder thrives off the satisfaction of completing a goal, attaining a certain ideal, adhering to a larger standard of beauty.

WORRIED ABOUT A FRIEND?

If you suspect that a friend suffers from disordered eating, keep on the lookout for her behavior. Watch for girls who suddenly become withdrawn, secretive, or moody. If you hear a friend making negative remarks about her body and/or image, idolizing or glorifying thinness, and you notice a shift in her behavior, then she may be suffering from a disorder. If a friend has a history of depression, physical/sexual abuse, or weight issues, she may be more at risk to rebound or partake in disordered eating. While it may be awkward to approach a friend about her eating habits, it's important to confront disordered behavior before it spirals out of control.

Set yourself up in a place that may be comforting to her, and be direct with your concerns. A simple "I've noticed you've been feeling down lately, and I haven't seen you eat much and I'm concerned." This addresses the behavior, but does it in a way where she doesn't feel attacked. Avoid blame or guilt, and just stick to your own observations and feelings. Present options to her to put her in control of the situation. If the direct approach is too difficult, frame it in the sense of a hypothetical issue. Ask for her reaction to a show on eating disorders or a special documentary. Expressing your support for this "hypothetical" situation may clue her in that you're a safe source for her to talk to. Be sure to follow up, and let her know that you're there to help in any way you can. What you want to do is offer a safe place and support.

Your own behavior

If you feel that your eating habits are sliding toward the unhealthy, try to assess what your behavior means. Recognizing disordered eating is the first step on the road to recovery. There are plenty of resources out there in order to understand your disease. Talk to a therapist about your behavior. They can work out a plan for you to understand and work with your disease. The best thing you can do is focus on your health and rebuild what the disorder damaged (self-confidence and self-esteem).

If you're unsure if you're experiencing disordered eating, listen to your body. Give yourself extra attention during periods of stress or depression. It's easy to feel trapped by fad diets and quick pills, but the results of these behaviors are long lasting and can have terrible effects on your body. If you're truly unsatisfied with your appearance, talk with your doctor and discuss healthy alternatives to weight loss and management. There are plenty of healthy ways to get big results. Be sure to tune in to the reasons why you want to lose weight. Weight loss other than for the sake of your health sets unrealistic expectations and can lead to dangerous behavior patterns. Consult a therapist to understand what such a change can do to your mental health.

If you are concerned about yourself or a friend, contact the National Eating Disorder Association's Helpline, at 800-931-2237. Other useful links include

- Anorexia Nervosa and Associated Disorders: Provides support groups, resources, and candlelight vigils around the United States. www.anad.org

- Eating Disorder Hope: An informational site about eating disorders. www.eatingdisorderhope.com

Insights provided by Aja Johnson,
University of Maryland–College Park

U Chic Essentials—Healthy and Happy

Listen to your body

College is the time to do anything and everything. But be careful not to overexert yourself. Take time to rest and rejuvenate. It will remind you that you are important, hardworking, and deserve to be pampered every now and then.

Remember that you are beautiful!

Cherish your unique beauty both inside and out. Ignore the tabloids that say all of Hollywood is getting plastic surgery these days. They are chasing an unreal beauty expectation that does not end up being beautiful but, well, boring.

Use your on-campus resources

From the campus health center to the fitness center, your university has fantastic resources created specifically for you. And you're paying for them, so why not use them? Your body and mind will thank you.

Looking for more great advice? Head to www.UChic.com for our fave resources and websites—they come highly recommended from our guide's contributors and editors. Be sure to leave your suggestions as well!

CHAPTER 9

Surviving Temptation Island

ollege is the ultimate Temptation Island. No curfews. No limits on alcohol or Facebook. No reminders to do homework. We could go on, but you get the picture. The only hard and steadfast rule is that you are in charge, and no one is there to help you say "no" to the many temptations that you'll face. Sometimes, it's not your own temptations that should be of concern. Your friends, a boyfriend, a guy you just met at a bar, and maybe even a professor will face their own temptations, and might drag you into situations you never had planned (or wanted) to be in. Taken too far, something that started out as innocent could end up being a disaster for all. Follow the advice in this chapter, and you'll learn how to not only survive but also thrive on Temptation Island.

over-the-top party pals
and ways to deal

Perfectly straightened hair? Check. Super-cute new outfit, complete with matching shoes and bag? Check. Your best friend completely plastered before you even head out the door? Uh-oh. Partying with the girls is a great way to de-stress after a tiring week of classes, papers, and exams. And if you haven't heard it before, "College is the time to try everything," and "Hey, you only live once!" While college is known as a time for experimenting, there is still work to be done and, well, embarrassing moments to be had.

Whether hitting a hot bar or club or hanging at a frat party, these moments, although fun, can also pose some challenges if you've got a friend who parties a little too hard. So maybe you're not the drunk girl dancing on the stripper pole, puking in the bathroom sink, or making out with a random stranger—*but what do you do if one of your friends is?*

Whether you're finally checking out the frat house down the street known for throwing killer bashes, kicking it with a few friends on the front porch, or hitting up the bar scene, keep these tips in mind when you're hanging out with a friend who tends to drink a little too much and take things a little too far.

SO, SHE'S EMBARRASSING YOU
You're at a bar

Is she letting a little too loose on the stripper pole? She might not be the sexiest chick on the dance floor after her seventh beer, but now probably isn't the time to discuss her not-so-suave moves. As long as she isn't popping, locking, and dropping in a way you know would embarrass her if she was sober, let it go. Everyone deserves the chance to go a little crazy on occasion. However, there's a fine line between being a fun drunk and a drunken mess. Use your best judgment in determining that line. If your gut tells you she's gone a little too far (i.e., taking clothes off), don't hesitate to let her know.

You're at a house/frat party with strangers

Is she making out with a dark shadowy figure off in a deserted corner? In college, a few random make-out sessions are almost a rite of passage. But if things look seriously wrong (for example, that guy she's kissing in the corner is twice her age, she's promising to go home with a boy from her English class, or announcing that she's driving home completely smashed), it's time for a chat. In these situations, it's OK to step in to help your friend avoid some potentially horrible consequences. She may drunkenly claim she hates you at the time, but she'll love you for it tomorrow.

DON'T, UNDER ANY CIRCUMSTANCES, LET HER LEAVE BY HERSELF!

Here are a couple of scenarios that you may face when partying with your over-the-top party pal.

If it's just the two of you

So that boy from her class? He says there's something going on at his house later and invites your friend, and you, along. You're tired and so ready for bed—but your friend obviously isn't. Make sure you let her know that you aren't going to follow her and that you don't think she's capable of going by herself. It may seem a little aggressive. But even if you weren't invited, it's still your responsibility to make sure she gets home safely. Offer an alternative: how about a few of you go out for some late-night pizza? The extra calories aren't half as dangerous as heading back to an almost-stranger's house.

If you're out with a group

Partying with a group changes the dynamic slightly. You should weigh all the options. Do you or any of your friends know this guy? Do you have any mutual friends? Does one of the other girls want to go with your friend, and is she sober enough to make rational decisions? Don't be afraid to play Mom in the group. Remember that nagging little voice you hear inside your head when you're about to do something you know is wrong? Be the one to speak the truth: going home with this guy is reckless, and could be dangerous.

If you just met up with her

Say you didn't spend three hours primping with her and didn't even know she was going to be at the same place, but you happen to bump into her at the party. Although there may not be an obligation, a good friend should keep an eye on her intoxicated girlfriend. Offer her the same options mentioned above and advise her as you would any of the girls you came with. If she does decide to leave with a guy she just met in her drunken state, check up on her later. For instance, give her cell phone a ring and make sure she doesn't need an easy out or somewhere else to stay.

If she's attempting to drive

The statistics are haunting—1,700 college students between the ages of 18 and 24 die each year from alcohol-related unintentional injuries. This includes vehicle crashes. Don't let your friend become a statistic! Offer to pay for a cab to send her home. Walk home with her and promise a ride back to her car the next morning. Do whatever it takes to make sure she doesn't get her keys in the ignition.

STAY CALM

You've decided to help, but what happens when your friend is not eagerly responding to your advice? Remember that your friend is in an altered state of mind. This means that anything you say or do at this point could be blown out of proportion. She might not take your advice so lightly, especially if she's intoxicated. Don't get angry with her or give up. Although she may not realize it, she probably needs your help. Explain that you are only letting her know because you are trying to be a good friend. Leave it at that. There's no reason to fight with her when she probably won't even remember why she was mad in the morning. Plus, no one wants to cause a scene when they're out having a good time.

NOW SHE'S PUKING ALL OVER THE FLOOR!

You've managed to talk your friend into doing the right thing in choosing to leave the bar and go home. But your job doesn't end there. If your friend is extremely wasted, don't leave your plastered pal passed out on the tile. Get her some water and hold her hair back. Then get her in bed on her stomach. Don't forget that she could possibly choke if she is lying on her back. She'll thank you in the morning, even if she's über-hungover.

YOUR FRIEND IS COMPLETELY WASTED AND NOW YOU'RE REALLY WORRIED

If her breathing slows, she appears unconscious, or her skin is cold and clammy, she might have alcohol poisoning. Don't hesitate to dial 911 or find a Resident Assistant who will do it for you. At Princeton, university policy requires that students help severely drunk people by contacting local medical or safety personnel or local police. And don't worry. Neither you nor the people you help will be disciplined for intoxication. Even if your school does not have this policy, always take care of a friend in need.

A COMMON OCCURRENCE?

People can develop psychological and physical dependency on alcohol, and alcoholism can occur in people as early as college. It's not uncommon at all. In fact, 31 percent of college students meet criteria for substance abuse and 6 percent meet the criteria for alcohol dependence. Everybody likes to have fun and relax in his or her own way after a long, stressful week. But if your friend is drinking every night, drinking alone, or can't control or stop herself while she is drinking, she could be developing alcoholism. You'll be doing her a favor if you sit down and talk to her about her drinking.

NEED MORE INFORMATION ON ALCOHOLISM?

Check out www.alcoholism.about.com for tons of information about alcoholism and other forms of substance abuse, including an Alcohol Abuse screening quiz.

Insights provided by Erica Strauss, Kent State University

dangerous dependency: prescription drugs

Between five-page papers, exhausting lecture halls, endless pages of math problems, and weekend road trips, the life of a college student can be overwhelming. There are lots of ways to reduce stress: exercise, yoga, meditation, writing, to name just a few. But some college students turn to prescription drugs instead. Bad idea. For one, they're illegal unless you're the one with the prescription. And two, they're incredibly addictive.

Need to get that paper done in an hour? Pop an Adderall. Want to unwind after a nerve-racking presentation? Try a Xanax. Have a few aches and pains? Vicodin will do the trick. OK, not really... "Marie" (not her real name), a junior fine arts major, takes Adderall, a popular prescription drug, for her ADHD symptoms. Adderall is a stimulant that affects chemicals in the brain and controls hyperactivity. "I take it because I can't concentrate without it," she said. However, many college students take drugs that aren't prescribed to them as a way to easily ace exams, chill out at a big frat party, or even clean their dorm rooms.

Over the years, students have started to use drugs in ways doctors never could have imagined. Adderall has been described as the drug for overachievers, and the side effects—including increased energy, ability to focus, and inability to sleep—sound like a miracle pill for the busy, hectic, fast-paced life of a college student.

"Whenever I have a paper due, I won't stress about it because I know I can take Adderall and get it done fast," said a freshman who wishes to remain anonymous. "It also helps when I pull all-nighters to study for exams." Adderall also suppresses the user's appetite, and many students, especially young women, enjoy that extra side effect.

"I like it because it's like taking Stackers or other diet pills, but you can also concentrate," she said. Not only will you get an A on your exam, but—hey!—you could even drop a dress size.

But Adderall is not the only drug abused on campuses. Xanax, Valium, and Vicodin—which treat anxiety, pain, and insomnia, among other ailments—are also college favorites. And with rising cases of generalized anxiety disorder on college campuses, according to the Anxiety Disorders Association of America, many students are finding themselves with easy access to these pills. Just ask the kid sitting behind you in psych, your hall-mate, or even that gorgeous girl in your sorority—one of them probably has a prescription to your drug of choice, or knows someone who does.

"People know I have a prescription, and I get phone calls all the time from people asking for it," Marie said. "I don't need them all, so usually I'll just give them away."

Marie isn't the only legally prescribed drug user who chooses to sell or give away her pills. A study conducted in 2008 by a Massachusetts psychopharmacologist reported that 11 percent of students surveyed who had prescriptions to Adderall XR sold their pills. Another 22 percent reported misusing their prescription and didn't take the pills when they were supposed to.

THE DANGERS

Although Marie is prescribed the drug, she can still see the many dangers of drug misuse. She feels not only physically, but also psychologically, dependent on the drug.

The drug becomes a crutch—an easy way to avoid a bigger issue. Didn't attend enough lectures? Take an Adderall and you can read the chapter in two hours. Want to calm your nerves before you get your drink on at the bars? Take a Valium to get an extra buzz. The problem is that once the drugs wear off, the real issues are still there. "I feel like I can't do my work without Adderall now," Marie said. "I think people who take drugs recreationally take the pills to escape their problems. They're just looking for a quick fix for whatever is wrong at the time."

Many students don't see the harm in popping a pill that is prescribed to someone else. People mistakenly believe that it's OK to take the drugs because they have been prescribed by a doctor, according to a study published in the *New England Journal of Medicine* in 2006. But when they are not prescribed to you in particular, you never know what kind of reaction your body might have when you introduce a new medication. Not only are there health risks involved, but addiction is another very serious side effect. "I've seen a lot of people, good friends actually, become addicted to drugs that weren't prescribed for them," Marie said. "I've seen it ruin their lives."

But prescription drugs don't carry the negative stigma like street drugs such as cocaine and heroin. You don't cringe to hear that a friend is taking excessive amounts of Adderall or Vicodin the way you would if they were hooked on cocaine.

"I take it to do better in school," said the same anonymous freshman. "It's not like I'm buying it off the street."

But getting caught with Adderall is just like getting caught with marijuana, since police can charge you with drug possession. And if you're caught selling your stash? Same deal: you can be charged with drug trafficking.

One acquaintance has never tried any prescription drugs because of the potential consequences. "I've heard of a bunch of people who do that stuff," she said. "I don't get it. I feel like if my doctor isn't the one who gave it to me, I don't want to take it." Goody-two-shoes? No. She's just smart. If you do not have a medical condition, you should not touch these things.

Despite the abuse of prescription drugs, the disorders mentioned here are real and do require treatment. If you feel that you suffer from ADHD or generalized anxiety disorder, make an appointment with your doctor.

Insights provided by Erica Strauss, Kent State University

facing sexual harassment on campus

"Sexual harassment on campus? That so does not happen anymore. Well, at least not to me anyway!" Does this sound like something you think when anyone mentions sexual harassment? Well, before you decide to skip to the next chapter, consider this: a recent research study by the American Association of University Women found that 62 percent of college women had experienced some form of sexual harassment. Surprised?

WHAT IS SEXUAL HARASSMENT, EXACTLY?

Before we dive any deeper into this discussion, it is worth asking what sexual harassment is in the first place. Definitions of sexual harassment vary depending on the source. I'm going to provide a definition from my own alma mater, California State University–Los Angeles, that provides a policy statement regarding students' rights on campus. This definition is pretty standard and comprehensive.

Sexual harassment includes but is not limited to

1. Unwanted sexual advances, requests for sexual favors, and other verbal or physical conduct of a sexual nature.

2. Any act which contributes to a workplace or learning environment that is hostile, intimidating, offensive, or adverse to persons because of the sexual nature of the conduct.

3. Conditioning an act, decision, evaluation, or recommendation on the submission to or tolerance of any act of a sexual nature.

So to make it clear, sexual harassment is any form of unwanted sexual advances—touching or otherwise—which can be anything from someone grabbing your butt to making a sexual joke. It can also be any sexual act that interferes with your college environment or routine. For example, it's that guy who constantly talks about inappropriate sexual stuff around you, so you leave your dorm a few minutes early every morning to avoid seeing him. And finally, it includes someone who holds authority in your life, conditioning your success or advancement on your participating in anything sexual. So, for example, you have a professor who puts his hand on your thigh in his office and insinuates that your A in the class is dependent on you responding to his sexual advances. In short, anything sexual and unwanted by you is sexual harassment.

Sexual harassment presents a unique problem for women these

days, especially since our culture tends to downplay the fact that it still exists. The college campus is no exception. Sexual harassment is common on college campuses, and women experience it in a distinctive way. According to the same AAUW study previously mentioned, women are more likely to be harassed through physical contact such as being touched, grabbed, or pinched. They are also more likely to receive sexual comments, gestures, jokes, or looks.

Bottom line: sexual harassment is not something that happens to other women somewhere out there. It happens to us—to you and me. Hopefully reading this will get you more informed and help you recognize it and know what to do when it happens.

A recent American Association of University Women research study found that 62 percent of college women had experienced some form of sexual harassment. Surprised?

DON'T BE AFRAID TO SPEAK UP

Not only will you possibly face a sexual harasser at some point during college, people are going to try to make you feel like sexual harassment isn't that serious. They are going to tell you to let it go, to just ignore it, to stop complaining. They are going to tell you that it's excusable for this reason or that, and they are going to tell you that it doesn't really matter. Well, I want to tell you that those are all lies, absolute untruths, falsehoods that perpetuate our society's belief that disrespecting women is excusable. We live in a culture that views women as sex objects and devalues women constantly. Some men think they have a right to women sexually as if they are possessions, and that sexual harassment is excusable. Well, it's not. Period.

Regardless of circumstances, please know that no one has a right to touch you, speak to you, or manipulate you in any unwanted sexual way.

> We live in a culture that views women as sex objects and devalues women constantly in the media. Some men think they have a right to women sexually as if they are possessions, and that sexual harassment is excusable. Well, it's not. Period.

Responding to sexual harassment

So what in the world do you do when you're being sexually harassed? Part of the answer depends on who the harassment is coming from. Often sexual harassment is student-to-student. If it's happening in your dorm, tell your Resident Assistant, or your Resident Director. If it's from a staff member like a professor at your college, then many campuses have a designated person who receives sexual harassment complaints. Explore your university website to find contact information for that person and reach out to them as soon as possible. The longer you let it go, the less likely you'll find the courage to speak up. The common thread here is that you say something. Otherwise, they will continue violating your right to a life without harassment and most likely the rights of other women just like you. Speaking up about sexual harassment can be particularly difficult when that person is a peer or someone you have to see regularly. Being scared of retribution is commonplace. In my opinion, the best way to deal with this is by finding support in community. Friends, family, even staff on campus can offer you great support and encouragement when it seems like it's just too hard to deal with sexual harassment. Some friends may discourage you but real ones will stick with you through it. Also, be confident in yourself.

Reporting sexual harassment is just plain hard. If the person you report is a peer then you will probably see them around campus but don't be intimidated. You don't have to address them or talk to them or argue with them or explain yourself if you're not comfortable. Seek support within your community. No one has a right to sexually harass you in any way, and you have every right to defend yourself against inappropriate sexual behavior. Assert yourself. Don't be scared. And now that you know what sexual harassment is and that it's serious, you know how to deal.

Even though sexual harassment seems like something that doesn't happen anymore, it's still a reality for many women in the workplace and on college campuses. But now that you have the info, you'll know what to do.

Insights provided by Monica Taylor,
California State University–Los Angeles

U Chic Essentials—Surviving Temptation Island

Be fearless

What you do and say influences your friends more than you think. When you fearlessly take the lead in defining your values and setting limits on drugs, alcohol, and other temptations, you'll find that those around you tend to follow. In the end, it helps everyone stay on track and out of trouble.

Sexual harassment can happen

It may come as a shock, but a recent study of college women found that more than 62 percent of respondents have faced some form of sexual harassment. Awareness is key, so read our chapter and be prepared in case you, too, ever have to deal with this unfortunate reality.

Take a self-defense class

This is a great way to prepare yourself for anything that can happen on campus or in your community. Look for these classes on campus first; your instructors will most likely spend some time talking about your campus specifically—important information that can help you become better aware of your surroundings.

Looking for more great advice? Head to www.UChic.com for our fave resources and websites—they come highly recommended from our guide's contributors and editors. Be sure to leave your suggestions as well!

CHAPTER 10

Money Matters

*P*aying for college, living on a budget, hunting for an apartment, staying on top of credit card bills: these are just a few of the "real world" (well, sort of real world) responsibilities and experiences that you'll face as an independent woman in college. On the surface, they don't sound like much fun. And when you consider how current economic challenges may have already impacted your college experience, things might look a bit tricky at the start. However, by taking charge of your life at an early age—whether by setting and sticking to a budget or getting a jump start on the financial aid search—you are guaranteeing yourself a bright future no matter what. On top of that, you'll develop a sense of pride, and more than anything, these good self-management habits will last a lifetime. Bottom line: this is definitely a chapter that you do not want to skip. So read on to get inspired with advice from other college women who discovered their inner diva by successfully pursuing the independent life.

the ins and outs
of financial aid

Our college years are full of building lifelong friendships, making memories that we will never forget, and gaining an education that can set us on the path to great success in life.

While most people will agree that college is well worth the money, it is still an expensive investment to make. With the cost of college tuitions skyrocketing, many students and families end up having to borrow thousands of dollars in financial aid just to pay tuition. The result? Students can expect to spend a good chunk of their adult lives paying off their college debt.

While we'd love to give you a tip that would help you avoid this scenario, unfortunately, it's just the nature of the system as it stands today. What we can do is shed light on the financial aid process to help alleviate some of the stress.

SOURCES OF AID

You're probably used to having your parents or older relatives remind you about all of the important things at this point in your life. That is about to change.

College is about claiming your independence, and along with that comes the responsibility of taking your future into your own hands. Now, your family will still be there to help guide you along the way, but they will not be able to keep your calendar updated or make sure you don't miss the various deadlines that will come up during your college years.

This is most apparent when it comes to dealing with the financial aid process and dealing with the cost of attending college. These things will be mostly up to you. So let's get started!

Financial aid is the primary way for you to receive financial assistance to help pay for higher education. Sounds great, right? However, wading into the financial aid waters can seem like a daunting task with all the options that exist and the hoops you have to jump through just to get funding. Consider this your cheat sheet to this complicated process.

According to Kiplinger.com, a business publication, the federal government provides the majority of financial aid—more than $100 billion a year. But your financial aid package can consist of a mix of funding from a variety of sources: federal or state agencies, private lending institutions, or, in the case of scholarships, your employer, club, or church.

Here's a quick snapshot of the various types of funding options:

1. **Federal and state aid:** Includes loans, grants, and campus-based programs and is based, for the most part, on financial need rather than scholastic merit.

   There are three types of loans: Direct student loans and PLUS loans for parents and Perkins loans for high-financial-need students. The Federal Pell Grant, which doesn't have to be repaid, usually is awarded only to undergraduate students based on financial need, cost of attendance, and other factors. To find out what your state may offer, check out your state's education department website.

   Also note that U.S. government agencies such as the Department of Health and Human Services, the Department of Veterans Affairs, and others provide a variety of scholarships, loans, and education benefits to families of employees, according to Kiplinger.com.

2. **Private loans:** Private loans used to fill in the gaps left by federal programs. Unfortunately, according to Kiplinger, these are harder and more expensive for students to get, as a result of the recent economic downturn. To get a private loan, you will need to have good credit and a creditworthy cosigner, typically your parent. Ask the financial aid office at your school for a list of preferred lenders. You can also

compare lenders and loan terms at FinAid.org to avoid securing an overly expensive college loan.

3. **Scholarships:** To uncover potential options, check with your high school guidance counselor, college financial aid offices, scholarship directories at your library as well as your employer, community organizations, advocacy groups, or associations related to your field of interest. According to Kiplinger, Sallie Mae's free CollegeAnswer.com scholarship database contains more than 3 million scholarships worth more than $16 billion in funds. Free sites such as Peterson's, the College Board's Scholarship Search, and FastAID also provide a host of options.

THE PROCESS

To get started with the financial aid process, it is important that you first find out all deadlines and write them down in one place that you will look at on a regular basis. Do you have a homework calendar? Make sure to include when the applications are due, when your tuition is due, when the loan money will be available to you, and the term limits of the loan, such as how much time the loan money will be available to you.

Now that we've got a handle on the basics of getting organized, the big question is likely some version of: What am I qualified for?

To find out, you will need to fill out a free FAFSA (Free Application for Federal Student Aid) form at www.fafsa.gov.

However, to ensure you get the most financial aid possible, we recommend that you first do some homework on your options before getting started with this admittedly tedious process. Head to www.studentaid.ed.gov, which has a ton of information on which types of aid you can get, how to apply, how to get started, and much more.

Don't miss those deadlines!

Don't delay in getting started. There is nothing more crucial than financial aid deadlines, especially when it comes to paying your college tuition on time. The deadlines for loan applications come a lot earlier than you think and may sneak up on you if you don't stay organized. These deadlines are strict, and you may not be eligible to receive any loan money until the next term if you miss the date. Staying organized is crucial.

An added benefit of staying on top of the process? According to a spokesperson for Sallie Mae (an education loan provider), as quoted in a Kiplinger.com article, students have a "better chance of securing cheap loans for college by completing the application early and in advance of state and school deadlines."

U Chic Tip!

What happens when it's time to pay your tuition and you don't have your loan money? Don't fret! Take a trip to the financial aid office. Most universities are already aware of the situation and have special deadlines and due dates for people who are waiting on their federal loan money to come in. They will definitely be able to fill you in on your deadlines, but make sure you don't wait until the last minute. You wouldn't want to find out that these special deadlines do not pertain to you on the day that tuition is due— another reason that there is nothing more important than paying attention to deadlines!

But beware!

One word of caution here. There are many scammers out there who will offer to complete your FAFSA form for free. Be sure that you go to www.fafsa.gov to fill out your FAFSA form, as this is a free service provided by the government.

Now, we know this process is not easy. If you need assistance with your FAFSA form, most colleges have a financial aid office that will happily guide you in the right direction, so don't hesitate to reach out and ask for assistance on any question you may have about the process. By tapping these resources that are available to you early on and staying on top of the deadlines, you should have no trouble getting through the financial aid process.

Insights provided by Kelly Leslie, San Francisco State University, and Megan O'Connell, University of Wisconsin–Platteville

finding scholarships in surprising places

Every spring, newspapers nationwide deliver stories of gradu-ating seniors who managed to earn a 4.0, start their own charities, serve as captains of the tennis team, and simultaneously master the trombone.

Not surprisingly, these students have no trouble nabbing full-ride scholarships to the most prestigious schools. In the fall, these students will attend Harvard or Yale, graduate with a 4.0, and will later run against each other for president. Nothing short of a superhuman feat.

But what about those of us who work just as hard but may not pull off 4.0s? The college admission game can be frustrating when you're having to compete with these overachievers.

On top of just getting in, there is also the added stress of having to come up with the funds to finance the cost of a college degree. Indeed, while financial aid does help ease the monetary pain of paying for college, some students do not qualify for financial aid, and, in many cases, the financial aid package does not completely cover the total bill.

So what are we to do? What other solutions might there be that can combat the rising price of a college education?

Well, first of all, if you think those shining star students robbed us of all the scholarships, think again! You need to stay positive. While they may have received the big-name, top-dollar prizes, an innumerable amount of smaller, often unheard-of scholarships are only an application away.

B-average student? There's a scholarships for that. Tall? There's a scholarship for that one, too. Good at duck calling? It's hard to believe, but there's a scholarship for that, too! You name it, there's probably some scholarship somewhere for it.

To give you a jump-start on these options, here's a quick list of resources you should have on your radar:

IF YOU'RE AN ATHLETE

The National Collegiate Athletic Association (NCAA) is a great resource to explore when on the hunt for a scholarship. Its website (www.ncaa.org) has in-depth details on the recruiting process, research on graduation rates, and access to athletic statistics. However, keep in mind that the NCAA does not itself offer scholarships, but its Division I, II, and III school members do.

For more information about athletic scholarships, check out the following websites:

- www.athleticscholarships.net

- www.finaid.org

- www.guidetoathleticscholarships.com

IF YOU'RE A MINORITY

Underrepresented minority groups, like African Americans, Hispanics, Asians, and Native Americans may be eligible for a wide range of scholarship opportunities. There are often strict guidelines and restrictions to these scholarships pertaining to your ethnic makeup, so remember to read scholarship criteria thoroughly!

One resource to have on your radar: The Gates Millennium Scholars Program (GMS). We're all familiar with the Gates family and their commitment to education through philanthropy. GMS provides significant financial help to thousands of outstanding minority students with undergraduate and graduate scholarships. For more information, check out www.gmsp.org.

If you identify yourself as a lesbian, gay, bisexual, or transgender student, you may also be eligible for a plenitude of scholarships. Consider the LEAGUE Foundation, which annually awards up to seven scholarships to individuals who have demonstrated involvement in their communities and who boast a strong GPA. For more information, check out www.leaguefoundation.org.

For more information on scholarships for African Americans, visit the following sites:

- www.thesalliemaefund.org

- www.4blackyouth.com

- www.oedb.org/scholarship/african-american

For more information on scholarships for Hispanics, visit the following sites:

- www.hsf.net

- www.oedb.org/scholarship/hispanic

For more information on scholarships for Native Americans, visit the following sites:

- www.catchingthedream.org

- www.nrcprograms.org

- www.oedb.org/scholarship/native-american

For more information about scholarships for Asian Americans, please visit the following sites:

- www.apiasf.org

- www.asianpacificfund.org

- www.awib.org

IF YOU'RE A LEGACY APPLICANT

Applicants considering attending their parents' alma maters often overlook the financial benefits of continuing a family tradition. Many universities offer financial incentives not just to children of alumni, but also to grandchildren, siblings, nieces, and nephews.

While I was not eligible for legacy scholarships, I have friends who benefitted from following their parents' and siblings' footsteps. The University of Virginia has a well-known legacy scholarship program that benefits first-year children of alumni. Awards are annually renewable and are given based on financial need and academic merit. The George Washington University also has a family grant program that offers half-priced tuition for an undergraduate sibling of a current undergraduate. Talk about an investment!

Universities are not the only institutions that award legacy scholarships. The Elks National Foundation Legacy Awards for the Children of Elks offers $1,000, four-year, renewable scholarships to children or grandchildren of living Elks based on good standing. Similar opportunities are also offered for children and grandchildren of Masons and Shriners.

IF YOU'RE CONSIDERING A CAREER IN SCIENCE, TECHNOLOGY, ENGINEERING, OR MATH

Women have risen through the ranks in the traditionally male-dominated industries of science, technology, engineering, and mathematics. If you aspire to be one of these inspirational women, there are many scholarships out there that can help cover the cost of an undergraduate or graduate degree.

1. **Science Scholarships:** The Association for Women in Science (AWIS) offers many grants and awards to undergraduates pursuing a science major. For more information, visit www.awis.org.

2. **Technology Scholarships:** The Vanguard Women in Information Technology Scholarship Program strives to assist junior and senior college females pursuing degrees in computer science, computer engineering, web design, and other IT-related disciplines. Annual scholarships of up to $10,000 are awarded based on academic merit. For more information, visit www.sms.scholarshipamerica.org/ vanguardwomenintechnology to find more information.

3. **Engineering Scholarships:** The Society of Women Engineers (SWE) awards scholarships to women pursuing engineering, engineering technology, and computer science at the undergraduate and graduate levels. In 2011 alone, SWE awarded 188 scholarships valued at $540,000. Wow! To find out about the extensive list of scholarships offered, visit societyofwomenengineers.swe.org.

4. **Mathematics Scholarships:** The Association for Women in Mathematics (AWM) awards the Alice T. Schafer Prize to an undergraduate women who excels in mathematics. The prize is named after founder and president, Alice Schafer, who promoted and supported women in mathematics. For

more information, check out https://sites.google.com/site/awmmath/programs/schafer-prize.

As you can see, you don't have to be the perfect, standout student to qualify for scholarships. There are thousands of scholarship opportunities at your fingertips. With a little research and a positive attitude, you, too, can uncover these gems.

Insights provided by Laura Iglehart, Georgetown University

avoiding the credit card black hole

Every time I dig up my mailbox combination and check my mail on campus, usually hoping for a new edition of *Glamour* or a postcard from my BFF abroad, I end up with dashed hopes and a ridiculous number of credit card offers. Even when I come home for Christmas break, my dad hands me a pile of envelopes from creditors who are just preying on young, presumably financially irresponsible students like me. But whose place is it to assume young adults can't manage credit? Some students are responsible for paying for their own tuition, board, and life's little incidentals and haven't depended on their parents for years. Other students appropriately manage their finances and know not to go crazy on $5-margarita night and buy a few rounds for the table. Many teenagers and young adults are perfectly capable of spending, swiping, and saving in measure. Right?

However, some irresponsible spenders have given young adults a bad rap, and new credit card regulations force adolescents and college students to give up some of their financial independence. Since February 22, 2010, individuals under the age of 21 have been unable to apply for a credit card unless they have a source of money that they can document, like a part-time job, or a cosigner on the account, most likely a parent. For most students, it really isn't that difficult to prove employment or find a parent or family member to authorize credit, but the fact that there are constraints on young adults' ability to secure credit is frustrating. Learning to manage finances on one's own at a young age is crucial to becoming an independent adult. In a time of economic uncertainty, it is vital that the next generation knows how to invest, save, spend, and support the American market economy.

NO CREDIT CARD? NO PROBLEM

Did your family decide that a credit card isn't a good idea for you this first year in school? Despite these new regulations, there are a few ways that students can learn to budget and start to build some financial savvy even without a credit card in their first years of college. Using strictly a debit card or cash can prove to be a safe way to manage money, although it will be more difficult to start building a credit history that will be crucial for mortgage interest rates in a few years' time. Students can also sign on as "authorized users" to their parents' credit accounts, so that parents can keep a watchful eye on spending. Or parents could simply act as cosigners, as required by the new law, and let their students have a margin of trial and error. In a time of "helicopter parents," where grown college students take their laundry home on weekends and call mom each morning and night, giving young adults free rein with credit may seem scary. However, financial education is crucial to (eventual) independence…just remember to keep calling mom daily after she gives you the go-ahead with the Visa.

TAKING THE PLUNGE

Have a job and want to take the plunge and get a credit card? If used wisely, credit cards can be a useful tool to have and help you manage your money. They also help you build good credit that can help years down the road when applying for a mortgage, but only if you pay your bills on time and in full. Rather than give up and resign yourself to a life of bad credit, use these strategies to prevent yourself from ending up like the countless thirty-something women still paying off the thousands of dollars of credit card debt they racked up during their teens and twenties.

U Chic Tip!

Credit card companies don't want you to pay your bill electronically because they will never get to charge you late fees or raise your interest rate when you miss a payment. One of their tricks is to initially give you a low interest rate, and then raise it through the roof as soon as you're late on a payment.

First up, make sure you do your research. And limit yourself to one card at a time, rather than opening several different ones; it will be easier to keep track of and pay one bill a month. When doing your research, pay attention to interest rates before signing a contract; credit card companies are not afraid to take advantage of students who don't read the fine print on their contract. Three of the features that credit card companies use most often to entrap students are low credit limits, low-income requirements (if any), and high interest rates. A Bankrate.com survey found that the average interest rate on a student credit card is 17.51 percent—ouch! Try aiming for a rate lower than 8 percent. For more info on common credit card terminology, visit the Adventures in Education website: www.aie.org.

No matter what, don't let yourself get tricked into signing up for a card advertising "low student rates"; make sure to read the fine print very carefully and make sure that low means low.

Really, using a credit card is no different from walking into a bank and taking out a loan for "entertainment expenses." It is way better to only use a debit card, which draws money automatically from your bank account, so you will never pile up any debt for items you didn't have the cash to buy.

A Spring Break Trip That Didn't Break the Bank
Nisha Chittal, University of Illinois

About a year ago, I was an inexperienced freshman, gearing up for a spring break trip to Morocco and Spain. I had never been to either of these countries before and was excited beyond belief to experience a new culture. The only problem? I had no money. I had borrowed hundreds of dollars already from my parents to pay for my flights and some hotel expenses, and they were refusing to loan me another cent. As the trip got closer, I started getting more desperate. I had a job, but $7.50 an hour wasn't going to be enough to cover my expenses. In complete desperation, I even tried to sell plasma but was told—much to my disappointment—that my veins were too small for them to take blood and I would not be able to sell my plasma! That's really bad.

At this point, it looked like I would be surviving on bread and water in Spain unless I came up with a better solution. So, I did what any utterly broke college student would do in my situation: I applied for a credit card, and a student card at that! It was one of the easiest application processes I had ever been through—a rushed process, in fact. However, the day it arrived, I had a strange sense of foreboding as I opened up the congratulatory letter from Citicards. For years, I had heard all the warnings about how I should be careful with credit cards. But I quickly forgot the nagging feelings of doubt as I prepared for my trip to exotic lands.

Well, the trip was incredible; I managed to make it out with only a hundred dollars in credit card debt, and my job helped me to pay it off quickly. However, most young women are not as fortunate when it comes to credit card debt.

GET A LOW LIMIT

Most reputable creditors will offer only very low credit limits to students who have little or no income and little or no established credit history. This is usually a good thing, since it acts as a built-in check to keep your spending under control. However, not all creditors are this kind; some are willing to give you credit limits of thousands of dollars. My first credit card, which I still have today, gave me a $4,000 credit limit from the day I signed up. Thankfully, I have never racked up more than a few hundred dollars at a time and have been able to pay off the balance each month, preventing a buildup of debt. But in retrospect, being handed that $4,000 credit limit as a naïve, inexperienced freshman was a potential recipe for disaster!

PAY IT OFF EVERY MONTH—ON TIME

One of the most important pieces of advice about credit cards goes without saying: pay off the balance in full every month before the due date or try to pay off more than the minimum payment if not the full balance. You have the option to pay late, but you'll also face penalties like finance fees ($30 a pop!) and the potential that the card company will raise your interest rate.

PAY YOUR BILL ELECTRONICALLY

The credit card companies make a lot of money off late fees, and off raising your interest rate when your payment is late. The best way to avoid this is to set up "automatic payment" from your bank account, so you will never be late with a payment.

WHAT TO WATCH OUT FOR

Credit card statements will offer to let you pay a minimum each month, which is just a small portion of the total bill—sometimes around $20–$50. If you're only paying the minimum, interest will accrue on whatever part of the balance rolls over to the next month and you may only be paying on the interest and not the original amount that was charged. The result? You actually end up paying the credit card company to hold your debt for you. Credit card companies are making enough; they don't need any additional help!

BUILD UP GOOD CREDIT

By paying off your bills in full each month on time, you will begin to establish a good credit history. This is extremely important in life—having a good credit history allows you to make large purchases like a house or a car, take out a loan, open certain types of bank accounts, and even apply for certain jobs. While it may seem boring and unnecessary to worry about now, women who neglected their credit scores while in college have regretted it for the rest of their lives when they weren't able to get a house, a car, or go on the vacation of their dreams! Sure, the "live in the moment" strategy seems great today, but you'll be sorry tomorrow.

PAY WITH CASH OR DEBIT CARD

Once that credit card is in your wallet, sometimes it's just difficult to resist the temptation to use it. So many things are available to you now! It's tempting when walking through the mall, or even down a shop-lined street off campus, to stop by and pick something up and come up with all kinds of reasons to justify it to yourself. (I just aced my exam! Or I just bombed my exam and need to treat myself!)

As you already know, college is a drain on your finances. You can work a part-time job for 30 hours a week and still feel like you don't have enough money to keep up with your rich friends or sorority sisters. But don't let credit cards get the best of you. Though it may seem hard right now to have an outdated wardrobe or have to skip your spring break with your friends (believe me, I know!), it's not worth getting drowned in debt that will haunt you for the rest of your life and make it difficult for you to buy a home or a car one day. If you're going to use credit cards, think smart and only buy what you can pay off at the end of the month. Don't let your credit cards control your life!

Insights provided by Kylie Thompson, Harvard University

living fabulously on a budget

If you haven't done so already, you'll soon be making the clichéd reference to yourself as a poor college student. I will be the first to admit that college can be tough at times—having to worry about grades, extracurriculars, working for low pay—all while trying to be trendy and up on the latest iPhone or other gadget that all our friends seem to have these days. Well, it's time for us to stop feeling sorry for ourselves for being financially challenged and start living fabulously despite our limited monetary possessions. Living the fabulous life on a budget is all about budgeting for your life, not your best friend's, not your parents', and definitely not those brats' on *My Super Sweet 16* (turn off your TV, now!).

THE B WORD: BUDGET

The first part in achieving this fabulous life is making a fabulous budget. Start your "fabulous financial budget" by recording all of your monthly expenses and due dates and then compare that to your projected monthly income. When writing down your expenses, also include things that are bought on a regular basis like gas, groceries, etc. Once you have your monthly budget set, limit your weekly expenses to whatever you have left over after taking into account your monthly financial goals.

If one of your goals is to save money, consider your monthly savings goals as part of your monthly expenses, and don't dip into your savings when spending your weekly allowance. One trick that can help (because we all have those days when an extra grande mocha with whip would solve everything) is what I call being "blind" to the savings—having money automatically moved into your savings account each pay period, whether each week or month. Sometimes it's easier to save if it's done automatically for you at regular intervals.

Now, if your monthly expenses are greater than what you make each month, you're a bit further behind in staying on a budget. However, no matter how far you may be behind in being financially responsible, it's never too late to get organized and headed in the right direction.

Last piece of advice: don't forget that budgeting has to be more than just a monthly occurrence. You must think about your budget on a daily and weekly basis.

WAYS TO CUT COSTS

If there is one thing that can't be emphasized enough it is to always pay your bills on time to avoid those unnecessary late fees and other charges. If you find that you are having trouble keeping up on your payments, contact your credit card company(s) or other creditors to work out a payment plan. These entities are willing to work with you, but you have to make the effort to stay in touch with them and let them know about your situation. When it comes to your credit cards, the obvious way to keep your fabulous financial budget is to not bite off more than you can chew and keep your debt down. If possible, make sure you pay your cards completely off and on time and only buy things that you know you can actually afford.

Also, if your annual percentage rate on your credit card is high and you're carrying a balance every month, it never hurts to call your credit card company and ask for a lower interest rate. To get them to deal, threaten to switch card companies if they will not give you a lower rate. Despite what you may have heard, credit card companies really do work with their customers and, more often than not, will come up with ways to help you pay your bills more easily.

Another place that you can easily cut costs is grocery shopping. Always make a list before you go, and follow the old saying "Never go to the grocery store hungry." When you're shopping on an empty stomach, everything looks appealing and you'll end up buying things that you don't need. The same thing happens when you shop without a list; having a list to follow when you grocery shop helps you focus on buying the things you need and helps prevent useless spending each month.

How I Managed School and a Part-Time Job

Rachael Smith, Radford University

If you're on a budget like most—if not all—college students are these days, there isn't a better way to supplement your income than from a job.

Luckily, my university offers work-study programs, and I got approved to participate. The Free Application for Federal Student Aid (FAFSA) offers qualifying students a work study scholarship of $7.25 an hour in exchange for 180 hours a semester of work. By getting approved for work-study, this meant I could apply for a job on campus. Since I had always wanted to work at the school's post office—it looked like such a fun place to work—I chose to apply there.

I have been working at the post office since my sophomore year, and for the two years I have been there, it has been the best part-time job I've had so far. The post office is a family, and we all joke that it is because the working atmosphere is so laid-back. I have made great friends with my student workers and supervisors. If a camera crew followed us around for a day, they just might have a new reality show. Instead of "The Office," we'd have "The Post Office" and it would be hilarious to watch.

Despite the fun, there are times when I resent it. Having a job means having to be responsible and show up on time. Of course, I love the positive impact it has on my bank account, but many times, it has prevented me from doing some of the fun things I want to do in college. There have been many times when my friends send me texts like, "Let's get lunch and go to the mall!" I hate telling them I have to work. It's the worst feeling being cooped up at work when you know your friends are having a great time.

And let's be honest. Having to "serve" the underclassmen at my school is occasionally no picnic (especially when they don't know how to address an envelope properly!). But you have to be polite to everyone at all times, even when your eyes are drooping and you want to take a nap after partying a little too late the night before.

There have also been some stressful days when I've had a major project or paper due and had to go to work instead. My boss will never forget the day when I had to go around campus, interviewing students with a digital recorder. I was already late for work when everything got deleted by accident! I was so paranoid about calling in to work to explain my absence that I had my mother call for me. It was such an embarrassment, but luckily one of my supervisors answered the phone with sympathy. I was a joke around work for a while, but I was thankful my boss understood that school comes first.

Working while in school can also be hard if you're feeling under the weather, if a friend wants to go do something fun but you have to work, or if you just want to sleep in. But I'm getting a taste of the real working world, and this experience is invaluable. After all, the reason you go to college is to find that dream job, and for most of us, that's a

9-to-5 gig. This job is teaching me how to learn to support myself without having to rely on Mom and Dad for everything.

I've never regretted picking up my job at the post office. I've met some great friends and am proud to say I can stand on my two feet while juggling classes, extracurricular activities, friends, and a job. If you have to work or are considering a part-time position for similar reasons as mine, embrace it. Find a job that interests you. It might end up being the best thing you do for yourself in college.

FABULOUS BUDGET-SAVERS

Now we can chat about the fun part of living fabulously on a budget—finding ways to cut corners and spend less money while still being utterly fabulous. You know how sugar gives you a little rush when the chemical dopamine gets released in your brain boosting your happiness level. The same thing can happen when you find great ways to save money! I call these happiness boosters "budget-savers." They can help you save a little or even a lot of money each day, week, and month.

One big budget-saver for me is investing in sandwich-sized storage bags and filling them each morning with snacks like almonds, Cheez-its, Chex Mix, or other little snacks to eat during the day to satiate my hunger. It prevents me from buying snacks from those overpriced student stores on campus. Also by having a little snack throughout the day, I can spend less money on lunch because I'm not as hungry.

Another great budget-saver for me has been to learn how to do a lot of things for myself rather than having to pay someone else to do them, like cutting or coloring my hair, basic manicures and pedicures, and waxing. The list goes on. You end up saving so much more money in the long run while learning a useful skill.

U Chic Tip! Great Budget-Savers

1. **Group your errands.** Make a to-do list of any errands within the same geographic locale. By running all your errands while you're out and about, you can save money on gas.

2. **Take the bus.** If you live on a bus line, try taking the bus to class once or twice a week rather than driving.

3. **Search the newspaper for savings.** No, coupon clipping isn't just for your grandmother. There is actually some good sale information in there that could be useful for a college chick on a budget.

4. **Invest in a wholesale store membership.** BJ's, Costco, Sam's Club—whatever it is—buy a membership. Buying in bulk can help you save a lot in the long run.

5. **Learn to cook.** Besides saving money, you'll be popular. Who doesn't like having a friend who can cook?

TREAT YOURSELF

What's a fabulous budget without the fabulous part? The most important part of maintaining a great budget, without going totally insane, is treating yourself with little things every now and then so the undeniable urge to splurge won't build. For instance, small treats like a movie or a magazine once a week or a new pair of shoes or purse at the end of the month should keep you satisfied to resist that dreadful urge.

BE THRIFTY!

Shopping at thrift stores or heading for the sales racks is a great way to save money while still being able to shop. Learn some basic sewing skills so that you can buy that ultra-cute dress with the missing button for half-off and fix the button later. Try making thrift store or sale rack shopping a special outing with your friends on a regular basis. Who's going to resist the opportunity to shop *and* save money?

There are so many ways to live fabulously while being on a budget. By mapping out your expenses and financial goals, finding budget-savers, and treating yourself every now and then, you'll not only be living fabulously on a budget in college, but you'll be living a fabulous life as well!

Insights provided by Lativia Jones Bolarinwa,
University of North Carolina–Chapel Hill

U Chic Essentials—Money Matters

Embrace your independence

You're in college, on your own now, and for most readers this is the first time in your life that you're in charge! Embrace this independence by establishing good money management skills, and you'll be setting yourself up for success not only in college but beyond.

Start a budget

The key to financial success is having a budget in place that is easy to follow. By knowing what your limits are ahead of time, you are more likely to not overspend. We know it's hard, but it will pay off in the end.

Cash only

When you're out having fun with your friends on a Friday night, you're less likely to want to stick to that budget that we discussed above. To prevent you from buying and drinking one too many, take a limited amount of cash with you. Your more rational self will thank you later! (You can even set this aside for your spring break trip.)

Looking for more great advice? Head to www.UChic.com for our fave resources and websites—they come highly recommended from our guide's contributors and editors. Be sure to leave your suggestions as well!

CHAPTER 11

The College Perks

ollege tuition is expensive these days. Sometimes you have to wonder where all of this money is going. Well, if you already are spending the cash on attending college, why not try to maximize all your opportunities while you're there—a surefire way to get a bang out of every buck going into your college's pockets. From finding internships to networking and reaching out to alumni to studying abroad, your school has a range of services, or as we like to call them, "college perks," set up to help you find your path in school and life. So what are you waiting for? Read on to learn about all the opportunities that await you in college.

secrets for landing that hot job or internship

If there is one piece of advice I have to pass along it has to be that internships are a must-do during college. They help you figure out your interests and can even land you a job right out of college— which is a key reason you're in school, anyway. I have many friends who worked at the State Department, Department of Homeland Security, and Congress right after college because they impressed their bosses during their internships and utilized the connections they made. Internships are simply the best way for you to gain professional experience while still an undergraduate. Bottom line: you really need to check out and take advantage of these opportunities.

BUT WHERE DO I BEGIN?

The process of finding an internship can potentially be daunting, but above anything else you must keep a positive attitude through the *entire* process, from rejection to rejection to finally an offer. Be excited by all the possibilities! Be open to exploring different areas. It is just as important to know what you don't want to do as it is to know what you do want to do.

Although you may not realize it, you already have access to a treasure chest of resources that can help you snag that hot internship opportunity. A good first step would be to drop by your university's career center. You can talk to a career counselor or review the school's database to see if your university has any established relationships with certain programs. Some may even keep satisfaction surveys from students who previously completed the same internship—another great way to figure out which internship is right for you. The counselors can also provide feedback on your résumé and cover letter.

In addition to the career center, don't be afraid to ask your professor, academic advisor, or teaching assistant if they have any recommendations. They may be able to directly connect you to an organization. If you haven't heard it already, connections really do matter!

U Chic Tip!

Sometimes an internship may sound great on paper, but the actual experience may be less-than-stellar thanks to a poorly managed internship program. How to avoid this? Track down people who have previously done the internship, and check for satisfaction surveys in your university's career center to help you better understand your options.

For those looking for advice for specific internships, here are some tips for you:

Want to work for a not-for-profit?

Looking for nonprofit work experience? You're in luck. There are many good websites such as Idealist.org that focus on posting internships and jobs, so check them out regularly and get on their mailing lists. In the nonprofit world, internships are like entry-level positions that often lead to a job afterward. But be prepared to work for free; it's a short-term sacrifice that can eventually land you a paid position.

For the corporate-minded

Want to work for an investment bank or a *Fortune* 500 company? As advised above, go to your college's career center and find out in advance about opportunities such as on-campus recruitment and local career fairs, company campus visits, and other unique programs they may have for the corporate-minded. Ask your relevant professors or mentors about potential opportunities. Take the initiative to thoroughly research the company by checking out their career or internship websites. Many companies have college recruitment programs and provide a lot of detail online to give you a sense of the corporate culture and opportunities for advancement. The company likely has established internship programs with set deadlines for which you will need to plan ahead to meet.

Interested in the government?

If you are interested in politics, you should definitely consider interning in Washington DC, whether on Capitol Hill, in a think tank, or at a nonprofit organization. Many colleges have established programs that will guide you through the process of finding an internship and may even help you find housing. For example, the Public Leadership Education Network (PLEN) is a national organization whose sole mission is preparing women for public leadership (www.plen.org). Participating in a program like PLEN can be an added credential that can help get you an internship.

Politics is all about networking and connections, so definitely take advantage of any personal connections you may have (family connections, professors' connections, alumni networks, etc.). For example, if you want to intern on the Hill, you should apply to multiple offices and not just those from your home state, even though you may have a better chance at getting one of these coveted spots from your home state. When applying to the Hill, prepare a succinct one-page résumé and make sure you comprehensively research the office before you interview. Ideally, it's preferable that you intern full-time rather than part-time, so you gain a better understanding of how things run day-to-day and your organization or institution gets to know you better (think future letters of recommendation).

> ## *U Chic Tip!*
>
> If you are aware that a particular congresswoman or congressional representative is interested in an issue that you are passionate about, consider applying to their office. In your cover letter, explain how you're passionate about the issue and include any specific experiences you've had that show this passion. For instance, did you organize a campus demonstration? Tell them and put this in your résumé, detailing the success you had in organizing a group of people.

For the budding young journalist or media maven

If you're considering a job in the media, there is no better time to start than now. And with the Internet, you can start as soon as you finish reading this chapter. Pick a topic that you love, and start a blog. Blog as often as you can (daily is most preferable to build a following), and you soon may be considered an expert on the particular topic you chose. As for other relevant experience, write for your college paper or even local newspaper during school. If you're interested in PR or marketing, join your campus organization for these careers, like the Public Relations Student Society of America (PRSSA; www.prssa.org) or the Society of Professional Journalists (www.spj.org), and aim to become a leader in the organization. These groups are a fantastic way to get to know the leaders in your industry through campus discussions, projects, and their close affiliation with their large parent organization. If these organizations do not have a chapter on campus, consider starting one! Nothing shows more initiative than getting a group off the ground and running on your own. When you are applying for internships in the field, be sure to call attention to your blog, campus paper clippings, and your involvement in campus organizations.

Dreaming of a job in medicine?

Medical school admissions offices like to see that you have clinical experience and are seriously interested in the profession. Volunteer in a hospital or clinic or become an Emergency Medical Technician (EMT). Participating in undergraduate research is another great way to prepare for medical school. See if your school has an established undergraduate research or independent study program. If such a program does not yet exist, feel free to approach professors whose work you are interested in. Think of a new project idea that you could collaborate on with them or think of a way you can assist them with a current project. Nothing shows more interest in medicine (well, a top grade in Organic Chemistry doesn't hurt) than conducting outside research and even getting it published in a medical or scientific journal.

No clue what you're interested in?

That's fine! College is about taking your time to figure yourself out and discover your likes and dislikes. Apply for an internship in an area that you are interested in. Who knows, you could love it or hate it, but you'll never know your preferences unless you explore different areas.

U Chic Tip! Using LinkedIn to Find a Job

Rachael Smith, Radford University

Have you tried LinkedIn yet? If not, you should. The goal of this social networking platform is to use the people you know to network and connect with the people you don't know for internship and job-hunting purposes. In fact, some employers have quit looking for applicants through traditional means and do their recruiting primarily through social media sites instead.

On creating your profile: make sure your profile is updated with the latest from your résumé, and that your portfolio and personal websites are up to date and professional. For advice on creating the perfect profile, check out sites like http://jobsearch.about.com/od/networking/a/linkedinprofile.htm.

Once you declare a major, join LinkedIn groups revolving around it. You may have to wait to be "accepted in" by an administrator, but some are open to anyone. You will also want to join your academic program's LinkedIn group, if they have created one, to keep up with any important announcements related to on-campus recruitment and networking opportunities you may want to participate in.

For the other LinkedIn bells and whistles, if you have work or internship experience, ask your former employer or mentor to submit a recommendation for you through LinkedIn. This way, potential employers can see your work ethic without even having to ask. You can also upload your résumé to your profile, which you should do if you're on the hunt for an internship and/or job. HR professionals are better able to get a good assessment of your potential for an open position if this is in place. You also cut out extra work that they would have otherwise to do.

In terms of building out your network, send invitations to only folks that you personally know. If you send too many LinkedIn requests to people you don't know (and especially to those who you haven't asked someone for an introduction to connect with), people may report you, forcing LinkedIn to block you from sending future requests…even to folks you know. Don't be that person.

After meeting a new professional at a networking event, it is completely appropriate to immediately add them to your network and send a note reminding them of your acquaintance with a note like, "It was great meeting and talking with you today at the seminar!" LinkedIn also has a "Jobs" board where you can find and apply to open job and internship positions nationwide.

LinkedIn is a great resource, so take some time to familiarize yourself with what it has to offer. And remember: it's not Facebook. So don't post about the crazy things you did with your friends last night!

BE PROACTIVE!

The Internet is your best friend. So love it and use it! If you are interested in a certain organization, check out their website, particularly the "About Us" section. This is where they usually state if they have current internship vacancies or regular internship application periods. Don't be afraid to call the organization and ask if there is a particular person you can address your application to. However, if the posting says "no calls," be respectful of that and don't call. Subscribe to as many listservs of organizations as you can, and you'll soon be amazed by all the opportunities you can randomly find out about from being on a listserv.

It's All about the Small Stuff

Harmony Haveman, Pacific Lutheran University

Internships will be your ticket to a job at the end of senior year when all of your friends are frantically searching for any job they can find. I had the most incredible opportunity to do three internships abroad thanks to networking and using the connections I had made along the way. I was able to intern at CNN International in London and MGM Television in London, and I also did an internship with the United Nations in Geneva, Switzerland. These experiences changed my life and paved the way for my career.

So how did I swing these fantastic opportunities? *It's all about the small stuff.* I went to every event that had anything to do with journalism. I was fortunate to get the internship at CNN International in London thanks to attending one of the many seminars about journalism at my university. It took being one of just a handful of college students to show up at an event to get my name out there. It was there that I met someone who worked for CNN. Because I was only one of a few students there, I had a great opportunity to talk about my future with this professional. After meeting with me and learning about my passion for journalism and my future, she said she'd help me get an internship at CNN in London. Those little connections make all the difference in the real world. I am a firm believer that it's a lot about who you know and even more about how to treat people.

USING SOCIAL MEDIA TO FIND A JOB

When you're on the hunt for that hot job or internship, social media can be extremely useful. Here's what you need to know:

LinkedIn.com, a social networking site for professionals, is a great way to find a job or internship. From personal recommendations to your connections, this platform shows—rather than tells—potential employers your worth. In fact, many employers now use the website to recruit potential employees. And career experts agree: it's never too early to start building your network on LinkedIn. To get started, first, create a profile, including employment (current and past), education, industry, and websites, and include a photo that looks professional enough, meaning no pics from the latest pub crawl. Next, include all your résumé keywords and skills in your profile, so your profile will be found. Now it's time to build your network, by connecting with contacts and friends and asking people you've worked with to write you recommendations. The more connections and recommendations you have, the more opportunities you have. When it comes time to searching for an internship or job, you can use the job search section to find listings of interest.

Twitter is a great resource for finding opportunities. First of all, it's home to several different internship-focused individuals, or "tweeters," who regularly put out job search advice that you can follow. How to find these like-minded individuals? Run a simple search for your profession, using a Twitter tool like TweetDeck, and then "follow" those with information on jobs and internships in your area. A personal favorite of mine is the "Intern Queen," which is very helpful for many different types of nationwide internships. The other reason we love it? When you're on the hunt for a job, tweets like, "Looking for a job, know of any leads in X industry," are a great way to connect with people in your field. But beware of using Tweets along the lines of "I hate my life, I can't find a job." Those tweets come off as whiny and don't show anything intellectual or positive about you or your potential for that dream job.

Facebook: Most career experts generally recommend that you not use Facebook for internship or career-building activities. It's obviously great for socializing, but it can present difficulties for you down the road when you're on the job hunt. Translation: future employers might not be too excited to find those photos of you and your friends from that raucous spring break trip. In fact, when it comes to posting anything on Facebook, here's our general rule of thumb: regardless of Facebook's privacy settings, don't post anything you wouldn't want your mom or that future employer to see. If an employer wants to find incriminating items on you, they will; so don't make it easy for them to do so.

Here's the bottom line on any of these social media tools: human resource departments and recruiting experts are less concerned with how many friends you have online and more about the qualifications and skills you bring to the table. A solid résumé along with stellar interviewing skills are the two most important aspects you should be focused on when conducting your job search. Sure, it's good to know which companies are more tech-friendly and open to social media job inquiries, but in the end, selling yourself on paper and in person is going to have the most impact on your future career goals.

TIMING AND FOLLOW-UP

Ideally, the goal is to plan ahead and apply to internships before the deadline. However, if you're like most of us, you get busy and may end up missing a deadline for an internship that you would have loved to have had. Don't be afraid to just go ahead and apply even if the deadline is close or has passed. Write in your cover letter that you are aware the deadline has passed, but you are still interested and available (this works especially well if you live near the organization). For example, toward the end of the spring semester, I finally decided I wanted to intern somewhere in San Francisco during the summer. I sent my résumé to many nonprofit organizations, even if they were not advertising an open position. I finally received a response from Greenpeace and interned there for the summer.

THE WAITING GAME

Don't be shy when going after something you want. Follow-up is a door-opening technique that can land you that great internship or job. If a decent amount of time has passed (use your judgment), it's definitely OK (actually, more like mandatory) to make a follow-up email or phone call. Keep it simple, "On April 10, I sent you my application for the summer internship. I am still interested in the position and would like to please check the status of my application." This worked for me when I landed a graduate internship at the United Nations. I applied for a summer internship and received an email from the UN saying that my application was still under consideration but they recommended that I apply again for a fall internship. So I applied again for the fall session but soon received a similar email. This time, I responded directly to this email, asking about the status of my application. I was told that the department I originally applied to no longer accepted applications, but if I was able to move to New York in the next few weeks, they would forward my information to other departments. Since I had good girlfriends from college whom I could indefinitely crash with, I was able to move from Los Angeles to New York immediately. So I asked them to please forward my information, and I quickly received a phone interview and an internship offer. I sent the follow-up email, and within a month, my dream came true of finally interning at the UN. The point of this story? Be persistent and your dreams will come true!

DON'T PUT ALL YOUR EGGS IN ONE BASKET

Don't be too emotionally attached to a single application; have faith that in the end it will all work out for the best. I applied to Teach for America twice, the first time during my senior year and then a year later when I was in graduate school. I was rejected both times. The first time I made it to the final stage of an interview; I thought it went really well, but I was not accepted into the program. I applied again a year later and was not even given a phone interview. Both times I got rejected I felt really bad about myself. My partner was accepted to Teach for America during our senior year. I hate to admit it, but initially I was really jealous. How silly was I! You should never compare yourself to anyone else! Everyone has a different life path. Reflecting back, I realized all the amazing things I have been able to do during the two years I would have potentially been in Teach for America. I volunteered in Kenya, lived in Egypt, got a master's degree, interned at the United

Nations, and did a fellowship in the United States Congress. In the end, it all really worked out, and as much as I wanted to do Teach for America during the times I applied, I truly believe things worked out for a reason.

DON'T LET HELICOPTER PARENTS HURT YOUR JOB PROSPECTS

Having parents who are invested in your future is great. But having parents that do all the legwork for you in regard to finding a college internship or your first real job? Ehh, not so much. The term "helicopter parenting" has become the go-to pop cultural phrase for the current generation of teens and college students who have moms and dads that are overly invested in making sure their child gets ahead in school and beyond. They "hover" around their child, emailing teachers at a moment's notice, researching every bell and whistle to get their kids into the right school, and yes, even going as far as to call prospective employers as to why Johnny or Sally would be the absolute best candidate for the job.

When to involve your parents in your internship or job search

Do ask your parents to supply you with their network of contacts if they have connections to your field or interest. It's fine to say you're "so-and-so's" daughter when sending an email expressing interest in an internship, but NOT OK to do so when it's a job. Talk to your parents' friends, see who they know, and feel free to ask for an introduction if they can put you in contact with a higher-up at the company of your choice. Just don't expect them to do all the legwork for you. It's up to you to send out your own résumé, follow up after an interview, and send out thank-you cards after the fact.

When NOT to involve your parents in your internship or job search

Under NO circumstances should your parents have any involvement in you finding your first job, beyond providing you with a contact, driving you to an interview, or footing the bill for a new outfit. Not only does it undermine your ability to project a confident and mature persona, it also suggests you're not really ready to be a professional candidate. Why should a company trust you with a million-dollar budget or a huge campaign for a client if you constantly have to run to mommy or daddy every time you need help with something? If you want to be taken seriously, sideline the helicopter parenting ASAP. Bottom line: it's OK to accept their help in some areas of your job search, but make sure it's limited to discovering new opportunities and providing contact information. Anything beyond that, and you run the risk of damaging your professional reputation before you even get your foot in the door.

APPLY, APPLY, APPLY!

Put yourself out there to the universe! People fear rejection, and this can prevent them from applying for multiple opportunities.

One friend applied for two internships and got one offer. Another friend applied for ten and got only three offers. That's a lower success rate, but she has three times as many opportunities as my other friend—three versus one.

A WORD ON UNPAID INTERNSHIPS

Certainly, college internships have long been viewed as the golden ticket to employment after college, or at least that's the thought at many universities where unpaid, for-credit internships are the norm. However, depending on what kind of work you do at your unpaid internship, it could actually be an illegal arrangement, says a U.S. Department of Labor ruling issued last spring. Why issue such a ruling? The Labor Department is afraid that these illegal situations—such as having an intern go on coffee runs, sit in the fashion closet for hours, or similar internship horror stories you have most likely heard from friends—are on the rise because of the bad economy and the need for cheap, or rather free, labor. You know the tasks; you've probably done them.

So how do you know if your potential unpaid internship is illegal? Basically the internship must contribute to your overall career goals in order for it to be legal. For instance, it should be run like a vocational or trade school, training you for future employment. If you're still unsure about a potential internship, be sure to consult with your career services center on campus, which can help you navigate this tricky issue.

U Chic Tip! Navigating Expensive Summer Internships

Kelly Leslie, San Francisco State University

If you're planning to do an unpaid or paid internship over summer, many companies require you to earn credit hours while you work for them, which means you'll have to pay tuition. For many students, this means taking out an additional loan to cover this extra expense.

Unfortunately, summer loans can get pricey because tuition at this time of the year actually costs more than the fall and spring semesters. And this doesn't even include the living and travel costs of completing the internship. Yikes!

To avoid taking out a loan for a full semester, try applying for a partial loan. Partial loans are available through private loan companies and can be given to students who wish to seek less than the full cost of their tuition, according to SummerInternships.com. This is a great option if you are able to hold on to some of your extra loan money from the previous semester.

Also, try to only take the minimal amount of credit hours for your internship. If you're able to get by with only taking one credit hour, that's a lot less expensive than having to pay for three!

Last piece of advice on finding that hot job or internship? Keep your hopes up! Honestly, ever since my senior year of college, every week (if not every day!) I apply to different opportunities. I have a solid résumé and cover letter (which I adapt to each posting) that I am able to send out as soon as I learn of opportunities. The more you put yourself out there, the more chances you have of things working out. Not applying is the only sure way of not landing that great job or internship.

Insights provided by Pamela O'Leary,
University of California–Berkeley

using summers wisely

It's that time of year when all of your exams have finished and this massive ray of sunshine is finding its way through your bedroom window. You reluctantly open your eyes, curl up in the corner of your bed, grab the blanket, and wonder what Mom's made for breakfast as you slowly roll your way out of bed and wander over to the bathroom to brush your teeth. You brush away diligently as you look at the clock hanging on the opposite wall.

What?

Noon.

No way.

You squint again, thinking that maybe your eyes haven't fully opened yet.

Noon.

Seriously? Then you look at yourself in the mirror and think. What am I doing with my life?

WHAT TO DO WITH THE SUMMER

Summertime for a college student can mean one of two things: (1) Sleeping and being a couch bum: this is probably not your best option. As tempting and easy as it is to stay put, let's be honest. You will get bored. You will regret it. And you have so much more that you can do with your time. (2) Getting up off that comfy couch and heading to work: although you are supposed to be getting an education in the classroom, one of the most valuable educations you can get is through a summer job. In fact, here's some shocking news: your summer job might be the only educational experience you'll need before graduation, as it will be teaching you more about something you will actually be *doing* when you graduate. Where else can you get this hands-on, practical experience?

If you're like most kids at the end of their teenage years and heading into their twenties, you have absolutely no clue what you want to do with your life. So, how does a summer job cure that? And what's the point of having a job if you don't know what job you want?

THE SIMPLE MATTER OF MONEY

Loans don't pay for themselves and neither do those movie tickets or those fancy-schmancy cocktails. There is only so long you can hold on to that cash that your grandparents gave you for Hanukkah or Christmas. Sooner or later, you won't be able to puppy-face your way into some extra money for your bank account and even if you could, do you really want to? One of the rewarding things of having your own money is that it makes you independent. You are your own person and you are one step closer to being a responsible adult. OK, maybe the word "responsible" doesn't make it sound *that* appealing, but trust me, it is. If you are actually going to dive into that world of responsibility, then why not use your summer wisely and get a job that not only makes you money, but also opens up opportunities for your future in a field you actually want to work in.

HAVING SUMMER JOBS IS KIND OF LIKE DATING

Thanks to this wonderful invention called an internship (or part-time job), you get to essentially date different jobs. You let the man (aka, internship) take you out for a drink or dinner and it's on him; and maybe you realize that perhaps he wasn't what you wanted. No worries; you're only there for a few more weeks. Or maybe you go out on that first date and realize that you don't know enough about him, so you plan for round two—another summer at the same place. Best-case scenario: you realize you really do like him and then not only have you gotten a nice drink or dinner, but you enjoyed it, too, and you are glad you went out and learned something about this guy. This might be the start of a lifelong relationship.

Bottom line: we, as students today, are very lucky. We don't have to just get thrown into any job and stick with it forever like our parents or grandparents did. Thanks to internships and summer jobs, we get a taste of what life is like in the real world, getting a teensy-weensy bit closer to that elusive dream of actually getting paid to do something we love to do. Everybody wants it. Hardly anybody gets it. Fact of life.

YOU'VE DECIDED TO DO SOMETHING PRODUCTIVE THIS SUMMER, WHAT NEXT?

So once you've peeled yourself off that couch and made the decision to use that summer wisely…what's next? Where to go?

Finding a summer job starts way before the summer sun shows itself in the sky. Most summer jobs and internships start recruiting for positions as early as the autumn leaves turn slightly orangey-yellow. So start looking early. It will pay off with a better opportunity in the end guaranteed.

Career fairs

Most colleges have career centers where you can find everything ranging from résumé help to career fairs and even summer internship recruiting. So step number one: find your college career center in person or online at their website and make an appointment. Go in and tell them that you've never made a résumé before and you're completely lost or—to be ahead of the game—go in with that résumé you've been hammering away at and ask them what they think.

Talk up alumni

Other useful college resources are the very people who used to be you—the alumni. Once upon a time, all those bosses and scary recruiters used to be college students just like you. They know finding a job is hard and, maybe even more importantly, they know you are smart. You go to the same school they went to! They know you will work hard and if you prove your commitment, they might even help you find a job.

The importance of persistence

Now, if you know what job you want, be annoying. Honestly! Just don't call every day, especially when on the job description they ask you not to. Find the place that you want to work at and email them or give them a call. Ask them if they are looking for interns or someone to help out or just ask for some advice about what kind of person they would want or what kind of internships you should take on before you apply for a job there. They might not reply, but if they do, you will have some valuable advice for your future or maybe even a job.

In addition, you can find that famous author or lab specialist you've been dreaming to ask for advice. Contact them. They are only human, and so are you. The worst thing that will happen is they won't answer. But if they do, it is really quite exciting.

Here's a basic summary on talking to alums or strangers who have your dream job: In the best-case scenario, you have contacted someone in the business that you want to be in and they tell you what kind of qualifications they think you would need and advise you on a good starting point. In the best-case, magical, and most amazingly amazing scenario, you get a job out of it.

Where else can you get a job?

Ask around. As much as we don't want to admit it, it's always about who you know. Ask your parents, ask your parents' friends, ask your friends' parents. Ask your professor. *Ask away.* Someone, somewhere must have an opening for the summer, and would certainly love to have an eager college student who knows how to use a computer better than some of the people in the office do. They may even like the fact you "get" the whole social-networking thing. Most companies today are interested in how they, too, can use Facebook to do better business. Make it known that you're an expert!

WHAT TO DO ONCE YOU GET THE JOB

Make sure to get to know the people at your office. Everyone around you can either be someone to learn from or a possible future contact for a job or recommendation. If you make the right impression and show that you are willing to learn, they will want to help you with your career and future.

Go to any of the lunches or dinners they have. Not only will you get a free meal out of it, but you will also gain a better relationship with a boss who you might want to write you a recommendation or offer you another internship or even a full-time job.

As we've already seen and admitted, it really is about who you know. The girl whose desk is next to yours might end up knowing a girl whose brother's girlfriend's mom works at your dream job and if you become good friends, she just might be the person you turn to for next summer's job.

Learn as much as you can. Always ask for more work or more responsibility. Use the fact that you are smart and skilled with computers and do twice as much work as they expect you to do. That way, when you leave at the end of the summer, they will realize just how indispensable you are and that they want you back as soon as you finish college. Even if you don't particularly want to have that job again, chances are that your résumé can use the boost of those new skills you picked up over the summer. Impress your bosses and coworkers. Show them that you are worth a stellar review or even a full-time job.

Last piece of advice? Meet up with your good friends—new and old. Let them ground you. Let them be there for you. Have a good time. Live.

Insights provided by Olga Belogolova, Boston University

what to do if you don't land a summer internship

Spending your summers between semesters at an internship may seem like a smart and logical choice, but for many students, landing that résumé-boosting position is not always possible.

Between scheduling, family vacations, cost-prohibitive locations, and those harsh rejections emails, there are a hundred reasons why a summer internship might not work out for you. No matter what the reason, "stuck" is definitely not the word you should use to describe your situation.

So how do you put those three months out of school to good use? We've got some tips for you.

GET A JOB IN YOUR FIELD OF INTEREST

Finding a job in your field of interest is the next best thing to getting an internship. Want to become a teacher but can't shadow due to summer schedules? Be a camp counselor. Want to go to medical school but can't find an internship at a hospital? Get a job with the types of people you eventually want to help, like at a daycare (pediatrics) or at a nursing home (geriatrics). Want to go to law school? Practice your organizational skills by getting a job at a front desk at a firm or as a secretary. There are so many opportunities out there that will allow you to gain experience in your field. You just have to be creative and persistent enough to look for them.

GET A "HARD-WORKING" JOB THAT PAYS

As unglamorous as a waitress or a cashier job may sound, there is no better time in your life to have get your hands dirty with an "on your feet" kind of job. Not only will it boost your bank account's bottom line, it will give you the ability to say to future employers that you know the value of hard work.

There are also a ton of people who say that some of their best memories are from their summer jobs. Between meeting new people every day and making friends, you will find yourself flexing those all-important responsibility skills while learning what it means to provide excellent customer service—something that any future employer will appreciate.

VOLUNTEER

Just the sound of this word may send shivers down your spine for a possible lack of a focused assignment. However, if you volunteer at a place of interest to you, you will not regret it. Volunteering, if done at the right place (i.e., one that is related to the field that you eventually want to work in), can be an incredibly rewarding and fun experience. In addition to the good you'll feel by giving back, you are gaining experience in a field that interests you—which is great for that résumé you are so worried about—while gaining experience in the real world.

TRAVEL

There is no better time to travel than when you are young and jobless. Start saving your money now and use your free time to go on some great adventures.

Nearby day trips with friends

You could:

- Have picnics in a park or go to the beach (if it's close enough).

- Visit the mall across the state.

- Have a fancy brunch at that restaurant you have been *dying* to go to.

- Walk around small towns and see what you can find.

Visit family members

Whether they live down the street or across the country, spending time with family members is a great way to spend your free time during the summer. It's something you won't likely have much time to do once you graduate. So why not do it now?

Go overseas

There are so many tour groups and packages created for a college student's limited budget. Round up a friend or two and spend time embracing the culture of another country. STA Travel (www.statravel.com) and Contiki (www.contiki.com) are two companies that offer many trip options for students to destinations all around the world and even in the States. If tour groups aren't your thing, consider taking a language class abroad or spending a week learning how to cook in Italy or France.

Another option would be to go on a service trip to places like Ghana or Beijing. There are tour companies that specialize in overseas service learning, but be careful when deciding as some options are way more expensive than others. No matter what, Internet research is your friend when it comes to trips overseas. Use it and find the one that is right for you!

Take a road trip

Road trips are as American as apple pie, and no college experience is complete without one. Get your map, pack a cooler, and hit the road with no plans but to have the time of your life!

GET CREATIVE

For those of you who want to put creative skills to work this summer, consider taking art or foreign language classes. For those aspiring writers, consider launching your own blog, as the benefits of consistent writing are numerous. Not only will your friends and family be able to keep up with your journeys and give you suggestions on what you can do next (maybe they will even join you!), you *just might* get discovered!

KNOCK OUT SOME CREDIT HOURS

You can never go wrong with taking classes at your own school or at a nearby university. Whether you choose a course that will get you ahead in your program or you take a class just because you have always wanted to but never had the time, you are guaranteed to gain from taking summer classes. Summer courses are known to move at a quicker pace and have longer sessions, but generally, they are smaller and students do quite well in them. This is a perfect way to boost your GPA, lessen your course load in the following semesters, and have the chance to enhance your learning by studying something that might not be offered during the school year. Check with an advisor first to make sure your credits will transfer over, though!

GET ADVICE

Still trying to figure out how to spend the next three months? Ask *everyone* you know for guidance. You never know which one of your friends, relatives, or mentors has a connection at a really cool PR firm or has a relative living abroad who needs help with a volunteer project. I asked my father if he needed help in his office at his fashion company. What started out as an unpaid, three-day-a-week position turned into a part-time job the next year. Don't be afraid to ask and look around. There are great prospects everywhere if you let it be known that you are open and willing to try anything.

FINAL THOUGHTS

Not having a summer internship is not the end of the world. If approached the right way, you can have just as enriching of a summer as you would have had with that "coveted" internship. Just plan ahead, think about all of your options, and relax. You'll end up having a great and productive summer in the end!

Insights provided by Amanda Ferrara, New York University

the ins and outs of networking

You probably have heard it many times before: networking can be the key to landing your dream internship or job. As a college student, worries about your future job can seem eons away. They're not. In today's work world, networking is the name of the game—even in college. It's incredibly important to your success and advancement in the workforce.

Did You Know?

Between 50–75 percent of people found their last job through networking, and so can you! People will be especially impressed and receptive when college students take initiative and reach out to them.

As a college student, you have tremendous access to resources and many different kinds of networking opportunities such as professors, campus lectures, career fairs, internships, student organizations, etc. Before you know it, graduation will be here, so you need to take advantage of these opportunities now! Simply put, networking is about connecting with people, knowing how to talk to them, and later utilizing those connections.

U Chic Tip!

Before you begin heading out to networking events, try making a list of your priorities. This will help focus your efforts when you begin making those all-important connections. Ask yourself:

1. What organizations or events are related to your interests, but you have not yet pursued?

2. What dreams do you have that you've always wanted to make a reality?

396 *U Chic*

3. What are your strongest skills that you can share with others?

4. What skills would you like to improve, and who could help you develop them?

5. How can you take more initiative in networking (maybe going to an event by yourself, checking out a new group, asking a friend to introduce you to someone, etc.)?

WHERE TO START

Networking can take place in person and (even more so these days) online. So, if you are on Facebook or MySpace, then you are already networking! Also, another important thing to note is that networking can be done with anyone around you at any time, not just in professional settings. You can network with your roommates, people who live in your residence hall, classmates, coworkers, friends of friends, professors, supervisors, members of clubs you are in, etc. I feel that I gained significant networking skills through recruitment for my sorority. So joining student organizations is a great way to hone your networking skills. If you are at a lecture on a topic you are very interested in, approach the speakers afterward and introduce yourself. Try to even get their email address for future questions. They could end up being a mentor. Also, it's important to build relationships with your professors and teaching assistants, as they, too, can help connect you with potential employers. So don't be shy. Visit them during their office hours so they can get to know you. These relationships are crucial to getting a good letter of recommendation when you apply to all those exciting internships.

PRACTICE MAKES PERFECT

Like anything in life, networking may be awkward at first, but know that your skills will grow with practice. If you are attending a networking event, first and foremost, have confidence and enjoy yourself. Don't think of it as "I am networking." This will make you nervous. Approach the event as if it's a new opportunity to meet new people. Most of all, don't doubt yourself; you are awesome, so act like it—*smile*! Have welcoming body language—make eye contact, don't fold your arms, and give a pleasant greeting with a firm handshake. Bottom line: be your confident self.

When networking, you need to take initiative. Sitting in a corner alone or clinging to your friends won't expand your horizons. Go ahead, approach others, and introduce yourself. A great icebreaker can be something as simple as "Oh I like your bag…where did you get it?"

Have a purpose to your networking—a concrete goal. For example, let's say you are interested in summer internship opportunities; this narrows the conversation and makes it less awkward. Ask open-ended questions rather than questions that evoke a simple yes/no response. Also, recognize that networking is just as much about how you can help them as they can help you.

Without even knowing it, you have something of value to them. Keep talking; you'll never know what you'll discover. It's like the idea of "to have a friend, be a friend."

U Chic Tip!

Networking is a two-way street. It's about giving and taking. Once you put yourself out there and help someone out, it will come back to you twofold in ways you could not imagine. Case in point, I was able to contribute chapters to this book because of networking.

And really try to build rapport. People love to talk about themselves. Let the other person talk, and listen intently to what they have to say (show this with positive body language). When the conversation ends, repeat their name when you leave: "It was great meeting you, Maria." People like to hear their name and will be impressed you remembered it.

UTILIZING YOUR CONNECTIONS

Make up some business cards so the people you meet can contact you later. This is probably the most important thing you should do in advance of any major networking events, and they don't have to be anything fancy. Your name, contact info, major area of study, expected graduation date, and school should appear on the card. Do you have an online résumé? Put the link on your eleven: the college perks   399

card too! You'll also want to be collecting theirs, or at least writing down their name and some form of contact information to get in touch with them later. Except for shipping and handling, you can get business cards made for free at www.VistaPrint.com or www.MOO.com. After you make a connection, write down some details about the person on the back of their card or wherever you record their contact info so you can remember details about them later.

The most important piece of advice? The great connections you just made do not go anywhere unless you follow up, and the sooner the better. Soon after you met them, within a day ideally, send them a quick email. Remind them who you are and where you met. Thank them for taking the time to talk with you. End with an action item of how to build your connection with them, such as getting coffee together. However, if you don't necessarily want to meet them soon to discuss a certain issue, then don't feel that you are obligated to do so. For example, if the person you met was a peer, you can add them as a new Facebook or MySpace friend, and later build the connection through those online social networking tools.

Sample follow-up email:

Hi Maria,

It was great meeting you at the UC–Berkeley environ-mental career fair. Thanks for talking with me about summer opportunities with the National Park Service.

I am very interested in learning more about your career as a research scientist. Please let me know if you are available for coffee sometime next week.

> Thank you,
> Sunitha

INFORMATIONAL INTERVIEWS

Believe it or not, you requested an informational interview with Maria and you got one! Richard Nelson Bolles, author of the career guide *What Color Is Your Parachute?*, describes the informational interview process as "trying on jobs to see if they fit you."

Did You Know?

Studies estimate that 1 out of every 200–1,500 résumés results in a job offer. However, 1 out of every 12 informational interviews results in a job offer. Truly, informational interviews are a great tool in landing your dream job!

Informational interviews are a first step to introduce yourself to an organization you'd like to work for in the near future, so be prepared to make a strong first impression. Everyone loves to meet with students, so don't be afraid to try to contact people you have never met before. For instance, you can call an organization and ask for someone by job title or search through professional organizations. Assure them that the purpose of your inquiry is to learn more about the employer and occupation rather than to haggle them for an actual job. Informational interviews are separate from you applying for a job, so don't make this the time you ask them for a job. Make sure to do significant research on the background of the organization and the person you are going to meet.

Since you requested this interview, you will be the one asking the questions. Make a list of questions you plan on asking. Dress appropriately, bring copies of your résumé, and be prepared to take notes. Listen intently to the person to fully take advantage of the knowledge they are sharing. At the end, kindly ask if they can give you referrals of other people in the industry that would be willing to meet with you. Make sure you send the person you met a thank-you note shortly after the interview.

The more people you meet, the more chances you have of making successful connections. Since you're investing in yourself and reading this book, you are already on your way to being a networking queen. Go out there, show the world how amazing you are, and meet tons of amazing new friends and colleagues! That's what college is all about.

Insights provided by Pamela O'Leary,
University of California–Berkeley

when to go abroad

One of the greatest perks you have these days as a college student is the opportunity to study abroad. And why wouldn't you? It almost seems like a requirement that you study abroad at some point during your time in college. What a great requirement! Who wouldn't want to study in some exotic place like Italy, Japan, or even somewhere in Africa? The decision to study abroad is the easy one to make. It's deciding *when* to study abroad that may keep you up at night.

The key to making this decision is to go when you are *ready*. What do I mean when I say ready? Ready means that you are academically, socially, and financially prepared for this adventure of a lifetime. So here's how you can get prepared.

GETTING ACADEMICALLY READY

Before you study abroad, I highly recommend that you first decide on your major. Some study-abroad applications will even ask you how you will use time abroad to gain credits toward your major. On top of that, several programs are actually targeted to specific majors, making it an added bonus to know your major before heading abroad. Think about it: there's nothing more relevant and fulfilling than going on an archaeological dig in Greece if you're an archeology or anthropology major.

After deciding on a major, try to complete at least one semester of major coursework. This may be difficult for those of you who have been itching to take your first-ever tango class in a bar in Buenos Aires. I completely understand this urge. But a semester of class is really the only way to make sure that you still want to pursue the major. After all, if you decide to change majors, you may need to stick around the good old USA for an extra semester—the one you would have spent abroad—in order to graduate on time.

Which year makes the most sense?

Deciding when to go abroad is a very personal decision, so I can't say what is right for you. From my experience, sophomore or junior year are more popular years to head to foreign lands, probably because most college students are more settled and ready for the experience of living abroad. Indeed, when I was in Florence, Italy, a large percentage of the students I met abroad were also juniors. As a freshman in college, you are still discovering your passions— who you really are. Going abroad during your first year may prevent you from making this all-important discovery. True, I did meet one freshman abroad, and from all appearances (dancing on tabletops at the local hot spots!) she was enjoying herself. But I think the important thing to understand is that college is your first opportunity to get a taste of independence. It is usually best to get comfortable in one new situation before deciding to put yourself in another one that involves a different culture and probably a different language.

Alternatives to Studying Abroad

Ashley Yenick, Merrimack College

Going on vacations when I was little was thrilling. I got to go to places I never thought existed outside my own little world. When I was younger, I watched Mary-Kate and Ashley movies all the time and wanted adventures like they had. Seeing other movies like *Sisterhood of the Traveling Pants* made me think about studying abroad in foreign countries when I was older.

But, to my own surprise, after going over my options for studying abroad and talking to other students about it, I realized that it wasn't for me. I realized I wanted a vacation instead of an education. I wanted to visit these places and not have to worry about doing schoolwork. After talking to the student involvement center at my school, I realized there were more alternatives than I had imagined.

Like most schools, my school offers "Maymester" trips. Almost every year, students can take a religious pilgrimage to Italy or go to London for a week-long course in a Shakespeare class. I've talked to students and professors that have been on these trips and they all say that it is life-changing and so unbelievably cool. Unfortunately, I was unable to go the dates that they had provided for the trips, but these opportunities are less expensive than studying abroad and still give you the experience of being in a foreign country.

There are also Alternative Spring Break trips (which you'll read more about later in the book) that you can go on if you want to have an adventure inside the United States. Every year, my school asks students to help build homes for people who are less fortunate, and it's a great bonding experience with your fellow students. My RA from last semester went on the trip and said that she had one of the greatest times of her life there. Staying within the United States can also turn out to be just as fun as going abroad.

These alternatives and others can prove to be just as fun and just as rewarding as studying abroad. I'm so glad that I went to my student involvement center because, if I hadn't, I wouldn't have known about any of the other options that they offered.

Don't wait until your senior year

I also feel strongly that you should not hold off on studying abroad until your senior year. Although you're nowhere close to being a senior yet, think about it: the last thing a senior college student needs is to come back from study abroad and have trouble transferring credits and then not be able to graduate on time. When I returned from study abroad, I was surprised when the office told me that it could take up to six months for the grades to come and credits to be transferred. Now, if you're on the five- or six-year plan, this probably doesn't apply to you so much. But for those of you who need to be out in four, I highly recommend that you avoid a senior semester abroad.

Not only can studying abroad put a cramp in your goal to graduate in four years, but your senior year in college is the last opportunity that you get to party and enjoy your best college friends. Most likely, you will all end up with jobs in different cities and states, so it only makes sense to spend your final year with them (especially when senior year gives you a little more time to kick off your shoes, relax, and have fun!). So stick it out and try staying put your senior year. You can always do your graduate degree abroad.

U Chic Tip!

Before choosing to study abroad, I highly recommend meeting with your academic advisor and mapping out what credits you still need in order to graduate. Tell the advisor that you are thinking of studying abroad, and see if they think it is possible for you to graduate on time. Then take that list of necessary classes and look at the possibilities offered to you by study-abroad programs. If you are extremely concerned, make an appointment with the study-abroad office and discuss whether or not studying abroad would stunt your academic progress.

Going after graduation

Don't forget that it is always possible to study abroad after graduation. Even better, there is also the opportunity to complete an internship while abroad that would provide you almost the same life-changing experiences as a study-abroad program. I met people abroad from the United States who found internships after graduation. One girl was a design intern for an architect in Florence (an incredible opportunity in a city known for its beautiful architecture) and another one was an intern for a company in Florence that organizes events and trips that are affordable for study-abroad students. Each seemed extremely happy with her decision to work abroad.

You can also go abroad for graduate school. This may be surprising, but there are some well-known foreign graduate schools that can provide equal or better training in your area of expertise. Schools like Sciences Po in Paris or the London School of Economics are top-notch training grounds for budding policy experts or politicians. If not completing your graduate degree abroad, you could get into a program at your college that will send you abroad for several weeks at a time. For example, the journalism school at UNC–Chapel Hill offers several trips to other countries for photojournalism graduate students. Your study-abroad office or website would have more information about the specific opportunities at your school, so be sure to look into these. And don't forget that you should also consider programs offered by other schools. I knew a girl from UNC who studied abroad in Italy through a program at NYU. The great thing about these programs is that they enhance your educational experience while offering something that is perfect for your résumé and for landing that dream job.

AM I SOCIALLY READY?

Besides academics, the decision to go abroad should also be based on when you're *socially* ready for the experience. For most people, studying abroad is a step way outside their comfort zone. Even the independence in college doesn't match the freedom of studying abroad. With this freedom also comes an element of responsibility that you've never had to face before: you are far away from your family and friends.

Some people long for that kind of independence, and the fresh new start that a semester or year abroad offers. But it is also important to understand exactly what you are leaving behind. To start, there are many aspects to a person's social life that you have to be OK with leaving behind for a bit: your family, friends, organizations or volunteer activities, and even relationships. Is there a boyfriend? Is a close family member sick? Are you a possible contender for a significant leadership position on campus? Bottom line: don't forget to consider your social life when trying to decide whether to go abroad, or you may end up spending your entire time abroad worrying about what is happening at home. And that would be a waste.

It is important to communicate with the significant people in your life before heading abroad, so everyone knows what the expectations will be. If you find that your boyfriend is not excited to be attached to a girl thousands of miles away, maybe it's time to take a break. But if the relationship means more to you, maybe you shouldn't hop on that plane (but I really do not encourage putting your boyfriend's wishes ahead of your life-changing plans!). Also, you need to be prepared for the reality that you will probably not be able to talk every day by phone. If this is a major sticking factor, try setting up a Skype account if you are going abroad. It is a program that you can download to talk to people over the Internet for free, like a phone or voice chat on AIM. The good thing about it is that if you get a web camera you can see each other as well.

Get your social life in order before heading out

To ensure that your study-abroad experience comes off without any social hitches, set aside time to keep up with friends at home, even if it means sending out mass emails to everyone. You'll be making a new life for yourself while abroad, and with it comes new challenges and stresses, but also incredible benefits. New friends, different roommates, and new dramas will appear. Prepare yourself for all of these experiences, and you will be certain not to run into any social difficulties during your adventure abroad.

AM I READY FINANCIALLY?

Last, but not least, your financial situation will also influence your decision of when to go abroad. This bit of advice should not surprise you: save up money before going abroad. Depending on the current currency exchange rate, it is entirely possible that everything you buy there will be more expensive than at home. Not a great thing. So if your dream is to be in the United Kingdom or somewhere in Europe, be prepared for a credit crunch. If having enough money is a concern, maybe choose to go somewhere with a better exchange rate. But don't forget that currency rates change often, so make sure that you look it up when figuring out your budget before heading abroad.

Save some cash

Saving up money before you head abroad will ensure you have a better experience. Wherever you end up going, you will have many opportunities to travel to other countries and cities that you may never have an opportunity to visit again. The summer before I studied abroad, I saved up a little over $1,000 for travel and souvenirs, and it's no surprise that I spent it all. Most of it went to my gypsy travels to other locales. In the end, I ended up traveling to six different countries! My favorite places that I visited were Dublin, Ireland; Barcelona, Spain; Nice, France; and Geneva, Switzerland. Having some money initially set aside for this extra travel guaranteed that I'd be able to see many places during my semester abroad.

Go for a few scholarships or even grants

Your study-abroad office should have a list of possible grants and scholarships for your study-abroad programs. Some scholarships are specific to programs or countries and others depend on whether or not you are eligible for financial aid. If you receive financial aid at school, you should be able to get help with study abroad as well. Your office can provide you with the proper forms to fill out for financial aid, but you need to be proactive in tracking down scholarships to fund your travels. With a little effort can come a big payoff. So don't forget to check out all options.

Working abroad

And don't forget that it is also possible to work abroad. One website, www.workingabroad.org, provides a long list of international internships and work opportunities that are available in many foreign countries. But don't forget to consider the legal restrictions that your host country might have in place. Most likely, the visa that you will receive to study abroad limits the hours you are allowed to something like 20 hours per week. But that amount a week could still provide you with enough spending money to really enjoy your experience. I knew someone abroad who scarcely spoke Italian when she got there, and she walked into a restaurant only knowing the word for work and the owner gave her a job. Moral of this story: if you want a job, even if there are language differences, it is very possible that you can land yourself with a sweet and, who knows, fulfilling job experience that you'll never forget.

Study abroad is a life-changing experience no matter how many times you've heard it. Step outside of the box and take a chance. Just make sure that you're fully prepared before you take the first step.

Insights provided by Kathryn Lewis,
University of North Carolina–Chapel Hill

spring break or bust!

The last section's focus on study abroad is a perfect segue to the last "college perk"—spring break! When else in life do you have the excuse to travel somewhere exotic for some fun in the sun? But wait. The stereotypical image of spring break is a mixed bag of fun and (sometimes) girls and guys behaving badly. This yearly pastime has been around since 1935 and is still going strong, thanks in part to highly visible media coverage and the many stories you find splashed across the TV throughout the months of March and April.

Sure, you may think it's a good time, but the experts don't exactly agree. In 2002, the American Medical Association actually put out a statement noting, "Spring break is no longer an innocent respite from the rigors of college academics; it's potentially life threatening." So why the hard feelings? Well to begin with, spring break isn't just a fun vacation you take with your friends—it's a huge moneymaking operation that generates more than $1 billion annually (and that's just counting Texas and Florida!). That averages out to about $1,100 a week per student, which means there are plenty of businesses out there willing to look the other way if things get out of control. In fact, some college tour companies have come under fire recently for encouraging reckless behavior like binge drinking and excessive promiscuity. It's become such a problem that some towns like Daytona Beach have tried to ban the practice altogether.

While spring break is certainly an important rite of passage for many coeds, putting your safety and health first should always be your top priority. Not everyone may agree, but trust us, the stats don't lie: taking things to an extreme will most likely land you in the hospital emergency room, or worse, cooling your heels in a jail cell.

If you're ready to take on the responsibility of a parents-free trip to an exotic locale, then the first thing you need to do is start researching now. Whether you're looking to kick back and relax or you're even exploring the idea of donating your time to a worthy cause, there's no time like the present to get your facts straight and make an informed decision about your first spring break experience.

Spring-Breaking for a Recharge

I'd never been on vacation with anyone but my family before, so when my sophomore year rolled around, I knew going away for a crazy week with my friends was a rite of passage I just couldn't miss. OK, so I never really saw myself as the typical spring-break girl who danced on tables and hooked up with some random guy I was guaranteed never to see again, but I figured as a college student, going on spring break was something I simply *had* to do. While Cabo was the hot spot for students at my school, my friends and I decided to hit the Bahamas instead, in an effort to avoid the entire student population.

My group of friends (four guys and five girls) settled on a nice, all-inclusive resort that was only a short two-hour flight from Washington, DC. Although the destination seemed like a no-brainer, determining the details of the trip (especially when trying to plan with such a large group) wasn't exactly a cakewalk. From deciding where to stay to figuring out how to get there, it seemed like everyone had an opinion! We all finally agreed on a nice, four-star hotel (always keep it classy, folks) that allowed us the opportunity to explore both the beach *and* the local culture.

For me, spring break was not only a time to spend with my besties, but also an opportunity to reconnect with one of our pals who had transferred schools. The Bahamas also served as a great meeting place for a reunion. It was less crowded, the vibe was pretty mellow, and we didn't have to deal with a bunch of drunk jerks hitting on us 24/7. While most people think spring break has to be all about partying, it can be a great time to rest, recharge, and spend time with the people you love the most.

PLANNING

Waiting until the last minute to plan your trip is definitely a big mistake if you want to get the best deals on hotels and airfare. About 1.5 million college students go away for spring break each year, which means rooms and flights fill up fast if you don't book at least three to four months in advance.

Typically, most college-aged travelers flock to popular spring break hot spots like Florida, Texas, Jamaica, Mexico, and the Bahamas. But don't feel like you have to follow the crowd to have a good time. Keep in mind you can have just as much fun (and score student discounts!) if you head to Europe, or skip the whole warm weather thing altogether and hit the slopes instead (Utah, Idaho, and Colorado are always an option).

Just remember, budget is key. If you're looking to save a lot and don't mind staying at a so-so hotel, then sticking to one of the more popular spring break destinations is probably your best bet, since there are quite a few packages to pick and choose from.

Breaking down your budget

Keeping on budget while lounging around on a beach is a lot harder than you think. Sure, hotel and airfare make up a big chunk of your trip expenses, but little things like food, drinks, car rental, cab/bus fare, tips, shopping, tourist excursions, and cover charges for bars and nightclubs can quickly add up. If you don't want to blow a lot of money all at once (or if you want to maximize your return), consider booking your vacation through a national travel agency.

Companies like Liberty Travel offer trips for various price ranges, easy layaway plans, and a trustworthy list of tour operators that circle the globe. While you might be able to snag a better deal with a college travel agency, that doesn't necessarily mean you can trust all the information you're provided with. Again, college travel agencies draw the most business from spring break, so they're eager to book as many people as possible so they can maximize sales. Regular travel agencies get business all year round, so they're less likely to pressure you into a package that doesn't fit your budget.

What's a realistic amount of money to spend? Again, $1,100 is the national average per student, but that can differ greatly depending on where you're going and how long you plan to stay. If that amount is more than you had in mind, you might want to consider traveling somewhere stateside that's not typically considered a spring break destination (but still caters to a younger crowd). For instance, Austin, New York, San Francisco, Seattle, or New Orleans are all great vacation options that offer up lots of culture, cool bar scenes, and shopping aplenty. Just make sure you hit travel websites like TripAdvisor.com or igougo.com first before you book anything. Both offer hotel reviews from travelers, pictures, ratings, and info on the age range of the average hotel guest.

So what's so great about an all-inclusive hotel?

Should you go with an all-inclusive package? Well, that all depends on what kind of vacation you're looking for. If you don't plan to spend any time at your hotel beyond sleeping and showering, then probably not. But if you're looking for a way to save money and get the most bang for your buck, it's a smart option. Hotel chains like Sandals, Beaches, and RIU Hotels & Resorts offer all-inclusive packages that cover everything from round-trip transportation to and from the airport, meals, drinks, discounts on travel tours, and free activities galore. Bonus: Tipping is generally discouraged at all-inclusive resorts, since gratuities are included in your stay.

U Chic Tip! Spring Break on the High Seas
Ashley Yenick, Merrimack College

So you are considering a cruise for Spring Break? Make sure you have a big group of friends that want to go. It will be so much cheaper if you go with a bunch of your friends, and, of course, it will be fun!

After you have your group of friends lined up, decide on a destination. A lot of cruise lines have tons of discounts for college students like meal and drink packages that can help save you a lot of money.

For those on the fence about even going on a cruise, know that they aren't for everyone. If you're prone to being seasick on boats or motion sick in cars, chances are that you'll likely find yourself seasick on a cruise. The good news is that you can prevent all of that with the right medication. Ask your physician, but a medication like Dramamine, which is available through prescription, can help prevent nausea and motion sickness. For other medical problems like food poisoning, there are over-the-counter antidiarrheal medicines you can take to prevent not-so-fun cruise experiences.

Concerned about unsafe cruise conditions? Lucky for us, the

Centers for Disease Prevention and Control (CDC) have a Vessel Sanitation Program that keeps track of safety issues on all vessels on its website (wwwn.cdc.gov/InspectionQueryTool/InspectionSearch .aspx). The CDC also has tips on cruise safety such as always washing your hands and reporting your sickness before your voyage or, if you get sick on the vessel, during your voyage (www.cdc.gov/ nceh/vsp/pub/cruisingtips/healthycruising.htm).

My last bit of advice? Cruises are a great option for students on a budget. By choosing an all-inclusive package on a cruise, you can save a TON of money because you don't have to pay for food and drinks every day. I've found that Studentcity.com has great prices for groups, but if you're more comfortable going through a travel agent, Liberty Travel has a great program where they beat the prices of hotels, cruises, and airfare as long as the trip is leaving from the United States. Enjoy your spring break and happy sailing!

Travel essentials—don't leave home without 'em!

No matter where you decide to go, there are certain things you can't live without. An updated passport is key if you're planning to cross the border, as is a copy of your passport information (it's generally recommended that you provide this to the nearest U.S. Embassy as soon as you arrive at your destination). Bringing along a copy of your medical records is also a good idea. You should also make sure that you fill all your prescriptions ahead of time,

and check the Center for Disease Control website (wwwnc.cdc
.gov/travel) to make sure you don't need any specific shots or
immunizations before you head out of the country.

You should also ask if your hotel has an in-house medical
staff. If it doesn't, ask hotel staff to provide information about
local hospitals or clinics that cater to tourists. If you plan to travel
outside the continental United States, purchase an international
calling card or plan for your cell phone. While some cell phone
providers, like Sprint, automatically update your phone to send
and receive international calls without operator assistance, others
still rely on the old method and will charge you a ton of money to
call home.

PLAYING IT SAFE

OK, you've seen the stories in the media featuring "girls gone
wild" during spring break. Since when did having fun become so
extreme? It seems like nowadays, it's not enough just to spend a
week in the sun with your best friends. Rather, it's become a game
of one-upmanship to see who can drink the most shots, pound the
most beers, and suck down the most umbrella drinks before the
week is over.

Unfortunately, binge drinking has become the social norm for
most college students, and while that in itself is dangerous for a
number of reasons, the consequences that can result from bingeing
on spring break can be even worse, and sometimes deadly.
First, there's the overexposure that videos like *Girls Gone Wild*

bring—something that may seem like harmless fun at the time, but is obviously not so smart when it comes to applying for a job a couple years down the road. And then there are other biggies like getting arrested, raped, contracting an STD, or even worse—a tragedy like the Natalie Holloway case. Most college students think it won't happen to them, but it's happening to someone because the numbers and statistics just keep growing and growing.

Indeed, according to a recent survey conducted by the University of Wisconsin, 75 percent of all college males and 44 percent of all college females were intoxicated daily while on spring break. Spring break is a time to have fun and celebrate, but it should also be a time that you want to cherish. While it may always be 5 o'clock somewhere, try to keep the margaritas at a minimum and your enjoyment at a maximum.

Hook up at your own risk!

A recent American Medical Association (AMA) poll showed that 74 percent of college students agreed that spring break trips go hand-in-hand with increased sexual activity. For some people, spring break takes on an "anything goes" approach that includes sloppy bar shenanigans, random hookups, and unprotected sex with strangers. Yes, it's inevitable that you're going to encounter cute guys while on vacation, but that doesn't mean you should do something that you'll later regret. Harmless flirting and a few stolen kisses are fun, but a one-night stand can come with some serious baggage. Be careful and use protection if you're dead set on taking it to the next level. After all, the only crabs you should run into are the ones hanging out on the beach!

The buddy system never goes out of style

It doesn't matter how cute he is, how close the hotel is to the bar, or how tired (or drunk) you might be feeling—never go anywhere by yourself! Bad things happen when groups get separated— especially when you add alcohol and out-of-control behavior to the mix. Map out a spring break buddy system before you hop a plane to your destination of choice. If you're going with a mixed group, make sure there's a guy for every girl, or team up into groups of twos and threes. The more people together the better. A big crowd not only provides a higher level of safety, it can also work in your favor. (Nothing says spring break sparks like a handy wingman ready and willing to help you make a love connection!)

ALTERNATIVE SPRING BREAK OPTIONS

Planning your spring break can quickly turn into a confusing blur of what to do, where to go, and who to go with. It seems like a daunting task, filled with way too many destinations to pick and choose from. If a wild week of sun and fun isn't exactly your thing, you might want to consider something a bit more rewarding.

Alternative spring breaks (or ASBs) have become increasingly popular, allowing students across the country to give back and help others. Why spend a week partying when you can make an impact in a community here or abroad? Not only does it look great on your résumé, it offers you a unique opportunity few people will ever get the chance to experience.

ASB options aplenty

How does building houses in a post-disaster zone like Haiti or teaching English to children in China sound? Of course, you may be thinking, "Hot days and hard labor—why would I want to spend my week off from school doing even more work?" Well, the benefits are nothing but rewarding. Think of all the places you'll get to go, the people you'll meet, and the culture you'll soak in from spending time outside your usual comfort zone. Plus, there are tons of programs, no matter what your interest. From building school libraries on American Indian reservations here in the states to joining an archaeological dig abroad, ASB excursions offer a "sky's the limit" opportunity you most likely won't encounter traveling to some crowded tourist destination.

Doing good in your own backyard

If you're not sold on the idea of traveling to some far-flung country, you can always stick close to home and offer your services to one of many student-driven nonprofit organizations here in the states. While Habitat for Humanity is always a good choice, other groups like Live United (www.unitedway.org/our-work) offer programs focusing on education, income, and health care, so there's something for everyone. The University of Nebraska in Lincoln, Lehigh University in Bethlehem, Pennsylvania, and the University of Wisconsin–Madison are just a few schools that offer service trips to desirable destinations without alcohol as the focal point.

Participating in an alternative spring break is both a rewarding *and* enlightening experience. While some people use it as a chance to immerse themselves in their field of choice, others simply enjoy the opportunity it presents to take a step back, learn something new, and help those in need. For more information on ASB opportunities, visit studenttravel.about.com/od/spring breakvolunteers/qt/alternate_sprin.htm or drop by the student activities or community service office on campus.

Insights provided by Erin Cunningham,
The George Washington University

U Chic Essentials—The College Perks

Use your summers wisely
We cannot emphasize the importance of this tip enough. Don't just go home and get whatever job comes your way. Be on the lookout during your freshman year, especially early on in the second semester, for a summer internship opportunity in your field of interest.

Network often
Getting serious about your future? Start going to as many networking events as you can. These events are definitely worth your time. It's

a great opportunity to speak one-on-one with recruiters, giving them a chance to get to know you and even end up being an advocate on your behalf. Why not look even more professional by having a business card handy? You can make one for next to nothing on the Web.

Don't forget about informational interviews
Most people aren't aware of this, but companies—even those that are not currently hiring—are willing to offer you an informational interview. It allows you to gain insight into an industry without having to commit just yet. And you're getting your name out there so when an internship or job comes open, you'll have someone to contact.

Looking for more great advice? Head to www.UChic.com for our fave resources and websites—they come highly recommended from our guide's contributors and editors. Be sure to leave your suggestions as well!

CHAPTER 12

What's Next?

S enior year is nearing, and you're starting to wonder, "What's next?" Great question. Maybe you're considering grad school. Or is heading to the real world the best next step? And some of you may have no clue. No worries—although we can't promise to help you figure it all out, we definitely have some great advice. So sit back, relax, and enjoy our last chapter and your time in college because the future is looking great no matter what you decide next!

getting into grad school

It's the last day of junior year, and you just hit the spell check button on your computer for the last time before submitting your final paper. Time to celebrate! Summer is finally here, but looking back, how did the last three years fly by so fast?

This is usually when you would throw on your bikini, hop in your car, and road trip to the nearest beach with all of your favorite girls. Not this year. The summer before senior year is a crucial time in determining where you are going to be once you have a degree in your hands. Do you plan on continuing with your education? Maybe an MA, JD, MD, or PhD is in your future? If so, today is just the beginning.

THE PRELIMINARIES

Applying to grad school is a lengthy process, so it's important to get an early start, even if it is just in the form of brainstorming. With your classes winding down and the summer internship several weeks away, May is an ideal month to begin researching the schools that have caught your eye. Are you looking to stay in the same city or are you ready for a change of location? A great way to start eliminating schools from your list is to determine exactly where you want to live and whether there are schools in that area that offer the program that you are looking for.

TEST TIME

The last thing on your mind after finals is testing, but now is also the time to take a practice test and see how you do. Whether it is the GRE, MCAT, or LSAT, it is important to know what to expect. Also realize that these tests come with a price, so you may need to start saving up.

Take a deep breath. Aren't you glad you got started early? Now you have the rest of the summer to prepare. Studying on your own can go a long way, but you may want to sign up for a test prep course along with it. It is definitely helpful to have someone who is able to give you tips on answering the extra tricky test questions. Make sure to get signed up right away, though. Your first attempt at the actual exam should be scheduled for some time in the late summer.

ESSAY TIME

August is when the real fun begins. Along with taking your exam, you should also start working on your statement of purpose. This is the essay you will be sending with your application to let the school know all about your intentions to further your education.

Where do you begin when it comes to writing a statement of purpose? The schools you are applying to will have different prompts for you to consider, so you won't be able to send the same essay to each school. The good news is that they all want to know the same basic information.

What do you want to study? Do you have any experience in this field? What do you plan on doing in your future that will require the use of this degree? If you can answer these basic questions about yourself, you will be able to compose an essay that will effectively address the important issues. Just make sure to pay attention to exactly what the prompt is asking.

Also, don't forget that it is also good to stand out! What makes you unique? Why are you the right person to do the job you want to do? You want to give them something to read that will make them remember you.

Last but not least, have someone you trust read it over and make suggestions before you send it. They may be able to help you add details about yourself that you didn't think of (and double check for grammatical errors).

IT'S TIME TO SUBMIT THOSE APPLICATIONS

Summer break is over, and it's time to get serious about your applications. By now, you have narrowed down the list of your top target programs and schools. Do you have a checklist of everything that they are looking for? This is a great way to stay organized. You wouldn't want to forget to send something crucial to the application process.

Between October and December, you will want to frequently go back and review your checklist to make sure you're not missing any crucial details. This is also the time to add the final details to your essay, take one last attempt at your exam, and order your transcripts. Have you worked on your résumé? Be careful that this doesn't slip your mind during the process because this is an important part of the application. You will also need recommendations. You may turn to a former professor or employer whom you had a strong professional relationship with to get these.

Make sure you know the deadlines for each of the schools you are applying to and try to send everything in as early as possible. Most schools will want you to have your applications in by December. It is important to keep copies of everything for your own records as well, in case something is missing from your application package.

Whew, the applications are in

While you've submitted the applications, it isn't quite time to slow down yet. Even though you aren't sure which school you are going to be attending, you should start considering how you are going to be paying for it. If you will be seeking financial aid, it is important to apply early for federal assistance.

If you don't want to rely solely on federal funding, start looking into different private loans, grants, and scholarships. One caveat here: watch out for private loans that have adjustable rates. Skyrocketing rates in the future may end up making the cost of your education greater than if you had stuck with a mix of fixed-rate loans and grants. And of course, keep track of these deadlines. They sneak up faster than you may think!

FINALLY, SOME PEACE AND QUIET

So you've taken care of everything. Enjoy some down time during the winter months while you are waiting to hear back from your top schools. Now you can take a breath and relax, but remember to keep up with your undergraduate classes! Your hard work will definitely pay off in the end.

WHEN THINGS DON'T GO THE WAY YOU'D HOPED

I've been waitlisted! What to do?

If you've been waitlisted, don't fret! The school hasn't officially said no to you yet. First, call the school's admissions office to find out why you were waitlisted. Maybe it was simply because you forgot to submit an important document. Send it right away.

You will also need to let the school know that you still want to be considered for the program despite being waitlisted. Sometimes updates on recent impressive activities, additional letters of recommendation, or phone calls from important alums who are close friends and/or mentors can help tip the balance in your favor. I heard about this one woman who'd been waitlisted by a top school. After waiting several weeks to no avail, she walked into the school's admissions office and asked to speak with the admissions director about her situation. She waited all day, and finally got the meeting. Guess what? Her tenacity must have paid off. Later that week, she received a phone call from the director who told her that she had been accepted into the program! Now, not all of us can walk right into the admissions office, but we can be persistent and unwavering in our commitment to getting in.

After you've followed up, expressed your interest, and sent additional material for consideration, the best thing you can do for yourself in this situation is to take a deep breath and patiently wait. Check in with the admissions office from time to time to find out your status. But don't make yourself crazy! You will find out soon enough. Did you get accepted to any other programs? If so, you may want to spend this time looking into what the other school has to offer. A definite yes is always better than being stuck in limbo without a sure answer from the school that waitlisted you.

You didn't get into any of the programs you applied to...now what?

Certainly, not getting into the programs you applied to can be very disheartening and confusing. But this isn't where your goals end. It is never too late to work toward what you want out of life, and the fact that you even applied means you are well on your way.

If you're still interested in attending grad school, the great news is that you can always apply again. The key to moving forward is understanding why you didn't get accepted and starting from there. You can retake tests for a higher score or head to the workforce to gain more experience, as schools take these things into consideration when choosing their next class.

NEED MORE INFO ON THE PROCESS?

That is the quick snapshot of the grad school application process. In need of additional information? The Princeton Review (www .princetonreview.com) is a great resource to check out for all things grad school. No matter what happens along the way, always remember to hold your head high and be confident. You can achieve anything in life if you are determined and have a little faith in yourself.

Insights provided by Kelly Leslie, San Francisco State University

the case against grad school

I've got bills to pay. A year out of school, I've realized that bills are what separate the grown-ups from the not-quite-there-yets. The sooner you have to pay them, the quicker you grow up. That's one of the reasons that I went straight into the workforce after graduating from The George Washington University, rather than piling on more student loans for another degree.

As a journalism student living in Washington DC, I helped pay my way through school by working for several publications while taking classes (and being extremely thrifty!), so I already felt very much a part of the working world by the time I graduated. A master's in journalism wasn't something I really needed to get a job, and after 16 years of education—well, I was tired. Tired of papers and research and required reading, when all I wanted to do was just get out there, write, and learn on my own terms. Some people say that going straight from undergrad to grad school will help you keep up a student momentum, but let's face it: most seniors, confronted with the prospect of quickly dwindling college days, are making the most of their friendships, not their final moments in the classroom. Senioritis beats momentum any day.

At the same time, the job search can be tough in competitive fields, which makes the idea of grad school very appealing. I spent three difficult months interviewing for every journalism job I could find, shuttling myself between friends' couches in Washington DC and New York and my parents' house in Pittsburgh, freelancing all the while. I am glad that I held out through those tough decisions, though—the job I ended up getting was a perfect fit for me.

Working is a welcome break from the classroom environment. It feels fantastic to come home from work and have my evenings to myself, rather than worrying about studying for a test or writing a paper. I feel challenged by my job, but without the pressure-cooker environment of exams and grades, my stress level has halved. I read books on my own timeline. The only thing I've envied my straight-to-grad-school friends for is the enhanced opportunities they have to meet new people, which can be harder when you've left the melting-pot environment of college. That and the leisurely winter, spring, and summer breaks, of course.

I'm not sure when I'll go back to school, or even what I'll go back for. I do know, however, that the continuance of my education will depend on that defining keystone of my grown-up criteria—bills. I hope to finish paying for my first degree soon, and then I'll be looking for someone else—an employer or a scholarship fund—to pay for the next one. It could be in two years or ten. I'll know when I'm ready. Until then, I'm reminded of a favorite quote from one of the chicest ladies, Dorothy Parker, on my chosen career: "I'd like to have money. And I'd like to be a good writer. These two can come together, and I hope they will, but if that's too adorable, I'd rather have money." College, straight to career—well, it's not too adorable for me.

Should you delay grad school for a job? If you agree with any of the following statements, a few years of work experience might not hurt.

I DON'T KNOW WHAT TO DO WITH MY LIFE

Every girl struggles with uncertainty in her senior year, but if you truly have no idea what you want to do, it's best to try out different careers before committing to several expensive years of school that you may not even like. I've known older friends to collect degrees like accessories. One girl toiled away at a master's in English, only to graduate and decide that her true passion was to be a personal trainer. Another friend got a degree in library science, and then took paralegal courses—neither of which has been very crucial to his current position as a marketer. And he still doesn't know what he wants to do with his life, but with so much school to pay off, he lives with his parents. A few years testing out library and legal careers would have saved him the costly decision. I know he doesn't feel he wasted the time—no time spent learning is wasted, after all—but he certainly doesn't feel like he has a head start on his peers.

Why Not Work for Yourself?

Terrified of finding a job after college graduation in this bleak economy? You're not alone. Many students are turning to entrepreneurship as a means of making a living.

Here are some tips on how to help your career take flight:

1. Look for service gaps in your community and brainstorm ways you can fill those holes with specialized goods and services that may not be readily available in your area.

2. Research costs involved in starting your own business. It could be cheaper to work as a consultant or freelancer than actually taking on the challenge of running something yourself.

3. Come up with a business plan and approach your friends and family about investing in it. One hundred dollars can go a long way if twenty people make a contribution.

4. Reach out to other small businesses both locally and online so you develop a successful referral network.

5. Create basic business cards (you can order a set of 500 for only $30 at Staples.com) with your name, address, phone number, email, and professional skills cited.

I AM UP TO MY EARS IN DEBT

So why add more? If you can get a full ride to grad school with a stipend, that helps—but they only go out to a select few. Grad school costs a lot of money, and can be way more intense than undergrad. You may find it difficult to hold a job while in school. Best to go to work and pay down your debt for a few years until it's manageable. Your employer may even help defray the cost of grad school with a tuition assistance program.

I DON'T NECESSARILY NEED THE DEGREE

In journalism, the number of degrees you've obtained doesn't entitle you to a higher salary—rather, it's the quality of your writing, and the reputation of the places you've been published. This holds true for several other professions. One friend got a master's in public policy, and later found himself working as a researcher at a nonprofit, where he was the only person with a higher degree on his team. After spending a lot of time and effort on a master's, he was frustrated and doesn't think he'll be there long. Ask other people in your field if they think a master's is crucial to getting your foot in the door, and if they say no, test the waters by applying for a few jobs. After all, you can always go back to school after a year or two.

FRANKLY, I'M REALLY BURNED OUT AFTER UNDERGRAD

One argument for going straight to grad school is that you maintain the habits and pace of student life. However, by the end of senior year, some girls just want to be out the door and done. There's nothing wrong with this—after all, you've spent the last 16 or 17 years of your life in school, and it's natural to want something different. If you're burned out but know that grad school is in your future, take a year off to travel, work, and learn for your own sake. Read all of the books that you were too busy to finish when you were in school. Do some additional research on your thesis, so you'll still be on top of your game when the application season rolls around next year. Figure out who you are outside of school. You'll be a far more well-rounded and polished candidate with a year or two of grown-up work under your belt, compared to the people who are applying straight out of school and know nothing outside of academia. Also, the mental break will refresh your brain and improve your attention span for school—and get you right back into your presenioritis momentum.

Insights provided by Maura Judkis,
The George Washington University

why I chose grad school

Should I go to graduate school? What is the best program for me? I'm not sure I want to go. What if I never go back to school? What if I get a graduate degree and then change my mind? Can I afford it? I'm tired of school; maybe I'll wait—is that OK? These questions plagued me incessantly in the months before college graduation. And I know I was not alone. Experts say that graduating from undergrad is one of the hardest times in one's life. It involves massive transition in almost all areas of existence: work, school, living situation, and the list goes on.

If you already know that you need an MA or a PhD to get your dream job, and you are certain that's what you want to do, then go for it! Do whatever it takes to get there. But if you're like me and think you should go to grad school but still have many unsettled questions, take your time, do your research, talk to your mentors and advisors, and then decide. You should not feel rushed or stressed at any point. The best decisions in life are usually made on your own terms. Here's how I made mine.

I went to California State–Los Angeles for my undergrad. I got a BA in history and a minor in women's and gender studies. I am in love with history, and if I could marry school, I would. I love class. I love reading. I love learning more than almost anything. Now, don't stop reading because I'm a nerdy bookworm and you're not. I'm just trying to set up the background. My plan was to be a professor—Dr. Monica Taylor, professor of U.S. women's and social history. At some point I began to wonder if that was what I really wanted. What if I went to the trouble to get an MA and a PhD, and then changed my mind?

My plan was to be a professor—Dr. Monica Taylor, professor of U.S. women's and social history. At some point I began to wonder if that was what I really wanted. What if I went to the trouble to get an MA and a PhD, and then changed my mind?

I was also scared that if I took some years off from school to decide, I would never go back. Both were very scary options.

So, with all this stress, how did I move forward? First, I decided that it was OK for me not to know or have a plan. I used to dread people asking me what I wanted to be in the future because I hated saying, "I don't know" or "Maybe a professor, most likely." Once I got past worrying so much what other people thought, I felt more at ease to make the decision that was right for me. So be OK with where you're at; you don't have to conform to anyone's standards or feel embarrassed for not being sure.

After I quit caring what others thought, I took an inventory of myself. It may surprise you, but this doesn't take as long as you would think. I sat down and made a list of what I'm good at. What are my skills and my natural talents? For me, they are academia, reading, teaching, and helping people. Next, I thought about what my passions were. After writing down social justice, education, history, and women's issues, I realized that my list of talents and passions made a pretty strong argument for going forward in my dream of being a professor. And I did. Currently, I am a graduate student at Cal State–LA, working on my MA in history.

Now, I am still not completely sold on being a professor. But taking the time to figure out my real passions has put me in a place where I know that whatever I do—whether becoming a professor or something else—will require maybe not a PhD but definitely a graduate degree. You can do the same thing. What are you good at? What are you passionate about? What direction does that pull you in? Start with these questions, and you are putting yourself one step closer to making the right decision.

I hate to break it to you: it's going to be a little scary no matter what you decide, grad school or not. There is always that little concern that you're not making the right decision, but that's life.

We can't predict the future, but we can make an informed decision. And remember, you're not alone; every graduating college student faces these challenging questions. But relax a little; take time to think and talk about it. You don't have to have everything perfectly planned out; the goal is to just figure out what is best for you.

Insights provided by Monica Taylor,
California State University–Los Angeles

moving in with the parents: how to make it work

Between the rising cost of living and the increasing amount of debt students accrue, moving back home after graduation is an increasingly popular money-saving stop on the way to your own place. How can you make living with the parents work?

R-E-S-P-E-C-T

The foundation of making life with the parental units work is respect. You're not in high school anymore; you are an adult now with a college degree. Show them how much you've matured in college by respecting their rules and their home.

Respect means cleaning up after yourself, being nice to your parents, and...honoring boundaries. Living at home shouldn't mean you put a halt on socializing and dating, but your parents probably wouldn't appreciate late-night callers. Move the party to his place if the occasion arises.

PLAY BY THEIR RULES

When you return home, it's important to sit down with your parents so they can put all their rules and expectations for you on the table. You've had years of freedom at college, but now you are a guest in their home.

It may put a damper on your social life when they expect you home by midnight, but that's a sacrifice you make to save up for a place of your own...and it will make you that much more motivated to get there.

PAY THEM BACK

Sure, the point of moving back home post-graduation is to save cash, but you can show your gratitude to your family in many ways. Offer to run errands for your parents. Go grocery shopping for your mom. Make dinner once a week. Baby-sit your younger siblings. Clean the house. By taking you back in, your parents are doing you a big favor; you need to show them your appreciation.

CONTINUE TO LIVE YOUR OWN LIFE

Just because you're stuck in your suburbs doesn't mean you should go into a self-imposed social exile! Make an effort to meet up with friends, get into the city if you're close by, and make new acquaintances if all your buds have flown the coop. Sequestering yourself at home will drive you crazy. You'll be much happier, healthier, and more motivated if you continue to have a social life.

YOU'RE NOT ON VACATION

Don't get too comfortable: this should be a temporary arrangement. Living rent-free with mom and pop is not an excuse to sit on the couch all day watching soaps. You should get into a productive routine: continue job-hunting, work a part-time or full-time job, and help out around the house. The more you put off making money and saving money, the longer you'll be forced to stay with the folks. No one likes a 30-year-old living in her parents' basement.

Insights provided by Alexandra Straka, University of Missouri

say bye-bye to graduation anxiety

Does the thought of graduation bring a rapid heartbeat or even sweaty palms? Or maybe it makes you a little nauseous? You might be suffering from a case of grad anxiety. Guess what? It's completely normal. Trying to cope with the stress of graduation is no piece of cake, but there are ways to take it in stride. Sure, leaving friends who have become your life for four years is hard enough, let alone trying to find a job or a new place to live or even adjusting to a move back home with your parents again. All of this can be super-stressful. It's important to remember that you're not in this alone. In fact, there are millions of college seniors across the United States facing the same pangs of anxiety that you're feeling at this very moment. The trick is to not allow the stress to take over and make you feel hopeless. This section is all about how you can relax and enjoy your final year even when the future is still a question mark.

RELAX A LITTLE!

First, take a deep breath.

In between preparing for the big move, a new job, or even simply the unknown, take time to *relax*. Whether it be exercise, television, writing, or just enjoying times with your friends, take advantage of any time that you have for yourself. The stress has been coming on fast and hard recently; I've taken all of the nervous energy and channeled it into exercise. Every time I start to feel overwhelmed with all of the work I have to do, I hop on the treadmill and work off those nerves.

Go brunching!

One of my favorite things to do during college was grab brunch with my girlfriends on the weekends at the school cafeteria. We would all roll out of bed, throw on our sweats, and meet at the café for a long, relaxing meal. There were never any time limits, nothing was rushed, and we could just sit there and gossip for as long as we wanted. You certainly won't ever get your college days back, so you might as well take advantage of the time you have left.

Pamper yourself

No matter how hectic your schedule may be or how much the stress is building, be sure to give yourself a little TLC once in a while. Consider going for a massage or having a spa day with your friends. It will be a great way to temporarily escape the stress. And who doesn't love a spa day? If you're like most college students and are low on cash, try something a little less expensive like a manicure or pedicure. And if you really have no cash, try creating a spa day of your own with your friends! I did this a few times with my girls. We'd paint each other's nails, try on new shades of makeup, and occasionally dyed each other's hair. After all of your hard work, be sure to treat yourself to something nice; you deserve it!

ENJOY THE MOMENT

The most important and fun factor in coping with your graduation anxiety is to focus on the *now* and really *enjoy* the end of your time at school. Make the most out of every aspect of college and save the worrying for tomorrow.

Take time to document the memories

I'm a huge fan of photographs. There is no better way to bring back a great memory than to look through old pictures of some of your favorite experiences. I suggest bringing your camera absolutely everywhere. I know we're all fans of taking pictures at the bar or at a party, but I mean literally everywhere. Are you having a movie night at a friend's apartment? Bring your camera! You'll find that it's those low-key nights that end up producing the most memorable moments. And then you can have a scrapbooking party at some point with all your friends to create something that will remind you of the fun you had for the rest of your life.

Get out and explore

Take a look around at your campus and the area that you are living in and really explore. It wasn't until the end of my senior year of undergrad that I realized how many great activities were being thrown at me, and for free.

Go out!

You're never going to have as much free time as you do in college. Take advantage of your schedule and go out once in a while. I'm not saying party like an animal, but just take time to enjoy yourself. Go out for martinis with your girls, or check out that frat party down the street. Some of my best college memories came from a night out with the girls. There was a bar down the street from CCSU—Elmers. Tuesday nights were "Bar Bingo" nights. We'd all walk down to the bar, play bingo, hang out, etc. It was so simple, but always so much fun.

Take a class for fun

After three years of sitting through several classes that were unrelated to your major, try taking something that really interests you even if it has nothing to do with what you're studying! As an English and journalism major, I took a *ton* of writing courses but was interested in psychology. During senior year, I took a great psych class the second semester that was really interesting. These amazing educational opportunities are right at your fingertips, so get out there and don't be afraid to try something new.

THE FUTURE IS UNKNOWN. SO WHAT?

Most of you have spent a good portion of your life planning for what comes next. However, when college graduation approaches, sometimes it is not always clear what the best next step will be. Although this realization can be a major stress, it really shouldn't be. After all the hard work that you've put in over the years, you owe yourself a break. Take some time. Travel. Live in a different city. No matter what, it's worth your time because every new experience is an opportunity for growth.

As graduation gets close, it's really important to cherish the friendships that you've built and appreciate everything your school has given you over the last four years. If you've made your best effort to prepare for the future, then there is really no need to worry too much about what's ahead after graduation. Prepare what you can, give yourself some time to relax, and truly enjoy the life that you have built for yourself as a college student. Your anxiety is certain to melt away.

Insights provided by Katie Reynolds,
Central Connecticut State University

U Chic Essentials—What's Next?

Don't forget your goals

A proven method for making your dreams come true is to self-actualize. What do we mean? Dream it, write it down, and go back to your goals over and over. The more you envision where you want to head, the more likely you're going to make it happen. And if your goals change, that's completely OK. That's the point of having goals in the first place—to always be in tune with what you really want and then not be afraid to change course if necessary.

Slow down a bit

As you near graduation, don't be in such a rush. Take time to relax and really make the most of your time in school. You'll have the rest of your life to work, but you won't be with these people forever. Brunch with your girlfriends. Visit those museums that you've always wanted to see but for some reason never found the time. Now is the time to really build bonds that will last a lifetime.

Go for nontraditional jobs

No one said that you had to put on a suit and go to a 9-to-5 job the next day. Consider living and working abroad for a year or moving to a place like New Orleans to get involved in the community for a year. These nontraditional experiences are great ways to make money (though maybe not quite as much as your accountant friends) while seeing a part of the world that many others never get to see. And who knows where it might ultimately lead you.

Looking for more great advice? Head to www.UChic.com for our fave resources and websites—they come highly recommended from our guide's contributors and editors. Be sure to leave your suggestions as well!

acknowledgments

This book is the product of a lot of hard work, support, and passion from a group of people whom I love dearly. Thanks must first go to my agent, Loretta Barrett, and my Sourcebooks editors for helping me turn the inspiration behind UChic.com into a book. Thanks to the team at UChic.com and our fantastic group of college writers. Many thanks, also, to Laurie Bainter, Director of Student Persistence at College Bound in St. Louis, Missouri. Laurie was a tremendous help in connecting with several of the contributors to this guide. I also want to thank my parents, Jim and Nancy, and my grandfather Bill for their endless support. You have always been there for me, reminding me that anything is truly possible in this life. Thanks to my lifelong partner and soul mate, Matt. You're a genius in every sense of the word.

contributors

Kara Apel, University of South Carolina

Olga Belogolova, Boston University

Maggie Biunno, Hofstra University

Janine Camara, University of North Carolina–Greensboro

Miryam Chico, Kean University

Nisha Chittal, University of Illinois

Johannah Cornblatt, Harvard University

Amanda Cross, University of Central Arkansas

Jessica Cruel, University of North Carolina–Chapel Hill

Erin Cunningham, The George Washington University

Allison Davis, Barnard College

Amanda Ferrara, New York University

Ikee Gardner, Duke University

Madeline Greene, Minnesota State University

Donyel L. Griffin, Kean University

Melanie Harris, Virginia Tech

Harmony Haveman, Pacific Lutheran University

Laura Iglehart, Georgetown University

Aja Johnson, University of Maryland–College Park

Lativia Jones Bolarinwa, University of North Carolina–Chapel Hill

Maura Judkis, The George Washington University

Emily Kaplan, University of California–Davis

Kelly Leslie, San Francisco State University

Kathryn Lewis, University of North Carolina–Chapel Hill

Rebecca E. Mill, Sweet Briar College

Krista Naposki, Elon University

Megan O'Connell, University of Wisconsin–Platteville

Pamela O'Leary, University of California–Berkeley

Briana Peppers, Spelman College

Anna Prestek, University of Washington–Seattle

Jill Ravae Scherr, Academy of Art University

Victoria Reitano, Quinnipiac University

Katie Reynolds, Central Connecticut State University

Alexa Rozell, Georgetown University

Jennifer Rubino, Kean University

Amanda Sandlin, Rider University

Kristyna Serdock, Stony Brook University

Rachael Smith, Radford University

Jillian E. Sorgini, Hofstra University

Alexandra Straka, University of Missouri

Erica Strauss, Kent State University

Monica Taylor, California State University–Los Angeles

Kylie Thompson, Harvard University

Ashley Tripp, University of Alabama

Alyssa Vande Leest, University of Wisconsin

Raneisha Williams, Ripon College

Ashley Yenick, Merrimack College

index

about the author

Christie Garton is the leading expert on the college experience for women. She is an award-winning social entrepreneur and creator of U Chic (www.UChic.com), an online magazine and merchandise brand for high school and college-aged women nationwide. With its "100% Behind You" commitment, the company gives a portion of its profits to the Open Door Foundation,

© Steve Attig

an organization that Christie founded to support young women in their academic and career pursuits here in the United States.

From founding Music Mentors, a youth-oriented music volunteer program that performed at the White House, to interning at *Glamour* magazine in Paris, Christie enjoyed the fabulous college life at the University of Kansas. While at the University of Pennsylvania Law School, she continued the quest for a fabulous grad school life by following her passion with the launch of U Chic.

Christie has also penned a daily online column on philanthropy for *USA TODAY* for several years and serves as a judge for the annual *USA TODAY* Academic All-Star competition, an award she won while in college, helping select the twenty "best and brightest" college students each year. As a writer, Christie has contributed to the *Wall Street Journal*, *The Huffington Post*, *U.S.News & World Report*, and *Seventeen*, among others. To learn more about U Chic and its foundation, visit UChic.com.

about u chic

· ·

The U Chic book series and product line was created by Christie Garton, founder of www.UChic.com—the #1 online resource for college women—to help young women succeed in school and life.

 U Chic: The College Girl's Guide to Everything
A fully updated guide for women to the entire college experience, from the day the acceptance letter arrives to graduation.
978-1-4022-8031-3 $14.99 U.S./£9.99 UK

 U Chic College Planner
A student planner to help you get organized and keep track of your fabulous college life.
978-1-4022-8345-1 $13.99 U.S.

 U Chic's Getting a Grip on Your Freshman Year: The College Girl's First Year Action Plan
A companion workbook focused on helping you take action during your freshman year to have a successful college transition.
978-1-4022-4398-1 $16.99 U.S./£11.99 UK

U Chic's Diploma Diaries: The Chic Grad's Guide to Work, Sex, and Everything in Between
An essential guide for college grads to creating a fabulous life in the real world, with stories, tips, and tricks from other successful young professionals like them.
978-1-4022-8061-0 $14.99 U.S./£9.99 UK